QUEER DHARMA

Volume 2

Statuette, Meditating Buddha, stone
Gandhara, India, 3rd cent. C.E.
Courtesy: Asian Art Museum of San Francisco,
          The Avery Brundage Collection B60 S541

QUEER DHARMA

Voices of Gay Buddhists

Volume 2

Edited by Winston Leyland

Gay Sunshine Press
San Francisco

LIBRARY OF CONGRESS CATALOGING-IN-PUBLICATION DATA
Queer Dharma : voices of gay Buddhists, volume 2 / edited by Winston Leyland.
    224 p.   23 cm.
    Includes bibliographical references
    ISBN 0-940567-24-5 (cloth : alk. paper).—ISBN 0-940567-23-7 (paper : alk.
paper)
    1. Homosexuality—Religious aspects—Buddhism.   2. Gays—Religious life.
 I. Leyland, Winston, 1940-
    BQ4570.H65Q84   2000   97-27590
    294.3'086'64—dc21   CIP

Gay Sunshine Press Inc.
P.O. Box 410690
San Francisco, CA 94141
website: http://www.gaysunshine.com
Write for free catalogue of books available, including how to order extra copies
of this book.

Table of Contents

ILLUSTRATIONS

Cover design/collage by Stevee Postman

The *Sutra That Perfectly Encapsulates the Dharma* says:

"Let those who desire Buddhahood not train in many Dharmas but only one.
Which one? GREAT COMPASSION.
Those with great compassion possess all the Buddha's teachings as if
  it were in the palm of their hand."

▼

"Always recognize the dreamlike qualities of life and reduce
attachment and aversion. Practice good-heartedness towards all
beings. Be loving and compassionate, no matter what others do to you.
What they do will not matter so much when you see it as a dream. The
trick is to have positive intention during the dream. This is the essential
  point. This is true spirituality"

—Chagdud Tulku Rinpoche

▼

*Short Practice for Drum and Bell from the Heart Treasure
of Dorje Gyurme*

> Rising as events
> But empty at their center
> May obstacles dissolve
> And accomplishments flourish.

Winston Leyland, San Francisco. Photo by Steven Underhill

Introduction

Winston Leyland

W hen *Queer Dharma* volume 1 was published two years ago, a reading/signing of the book was held at A Different Light Bookstore, San Francisco—with several of the authors present as well as myself as editor/publisher. To my great astonishment, the bookstore was packed for the reading—more people than I've seen for any other Gay Sunshine Press book signing in the past twenty-odd years. At that point I realized, surprisedly, that the book was going to do very well: it was obviously meeting a deep need among gay men.

I edited and published *Queer Dharma* knowing that it was a very catalytic, insightful collection but thought it might just be too specialized to reach a wide audience. I was wrong. The book indeed went on to find many readers (for a small press book, that is; we aren't talking of mass market paperback sales) and was enthusiastically and sensitively reviewed by both the gay and Buddhist press (see the back cover of the present volume for quotes from some of those reviews; also the Gay Sunshine Press website: www.gaysunshine.com).

And the reason for this modest success? Gay people, matured and deepened by having to deal with the AIDS crisis and other crises of the past decade (most people have lost lovers or friends), and many traumatized in their youth by the shibboleths, dogmas and quasi-fascist fulminations of the extremist right and the smug homophobia of the established Christian churches, are looking for a spirituality with depth, one which is accepting of gay sexuality/culture. And Buddhism most definitely *has* such depth and *is* so accepting, even though one can still find homophobia among some American Buddhists—see the sensitively written article, "We Two Boys Forever Non-Clinging," elsewhere in the present volume (p. 191) for more on this.

The response to volume 1 energized me to prepare this second volume. I asked each of the writers to focus on Buddhist practice and gay male sexuality/relationships. You will find the results in the ten in-depth articles which follow.

Michael Sweet, a psychologist and scholar of early Buddhist Sanskrit texts, presents here the results of his researches on Ānanda, the Buddha's loving disciple: a very erudite but charming essay on a man of homoerotic orientation and his relationship to the Buddha.

Finally, Japanese Ph.D. student Jeffrey Angles has done a superb, fluent translation of part of Mutsuo Takahashi's novel *Zen's Pilgrimage*, a selection which can stand on its own with literary/spiritual integrity. Takahashi has been one of my favorite writers for over two decades, and I've published him often, beginning in the 1970s. Most recently the book *Partings at Dawn: An Anthology of Japanese Gay Literature* (Gay Sunshine Press, 1996) features a hundred pages of his work. The piece here is, on the surface, pretty wild, yes; but read it twice and savor the depth and brilliance of his writing.

I asked each of the contributors to allow a recent photo of themselves to be used in the book, feeling that this would add a more personal touch to their articles. I also made a special trip to San Francisco's Asian Art Museum, the Avery Brundage Collection, to research and locate Buddha heads/statuettes for publication in the book. Again, as in volume 1, I chose heads and statuettes mostly of the Gandhara period in India, only a few centuries after the Buddha's *Parinirvāna*. Their Graeco-Roman-Asian sensibility has a special aura of appeal to western gay Buddhists: we have here handsome Buddhas of spiritual presence (pp. 2, 12, 31); while the Javanese Buddha from the 9th century C.E. (unusually seated) projects strong virility (p. 51).

I would like to share with you excerpts from a few of the letters I received from readers of *Queer Dharma* volume 1 after its publication:

From New Zealand: "I am writing to you from the other end of the Pacific Ocean, after buying a copy of your book *Queer Dharma*; it's becoming a smaller world when in New Zealand I can walk into a bookstore in town and pick up a book just published. Awesome book . . ."

From Pennsylvania: "I have just finished reading *Out of the Blue* [Gay Sunshine's book anthology of Russian gay literature] and *Queer Dharma*. As a gay man of Russian descent, who has been a practicing Buddhist since the age of 15 (I am now 30), it was with tremendous joy that I read these books."

From Brooklyn, N.Y.: "I found the variety and scope of the book *incredible*. It encompasses so many aspects of queer life, sexuality, psychology and spirituality that it's going to take me a long time to digest it. The amount of effort, thought, sincerity, generousness and (even) tenderness and humor that went into writing and compiling such a volume boggles me. . . . Enormous gratitude to the individual authors and the editor."

What I wrote in the introduction to *Queer Dharma* vol. 1 holds true here also: I welcome comments/feedback from readers. It is a "loving-kindness" thing to do, and I hope to hear from you: Winston Leyland, P.O. Box 410690, San Francisco, CA 94141.

I

HISTORICAL ESSAY

Do not believe in anything (simply) because you have heard it. Do not believe in traditions, because they have been handed down for many generations. Do not believe in anything because it is spoken and rumored by many. Do not believe in anything (simply) because it is found written in your religious books. Do not believe in anything merely on the authority of your teachers and elders. But after observation and analysis, when you find that anything agrees with reason and is conducive to the good and benefit of one and all, then accept it and live up to it.

—Buddha (Anguttara Nikaya Vol. I, 188–193 R)

Head of Bodhisattva, stucco
Gandhara, India, 4th/5th cent. C.E.
Courtesy: Asian Art Museum of San Francisco
　　　The Avery Brundage Collection B60 S78 +

Pining Away for the Sight
of the Handsome Cobra King:
Ānanda as Gay Ancestor and Role Model

Michael J. Sweet

Human beings appear to have a deep propensity toward locating their roots in the past, finding or creating a lineage, to use the Buddhist term, of others who have come before us whom we can view as exemplary precursors. Some have found their rootedness in biological family, conducting genealogical researches. Others have preferred to find spiritual or intellectual ancestors: the Romans looked toward the great philosophers and statesmen of classical Greece as their role models, the Founding Fathers of the United States Republican Rome, and the Chinese the idealized emperors and sages of the past, such as Yao, Shun, Confucius and Lao Tzu. The need for ancestors is especially strong for many gay men, who are often alienated from or rejected by their biological families, and many of us have found a bond of spiritual kinship with notable same-sex lovers of the past such as Socrates, Michelangelo, Leonardo da Vinci, Rumi and Oscar Wilde, to name only a few. Perhaps the outstanding example of this tendency in Anglo-American gay male culture is the oft-told story of having slept with someone who had slept with Allen Ginsberg, following the generational daisy chain four links back from Ginsberg to the great gay sage Walt Whitman (see "The Gay Succession" by Gavin Arthur, himself a link in this chain, found in Winston Leyland [ed.], *Gay Roots: Twenty Years of Gay Sunshine*, San Francisco: Gay Sunshine Press, 1991:323–25).

For Buddhists of all times and cultures, the Buddhas, bodhisattvas, yogis, saints and scholars of the past have served as a source of inspiration and spiritual kinship. The present essay is an examination of one of the key early figures in Buddhism, Ānanda, the chief attendant of the historical Buddha Śākyamuni, viewed as a possible spiritual ancestor and role model for Buddhist gay men. The textural sources of this

MICHAEL SWEET (Monona, WI) received doctorates in Buddhist Studies and Counseling Psychology, both from the University of Wisconsin–Madison. He is clinical assistant professor in the department of psychiatry at the University of Wisconsin–Madison, and a psychologist in private practice. He has published on Buddhism, psychotherapy, Yiddish, and on sexuality in premodern India in collaboration with Leonard Zwilling. He is currently working with Geshe Lundub Sopa on a translation and study of two Tibetan Buddhist meditation texts.

paper,[1] mainly from Buddhist scriptures preserved in the Pali canon of the Theravada or Southern school of Buddhism,[2] have long been known to Western scholars. However, in reading these texts, the queerness of the figure of Ānanda, whose name can be variously translated as "joy," "bliss" or "happiness," fairly leapt off the pages at me; it is in light of such a reading that he will be discussed here. I make no claims of "historical accuracy," because, regarding Ānanda, there are no "facts" which can be established with any certainty or probability, given the late date and the diversity of the writings about him. What we do have are a series of discourses about a figure named Ānanda, and what I propose to show here is that these discourses are particularly susceptible to a queer reading both in the context of the sociocultural world in which they were created, as well as from a contemporary point of view. I will also look at the practical implications for gay male Buddhists of such a view of Ānanda and briefly take up the problematic of sex and affection for Buddhist practitioners.

Ānanda is one of the more attractively human figures found in the Buddhist scriptures; this in itself suggests that some faint memories of an actual personage may have survived, since beneath the usual hagiography the various accounts present him as having personality traits that are highly at variance with the rather dry detachment of the ideal saint (*arhat*) described in the Pali canon. Ānanda is depicted as a tenderly emotional person, with a human love for others, despite his unequalled command of the Dharma and insight into its wisdom. The foremost aspect of his personality was his devotion to the Buddha. When the Buddha was dying, Ānanda became vicariously ill out of his extreme empathy for his beloved Master: "When he saw how badly ill the Buddha was his body became weak, the horizon became dim, and his senses were not clear"[3] and he burst into tears, prompting the Buddha's sermon on impermanence.[4] As one writer put it: "Ānanda's words at the death of the Master were not those of a saint risen above everything worldly. They were the words of a man mourning the loss of a beloved Master, friend, and companion."[5]

In fact, according to tradition Ānanda's attachment to the Buddha prevented him from attaining sainthood ("arhatship") during the Buddha's lifetime—he could only achieve that after the Buddha's earthly passing, the *parinirvāṇa*—and he was initially refused admittance to the first monastic Council because he was not free from all the "passions" (*kleśa*). Nor were his feelings exclusively for his Master, but also for peers, such as his best friend Śāriputra. When he heard of Śāriputra's death, Ānanda felt as though his whole body was drugged, his senses were confused and his mind became blank.[6] A commentary adds that Ānanda was trembling like a bird escaping from a cat's mouth.[7] In verses attributed to Ānanda after the Buddha's death,[8] he expresses his sadness at the loss of both Śāriputra ("my companion") and the Buddha:

> My companion has passed away,
> The Master, too, is gone.
> There is no friendship now that equals this:
> Mindfulness directed to the body.
>
> The old ones now have passed away,
> The new ones do not please me much,
> Today I meditate all alone
> Like a bird gone to its nest.

This beautifully expresses his grief at the loss of beloved persons, readily understandable to any of us who have lost dear friends, lovers, or family members; it is certainly not the more-than-human detachment of the perfect saint.

The relationship of the Buddha and Ānanda can be viewed in light of the ideal of the lover and the beloved (*erastes-eromenos*) presented by Plato—the non-sexual, non-possessive love between an older and a younger man, the older leading the younger to wisdom through his teaching and example (see for example the Platonic dialogues *Phaedrus* and the *Symposium*). In fact a seventeenth century Japanese work presents the Buddha and Ānanda as such a pair of idealized lovers [see Bernard Faure, *The Red Thread: Buddhist Approaches to Sexuality* (Princeton, Princeton University Press, 1998):235]. Ānanda is usually described as a cousin or other kinsman of the Buddha; in the Pali texts he is said to be the same age as the Buddha, but in works of the Mahāyāna and other schools his birth occurs on the day of the Buddha's enlightenment at age 35, making him a generation junior.[9] The Buddha-Ānanda relationship has served as a paradigm for the Buddhist student-teacher relationship down through the ages, and it is this sense I think, that a late friend of mine, a Buddhist monk and neo-Platonist of bisexual disposition, stated that "homosexual relationships can be good, if they lead to spiritual goals." This view is very much in the spirit of Buddhism as a living religion, and indeed of the Indian tradition as a whole, which, as J. Garrett Jones puts it "has never seen warm, tender, loving feeling between males as anything but good—so long as the males concerned were mutually motivated towards the good, and were not, either one of them, gravitating towards the evil." [Jones:113].

Certain other aspects of Ānanda's legend point to a definite queerness, that is, gender/sexual non-conformity, in his personality makeup. He challenged the patriarchal and misogynistic assumptions of his time in his tireless and ultimately successful advocacy for an order of nuns, and was in this more progressive (from a present-day liberal point of view) than the Buddha himself, who only reluctantly and with serious misgivings finally agreed to its foundation. There is also the curious accusation made against Ānanda by Mahākāśyapa after the Buddha's passing, that he showed "bad-acting women" the genitalia of the Buddha, concealed by the sheath which is one of the marks of the body of the Great Man, after the latter's death.[10] Ānanda's response to this charge was even more remarkable: he justified his action by stating that the women in question had only common merits, and that "I wanted to show them the sexual mark of the Buddha, in order that the sight would inspire them with disgust and aversion for the female body, and they would then obtain male bodies."[11] In one version Kāśyapa's response to this perhaps proto-Mahāyāna viewpoint[12] was an astonished and sarcastic question, asking Ānanda how "such excellent wisdom" could have occurred to him.[13] Furthermore, Ānanda is accused of having shown the Buddha's body first to the Malla women, thus allowing his feet to be soiled by their tears.[14]

Ānanda was also described as being quite handsome and charismatic, and a very popular preacher with female devotees. Legends suggest that his sympathy for women originated with his own previous births as a female, which were seen as a punishment for his having committed adultery.[15] This interpretation is found in one of the birth stories (*jātakas*) of the Buddha's previous lives as a bodhisattva (Jātaka story [JS] no. 544), in which the virtuous princess Rujā relates how she long ago was a blacksmith's son in Rājagṛha and had fallen into bad company, corrupting other men's wives. Therefore she (actually, the future Ānanda) will have to complete six more births as a woman before being born again as a man. This birth story also recounts Ānanda's lives before those as a woman, as a punishment for the sexual sins described above. Proceeding in a karmic evolutionary order, from lower to higher, these began with his life as a castrated goat and continued as a monkey who was castrated by his father,[16] as a handsome but castrated ox, and finally as a *napuṁsaka*, that is, a third sex person, one who was neither woman nor man.[17] This legend has in fact been rather influential, being cited, according to Peter Jackson, in Thai accounts of homosexuality in support of the view that it is an innate condition resulting from previous karma, and is, therefore, to be treated with acceptance.[18]

In the birth stories "there *is* a constantly recurring friend for the bodhisattva and the friend, unlike the wife, always has a predictable fidelity. In story after story the bodhisattva's friend plays a significant part, and in nine cases out of ten the friend will be identified as Ānanda." [Jones:105]. JS no. 498, for example tells of three former births of the bodhisattva and Ānanda, first as two outcastes, then as two deer, who ". . . always went about together . . . ruminating and cuddling together, very happy, head to head, nozzle to nozzle, horn to horn," [Jones:107], then as two osprey, similarly devoted.

The birth story with the most clearly homoerotic content concerning Ānanda is that of Jewel-neck (*Maṇikaṇṭha*; JS no. 253).[19] In this story, Jewel-neck, a *nāga* or divine cobra, came out of the Ganges river "disguised as a Brahman youth," and approached the younger of two brother ascetics, who was in actuality the future Ānanda. This young man and his brother had adopted the life of hermits out of disillusionment with the world after the death of their royal parents. The serpent/youth talked nicely to the ascetic and they became "intimate and could not live without each other." Jewel-neck would repeatedly come to the hermitage of the younger ascetic, sit down and converse with him. When it was time for him to go, out of affection for the ascetic he would lay aside his human form, encircle him with his coils, and embrace him, holding his huge hood over his head.[20] This image, with its clearly phallic connotations, is also reminiscent of the great ideal ascetics of the Buddhist, Hindu, and Jain traditions who are depicted as protected by the cobra's hood: Śākyamuni, Viṣṇu, and Parśvanātha. Having remained in this position for a time, and having "satisfied his affection" in Rouse's translation,[21] or more graphically in the original *sineham vinodetvā*, "having released his lust or desire" (literally a "sticky love fluid"), he would unwind his body, bow to the ascetic, and go back again to his own abode. The ascetic became frightened by these amorous encounters, and took sick, becoming yellow and emaciated, and thereupon visited his older brother to seek his advice as to what to do. Without delivering himself of any moral judgment on the relationship, the elder simply asked his sibling whether he wanted the cobra king to continue his visits or not. When told that he did not, his elder brother advised him with the worldly wisdom that he could discourage the cobra's attentions through pretending to be a gold-digger, by asking the cobra king for his prized neck jewel, in Pali *maṇiṃ me dehi*, which can be loosely translated by the immortal campy line of María Montez: "Gif me the Cobra Chewel!"[22] The younger ascetic takes his advice and on three occasions asks Jewel-neck for his jewel, which the cobra king refuses, finally telling the ascetic that he is "asking too much" by demanding this jewel which is the source of his wealth—and he then disappears into the Ganges, never to return. However, this resolution fails to make the ascetic happy; on the contrary, he becomes sickened with grief, becoming once again very wan and jaundiced "because of not seeing the handsome cobra king." He once more visits his older brother, who concludes that "This ascetic cannot live without the nāga king," and then related the ostensible moral, in Rouse's lovely Victorian rendering: "Importune not a man whose love you prize/ For begging makes you hateful in his eyes" (Cowell:199). The story concludes by having the older brother console the younger, and with their return to their spiritual practices, ultimately attaining a high heavenly state. This tale has been fairly well-known in the Buddhist world; it is found on a stone relief at the early Indian Buddhist site of Bharhut, in which "the ascetic with hair tied in a knot at the back is shown seated in front of his hermitage with a five hooded snake coiled in front of him, raising his hood."[23] It is also represented in the plaques depicting the lives of Ānanda to be found on the terrace of the Ānanda temple at Pagan and at other Burmese temples.[254]

What is this very strange tale really saying? A worldly and facetious person might phrase it as "boyfriends, can't live with 'em, can't live without 'em." Indeed, it expresses the dialectical tension inherent in the Buddhist view of same-sex love and friendship; male friendship is okay up to a point, but when it becomes too "sticky," too personal and exclusive, it poses a danger to the spiritual life, toward obtaining that freedom from pain which arises from thoroughgoing detachment. It is noteworthy that the relationship between Ānanda and the cobra king appears unproblematic as long as they are "dating," but changes when the handsome Brahman youth reveals himself as a phallic and sexual being. Non-sexual homosociality is approved of and reinforced; in one famous passage the Buddha rebukes Ānanda, who has said that "good friendship is half the holy life" by trumping him: "Do not speak thus, Ānanda! Noble friendship is not half the holy life. It is the entire holy life."[25] However, even the homosocial could get out of hand, as when Ānanda organized a sewing circle among the monks to mend the hems of their robes, which led to "frivolous chatter." The Buddha condemns this unmercifully: "A monk does not deserve praise who enjoys socializing, who finds joy in fellowship [etc.]. . . . That such a monk should attain the bliss of renunciation, the bliss of solitude, the bliss of tranquillity, the bliss of awakening in their totality, that is impossible."[26]

Psychodynamically, we might view the ascetic retreat of the brothers in this story as a radical defense against the pain of grieving for their parents, and a guarantee against the anticipated distress of future losses. This defense, which would have also protected them against fears of sexuality, is undermined for the younger brother by his love for Jewel-neck, precipitating his psychogenic illness. Despite his attempt to opt out of emotional attachments, his entanglement with the cobra king was already so strong that the loss of his beloved and handsome friend was extremely painful, the ascetic's wasting away suggesting a life-threatening melancholic depression. The solution presented in the story is the renewal and buttressing of his previous defensive strategy, that is, a retreat into solitude and detachment once and for all. From the Theravada Buddhist point of view such a withdrawal from the world is admirable and is necessary for the creation of karma favorable to the eventual achievement of liberation, but it hardly fulfills the emotional need that the story reveals.

In short, Ānanda, a beloved figure in Theravada Buddhist cultures, is seen as the paradigm of selfless love and devotion to the Buddha and a model for all future disciples. At the same time, and without any contradiction, he is revealed as a person who had a very human attachment to his dear friend Śāriputra, as well as to his Teacher. His legend presents a gender-atypical individual, especially empathic toward women, having experienced in his past births lives as a woman and as a third sex person, and as a man who had an erotic attachment to another male (and of a different species at that). In his position as chief attendant he enacted an archetypically nurturing, female role; he cared for the Buddha "like a good mother or a caring wife."[27] The question is whether, without doing violence to the tradition, Ānanda could become an exemplar, a role-model, to employ an overused but nonetheless meaningful social-psychological term, for gay male Buddhist practitioners?

Some things would seem to argue for such an appropriation of Ānanda as an honored ancestor by gay male Buddhists, just as some gay Christians have appropriated Jesus' Beloved Disciple,[28] as well as St. Sebastian and lesser-known figures such as Sts. Sergius and Bacchus.[29] The story of Ānanda's devoted service to the Buddha and the sangha is totally in accord with Buddhist ideals, and also speaks to the well-known over-representation of gay men in service professions which are focused on promoting others' happiness and well-being, such as nurses, waiters, therapists, shamans, entertainers, social workers, priests, flight attendants, masseurs, hairdressers, and teachers. The model of selflessly virtuous friendship exemplified by Ānanda is certainly a potential source of inspiration to gay male relationships, and can serve as a much-needed corrective to the superficial, hedonistic, and interpersonally exploitative personality models promoted by the hyper-commodified gay consumer culture of the developed world.

It must be admitted, however, that there are problems inherent in the above picture. Ānanda had after all to eventually sever the last vestiges of his emotional attachments after the deaths of Śāriputra and the Buddha in order to attain sainthood, and there is an inherent contradiction between "particular friendships," as they are called in Catholic monasticism, and the ideal of universalistic and detached benevolence expressed in the Buddhist concepts of love and compassion. Even in the optimal gay male relationship, from a Buddhist standpoint, in which two friends live together and devote themselves to religious practice, as the Buddha and Ānanda are represented as doing in some of the birth stories, any sexual contact would create an impediment to spiritual growth, since it would inevitably increase the desire and attachment that are considered to be the causes of suffering in this life and in future lives. The dilemma that gay male Buddhists face was expressed by the character of Professor X in Irving Rosenthal's underground classic *Sheeper*, when he said that he believed in all of Buddhism "except for the giving up of desire."[30] It is out of such contradictions that gay men are challenged to create a viable new synthesis. Perhaps the example of Ānanda may serve some of us as a useful guide in this endeavor.

FURTHER READING

Burlingame, W., *Buddhist* Parables (New Haven: Yale University Press, 1922).

Cowell, E. B. (ed.)., *The Jātaka, or Stories of the Buddha's Former Births* (1895: rpt. Delhi: Motilal Barnarsidass, 1990).

Jones, John Garrett, *Tales and Teachings of the Buddha: The Jātaka Stories in Relation to the Pāli Canon* (London: George Allen & Unwin, 1979).

Nyanaponika Thera and Hellmuth Hecker, *Great Disciples of the Buddha* (Boston: Wisdom, 1997).

Witanachchi, C., "Ānanda," in *Encyclopedia of Buddhism* (EB), vol. 1, fasc. 4 (Colombo, 1965):529–36.

Zwilling, Leonard, "Avoidance and Exclusion: Same-Sex Sexuality in Indian Buddhism" in Winston Leyland (ed.). *Queer Dharma: Voices of Gay Buddhists* (San Francisco: Gay Sunshine Press, 1998:45–54).

NOTES

[1] This is a revised version of a paper presented at the annual meeting of the American Academy of Religion, San Francisco, November 24, 1997. My thanks to the participants in this panel, as well as for the extremely helpful suggestions and ideas of my partner, Dr. Leonard Zwilling.

[2] However, Buddhist terms and names will generally be given in their more familiar Sanskrit rather than Pali forms, for example, bodhisattva rather than bodhisatta, Śāripūtra rather than Sāriputta. The exception will be quotations from secondary sources, and one time direct quotation from Pali sources.

[3] *Dīgha Nikāya* 2:99.

⁴*Dīgha Nikāya* 2:143ff.

⁵C. Witanachchi, Ānanda in *Encyclopedia of Buddhism* (EB), vol. 1, fasc. 4 (Colombo, 1965):531. Ānanda's reaction to the death of the Buddha is found in the *Saṃyutta Nikāya*, 1, 58.

⁶*Saṃyutta Nikāya*: 5, 16. See also *Theragāthā* 1034, trans. by Bhikkhu Bodhi in Nyanaponika Thera and Hellmuth Hecker, *Great Disciples of the Buddha* (Boston: Wisdom, 1997):158:

> All the quarters have become dim,
> The teachings are not clear to me;
> Indeed my noble friend is gone
> and everything is cast into darkness.

⁷*Saṃyuttanikāya Aṭṭhakathā*. 3:223. This interesting image suggests that Ānanda may have felt some unconscious relief "Śāriputra is dead, but I'm still here." This is, of course, purely speculative, and in any case would relate to the commentator's state of mind, and not "Ānanda's."

⁸*Theragāthā* 1035-36. Translation by Bhikkhu Bodhi in Nyanaponika and Hecker:179.

⁹EB:529. There is also an indication that he was younger than the Buddha in the Pali canon itself; see *Suttanipāta* 16:11, where he is rebuked by Kāśyapa as a "youngster." Cited in Nyanaponika and Hecker:144.

¹⁰This is found among the accusations made by Mahākāśyapa against Ānanda during the first Buddhist council at Rajagṛha. It is not recorded in the Pali scriptures, but is found in the *Vinayakṣudraka-vastu* of the Mūla-Sarvāstivāda Vinaya, preserved in Tibetan translation (*'Dul ba phran tshegs kyi gzhi*) in the *bKa' 'Gyur* Vol. 2,271.7.2–4 of the Taipei Edition of the *Tibetan Tripiṭika* (Taipei, SMC Publishing Co., 1991). This corresponds to f.308b.2–4 in the Derge edition, vol.da. It is also found in the Vinayas of the Sarvāstivāda and Mahāsāṅghika schools, and in the *Da zhi du lun* (*Mahāprajñāpāramitāśāstra*) of Xuan-zang; see André Bareau, *Les Premiers Conciles Bouddhiques* (Paris: Presses Universitaires de France, 1955):9–11.

¹¹From the Sarvāstivāda Vinaya, translated from the Chinese by Jean Przyluski, *Le Concile de Rājagṛha: Introduction a l'histoire des canons et des sectes Bouddhiques* (Paris: Librairie Orientaliste Paul Geunther, 1926):233–34. Other versions of this episode, in the *Da zhi du lun* and the Mahāsāṅghika Vinaya, are translated in the same work, pp. 64, 215. The belief that females can and would change their sex, either immediately in this life, or in their next rebirth, in order to achieve spiritual rewards barred from those with a "female nature," is widespread both in Pali and Mahayana sources; see Diana Y. Paul, *Women in Buddhism: Images of the Feminine in Mahāyāna Tradition* (Berkeley: Asian Humanities Press, 1979): 166–211. The belief expressed in this passage, that seeing the genitalia of the Buddha would inspire the women with disgust for their own genitalia, seems parallel to Freud's now discredited theory of "penis envy."

¹²For example, the story of the Bodhisattva Priyaṃkara ("Pleasure-Giver") in the Mahāyāna *Upāyakauśalya Sūtra*, quoted in Śāntideva's *Śikṣāsamuccaya*: "By the vow of Priyaṃkara, the noble woman who would look upon him with a lustful mind would cast off her female nature and become a man, a truly exalted being" (see translation in Cecil Bendall and W. H. D. Rouse (trans.), *Śikshā-Samuccaya: A Compendium of Buddhist Doctrine* (rpt., 1971: Delhi: Motilal Banarsidass):164. The full story of this Bodhisattva, in which the idea of a spiritually propitious sex change through the sensual gaze is presented (perhaps not coincidentally, by the Buddha to Ānanda), is found in the translation of this sūtra in Mark Tatz, *The Skill in Means Sūtra* (Delhi: Motilal Banarsidass, 1994):40–45.

[13]In the Mūlasarvāstivāda Vinaya, Taipei edition of the Tibetan Tripitika, vol. 2,271:7:3.

[14]For the Pāli account in the *Cullavagga*, see translation in Przyluski:157. Ānanda justified this action on the ground that he didn't want the women to have to stay too long. Other versions are found on pp. 187, 215.

[15]*Dhammapadaṭṭhakathā*. 1:327.

[16]Yet another example in which the Pāli texts seem to adumbrate Freudian theories: in this case, that of Oedipal castration anxiety.

[17]"*n'ev'ittī na pumā āsiṁ*. Fausböll, *Jatakas* (1877, rpt.: Oxford, Pali Text Society, 1990) vol. 6, p. 238, v. 121.

[18]Peter Jackson "Male Homosexuality and Transgenderism in the Thai Buddhist Tradition," in Winston Leyland (ed.), *Queer Dharma: Voices of Gay Buddhists* (San Francisco: Gay Sunshine Press, 1998):56, 72.

[19]*Maṇikaṇṭhajātaka*, Fausböll, vol. 2, 282–86. A shorter version of this story is found in the Pāli Vinaya 3:145, as the story of the Nāga Kaṇṭhamaṇi. This is translated in W. Burlingame, *Buddhist Parables* (New Haven: Yale University Press, 1922):68–72.

[20]Nāgas were believed to reveal their true form on only two occasions: when asleep and when having sex: Vin. 1:86–88, cited in Richard Gombrich (1996). *How Buddhism Began: The Conditioned Genesis of the Early Teachings* (London: Athlone Press):73.

[21]In his translation in Cowell, E.B. (ed.), *The Jātaka, or Stories of the Buddha's Former Births* (1895: rpt. Delhi: Motilal Barnarsidass, 1990), vol. 2:198.

[22]In the movie *Cobra Woman* (1944), directed by Robert Siodmak. This was an icon of camp, particularly in the 1960s, when it received *hommages* from such diverse figures as the avant-garde queer film-maker, Jack Smith, and Gore Vidal (in *Myra Breckinridge*).

[23]Nagar, Shanti Lal *Jātakas in Indian Art* (Delhi: Parimal Publications, 1993): 97 [depicted in fig. 63 and Plate 28].

[24]See Guillon, Emmanuel, *L'Armée de Māra: Au Pied de l'Ānanda (Pagan-Birmanie)* (Paris: Editions Recherche sur les Civilisations, 1985).

[25]*Sutta Nipāta* 45:2, in Nyanaponika and Heckel:162.

[26]*Vinaya* 1:287, cited in Nyanaponika and Heckel:146.

[27]H. Hecker, in Nyanaponika and Hecker:148. See also ibid., 158, in which his "motherly and preserving" personality as the guardian of the Dharma (*dhamma-bhaṇḍāgārika*) is contrasted with the much more active role of Sāriputra, the general of the Dharma (*dhammasenāpati*).

[28]Recent Biblical scholarship has identified the Beloved Disciple with the disciple Thomas: see James H. Charlesworth, *The Beloved Disciple* (Valley Forge, PA: Trinity Press International, 1996):225–86. The parallels between the Beloved Disciple and Ānanda are numerous, and some scholars have even suggested that the Christian accounts were informed by Buddhist models transmitted along the caravan routes (Charlesworth, *Disciple*:131–32).

[29]These two saints in the Orthodox tradition have gained recognition among American gay men because of their association with religious ceremonies claimed by John Boswell to have celebrated a sort of same-sex marriage; see his *Same-Sex Unions in Premodern Europe* (New York: Villard Books, 1994):147–51, 375–90.

[30]*Sheeper* (New York: Grove Press, 1967):145. Rosenthal was an editor of avant-garde literary journals, who became associated wtih Ginsberg, Burroughs, and other early Beats. *Sheeper* is a quasi-memoir; the character of Professor X appears to be based on A. L. Rowse, the eminent Shakespearean scholar and early vocal advocate of gay pride.

II

THE DHARMA AND PRACTICE:
GAY PERSPECTIVES & PERSONAL ACCOUNTS

What the world needs more than anything is bodhisattvas, active servants of peace, "clothed," as Longchenpa said, "in the armor of perseverance," dedicated to their bodhisattva vision and to the spreading of wisdom into all reaches of our experience. We need bodhisattva lawyers, bodhisattva artists and politicians, bodhisattva doctors and economists, bodhisattva teachers and scientists, bodhisattva technicians and engineers, bodhisattvas everywhere, working consciously as channels of compassion and wisdom at every level and in every situation of society; working to transform their minds and actions and those of others, working tirelessly in the certain knowledge of the support of the buddhas and enlightened beings for the preservation of our world and for a more merciful future.

—Sogyal Rinpoche
(from *Glimpse After Glimpse*)

Mark Marion, San Francisco

The Bad Buddhist and the Good Gay Heart

Mark Marion

I'm a "bad" Buddhist. I get lazy about meditation practice. There are days and weeks at a time when my daily sitting practice—when I do sit—seems to be nothing more than either trying not to drift into sleep or getting swept away on a mental/emotional roller coaster. While I deeply believe in loving kindness and nonviolence as a way of life, I sneer and bark at other drivers on the freeway, especially the ones going 50 miles-an-hour in the left lane. As for people who run red lights, I'm designing a hell realm especially for them. I relish the occasional steak—blood rare. While I accept that too much desire or aversion is not a good thing, I unapologetically hate bigotry of any kind, television, and slow salespeople. And as for desire, didn't someone promise that it would naturally decrease with age and spiritual practice? Yeah, right. Contemplating the four noble truths, I don't always feel so noble. It's like there's this voice in my head that talks to me like it's talking to a big, clumsy Labrador puppy that's failing house training, "Bad Buddhist, *Bad!*"

While in my more spacious moments I can chuckle about this, it does create a quandary. What drew me to the Dharma in the first place was that Buddhist teachings are more about acceptance than moral judgment, more about opening to all experience rather than contracting away from whatever is wrong. While I'm sure some schools or interpreters of the Buddhist words have tried to turn them into another catechism, something about the Dharma seems to dissolve this kind of hardness like water around a stone. What drew me to the Buddha's "middle way" is that it doesn't promote guilt and shame in the name of love. But now, that old Judeo-Christian guilt was sneaking into my Buddhist practice and getting a foothold.

"Nonduality" is a concept that's relatively easy to grasp intellectually, but it's difficult, especially for westerners, to truly understand. We are so immersed in a dualistic world: it's encoded into our language so that every sentence splits or fragments experience. It's an essential part of

MARK MARION (San Francisco) was born in 1959. He is a psychotherapist, whose Buddhist practice is in the Vipassana tradition. He has written a chapter about coping with multiple loss in the gay community for the book *Gay and Lesbian Mental Health: A Sourcebook for Practitioners* (New York: Haworth Press, 1996). He also participates in the Bay Area's Gay Buddhist Fellowship.

our philosophy from Aristotle to Adam Smith to Freud: You versus me. Us versus them. Good versus bad. Right versus wrong. Light versus dark. Male versus female. Body versus soul. Beginning in early childhood, we learn to divide and separate apples from oranges and then later graduate to separating the good little boys from the bad little boys. By the time we are adolescents, we are completely programmed to perceive the world dualistically. At this point, the mind can separate, categorize and evaluate so efficiently and automatically that we cease to be aware of it.

Our society operates from the assumption that if right versus wrong and good versus bad are not dramatically polarized and then drummed into the developing mind of a child—barbarianism and debauchery will reign. Dualistic perception is thus seen as an essential part of moral development. Some scientists believe that dualistic thinking is even coded into our brain structure, viewing the human brain from an evolutionary context, with a cerebral cortex—as the most complex and therefore most evolved part of the brain.

Underneath the cerebral cortex are other more primitive layers of the brain, having to do with earlier stages on the evolutionary ladder. One of these is the "reptilian brain" which perceives the world according to only two categories: "similar to me, familiar = ally and good" versus "unfamiliar, different from me = enemy and bad." We can see the simplest and crudest form of duality operating in the world and ourselves today.

Duality is a profound cause of suffering. When we perceive the world dualistically, we lose a sense of interconnectedness with it—we become separate from part of it, polarized from some *other*. Our internal world will reflect this loss of interconnectedness also, as we become separated, alienated from part of ourselves. Then, we are forever identified with a tug of war between conflicting voices inside as well as outside. Without a perspective that transcends dualism, there is no place to rest, no equanimity.

Part of the quandary that I feel about being a bad Buddhist, of failing "Buddhism 101," I know has something to do with the concept of nonduality. This sense of failure, and the profound self-criticism arising from it, is now giving me the opportunity to see how immersed I am in dualistic perception and the suffering this is causing.

In our society, the striving to be *good* casts a long shadow of suffering. It requires a rigid division of the world and the self into the *acceptable* and the *unacceptable*. In this divided experience, we are encouraged to grasp toward good and have aversion to evil. The rigidity of the pattern of clinging to goodness and rejecting badness means compassion is lost for the whole self and the whole world. An enemy is created— whether it is Satan or unwholesomeness or the unknown. Then, inevitably, certain individuals, groups, and normal human qualities (like sexuality) become identified with this enemy. Then this enemy must be sought out and destroyed. Sadly, much of the harming ideology comes from religious and political institutions caught in the "mission" to destroy the bad and promote the good at any cost, including their own compassion and humanity. The trap of good versus evil dualistic thinking is finally its heartlessness. The Holocaust, Croatia, Kosovo, hate crimes.

In my own practice, I am facing the heartlessness of rigid good versus bad, right versus wrong thinking. I recall a story told by gay spiritual seeker and author, Mark Matousek. He tells of meeting a close disciple and personal attendant of the late Meher Baba in India, at a particularly discouraging low point, after years of unsuccessfully trying to perfect himself on the spiritual path. Seeking out the wise man's advice, the seeker began to recount his failed attempts at avoiding temptation and becoming more pure. The old man interrupted him and began speaking of his beloved teacher, "Baba loved scoundrels. Of course, Baba loved everyone, but scoundrels were his special children. . . . Remember, God does not need your virtue. God will take the worst of you. Never try to be too good."

This story speaks to my quandary of being a bad Buddhist. I have been trying to be "good enough" for the Dharma, trying to divide my behavior into good Buddhist and bad Buddhist traits. As a result, compassion, interconnectedness and equanimity are getting lost. *Metta* or loving kindness, the heart of compassion, does not pick and choose. Like rain or sunshine it covers everything. The Buddha doesn't need my virtue, my trying to be good:

> Both gain and loss, and right and wrong—
> once and for all get rid of them.
> Delusion spawns dualities—
> these dreams are nought but flow'rs of air—
> why work so hard at grasping them?
> —*Xin Xin Ming,*
> 3rd Zen Patriarch, 7th cen. A.D.

Part of the reason I project this good-bad dualism onto the Dharma comes from the Dharma itself, or rather the translation of the Dharma. Translators who have grown up in a dualistic culture have translated the Dharma into a language that favors duality. As a result, we hear the fourth noble truth usually translated as right understanding, right thought, right speech, etc., which implies that there must be an opposite, polarized wrong thought, wrong speech, wrong action, etc., that one should resist with all one's might. This fed right into my categorizing of good and bad Buddhists. So it was a revelation for me to learn that the use of *right* to translate the original Sanskrit was less accurate than the word *whole*. Then the fourth noble truth would be heard *as whole thought, whole speech, whole action, etc.* "Wholeness"—not only evokes an entirely different response than "right," but is also consistent with the Buddhist teaching of nonduality.

Nonduality. This concept not only keeps me from reducing the Dharma to a list of "dos" and "don'ts," but also seems to be speaking to something deeper . . . the possibility of relating to the world differently. But how to explore nonduality given my conditioning, my thoughts, when even my language for communicating can so easily fragment and polarize?

It's as if I live in a two-dimensional world like a stick figure drawn on a flat piece of paper. As this two-dimensional man, I can move right and left and up and down on the paper, but jumping off the page—out and in—are three-dimensional concepts that I'm unable to grasp. But the truth is that the flat, two-dimensional world that I know is an illusion. I fact, I live in a three-dimensional world but I don't know it. I've been trained since birth to ignore and deny out and in, to not see the third dimension. "It doesn't exist," my two-dimensional parents told me. My language only acknowledges two-dimensionality and has no words or definitions for out and in (except at church where my stick family worships a god that is three-dimensional but this is never really explained, just described as a *mystery*.) The truth is, three-dimensionality is all around me, is me; I am three-dimensional myself but I have been programmed to only see two dimensions. Now imagine that it's your job to explain to me that I'm really three-dimensional. So you sit down with me and start describing out and in and I look at you like you're crazy or speaking gibberish. So finally you both get exasperated and you take me by the hand and slowly move me out of that flat world into the experience of out and in. It's as if I'm being pulled off of that flat piece of paper into another universe. I'm amazed by the reality of out and in which I had been taught didn't exist and I begin to understand three-dimensionality, not from your explanation but only from my experience of it.

It is difficult to turn any Buddhist teachings, such as nonduality, into a dictionary definition. It often misses the point and frustrates as much as it enlightens. Yet, this is the way we are taught to learn, to define experiences into ideas and concepts which we can then analyze. Buddhist Dharma is not an idea or a concept. It is an experience. And practice allows and invites the "a-hah!" experience of discovering non-duality, whch we are all already immersed in, and in fact is who we are. But, like the two-dimensional story, we've been taught to not see.

I remember giving a talk on non-separateness and interconnectedness one day at the Gay Buddhist Fellowship, and one of the men attending was getting really exasperated. "But what *is* interconnectedness?" he asked. I answered that it wasn't a concept but an experience and went on to share stories and experiences that can convey interconnectedness: intimacy, nature, single-minded attention, meditation, or any moment of such fullness—whether it be a moment of great beauty or horror, joy or grief, that the ordinary mind cannot comprehend it and the separate "I" is consumed for an instant into that moment.

This explanation simply made this man more annoyed and his face began to turn red with frustration. "But what *is* non-separateness?" he repeated. "I still don't understand what this experience you are talking about is. Define interconnectedness!" he demanded. If I'd had the guts or the chutzpah of a Zen teacher, I might have slapped him hard across the face or kissed him deeply and passionately. In either case, so quickly that he couldn't prepare for or anticipate the experience. Before he could compose himself from bewilderment or shock, I'd point to that shock, that space between his thoughts where he sat there slack jawed and say, *"That* is interconnectedness."

Interconnectedness, impermanence, non-duality, equanimity are all basically pointing to the same thing: our own essential nature, the way things are, but we are all so caught up into the trance of duality, separateness and grasping that we are like the two-dimensional stick man perceiving a very flat world. So all we can do is tell stories and recall experiences that evoke non-dualistic perception. When, for a moment, the flatness of our perception inexplicably opens to depth and breadth —peaks and valleys. Spacious skies and fathomless oceans reveal themselves in what we once thought were only lines and points on paper.

Of course then they disappeared again and we say, "I had a religious experience" or "I had a drug trip" or "I saw the face of god in meditation" and go back to our two-dimensional world a little inspired, but also a little frightened of three-dimensionality. But at least we know, at least we get a taste, like a beacon on the dark sea samsara.

Nature is one of my favorite sources of Dharma. It is a wonderful source for contemplating Buddhist teachings, including nonduality. I suppose if you lived your entire life in downtown Manhattan this wouldn't work for you but for a country boy like me nature abounds in the Dharma. I can go anywhere in nature and simply observe. Give it some time for any internal chatter to fade or recede and ease into the rhythm and subtlety of nature: sound, smell, sight, sensation. Relax. Then I can contemplate nonduality. I can look around me and wonder where are the good and the bad here? Which part of nature is right and which is wrong? Which is better and which is worse? I can choose any sentient being that I see, from an insect to a tree to an animal and observe whether it can exist separately or independently from another sentient being . . .

This contemplation on nonduality in nature is simple, ordinary. But I'd never taken the time to comprehend the experience. Feel free to give it a try. Whether you are a tree-hugger or not, non-duality awaits you. Or as Madge, the woman on the old Palmolive commercials used to say, "You're soaking in it, honey."

So I'm a "bad" Buddhist. With even just a taste of nonduality, a warmth and compassion begins to permeate all the so-called successes and failures. Zen Master Hui Neg said, "As far as Buddha nature is concerned, there is no difference between sinner and sage . . . one enlightened thought and one is Buddha, one foolish thought and one is an ordinary person." My practice reminds me daily of my ordinariness but at least with less inner conflict, less self-condemnation. That, in itself, is a kind of liberation.

*　*　*

I remember being in Sunday school at about age six or seven, staring at this framed picture depicting a blonde, blue-eyed Jesus with lustrous hair draped over one eye and a form fitting beige tunic. Jesus is sitting in a meadow surrounded by children, some of whom are on his lap or under his feet. The picture both fascinated me and made me feel slightly queasy. Not only because it seemed fake. ("He's Jewish," I told my mother, "like Ethan," who was my best friend at the time. "Jesus is not supposed to look like Veronica Lake!" My mother was not amused.)

The queasiness I felt was not so much for questioning depictions of Jesus, as for believing that Jesus would never permit someone like me to sit on his lap or play at his feet. Even then I knew only good kids get to romp in the meadows of heaven with Jesus. And little boys who like other little boys and want to get to know other little boys (in the Biblical sense of *know*) were not welcome.

A flash of memory, like this, will sometimes spontaneously appear in my meditation practice. On longer meditation retreats, but occasionally in daily practice, images from the past (often long forgotten mem-

Buddha head, stone
Gandhara, India, 3rd. cent. C.E.
Courtesy: Asian Art Museum of San Francisco
The Avery Brundage Collection B60 S542

ories) will pop up without any conscious intention. I am doing sitting meditation, just watching my breath, and then this film clip from my life will begin to play. So, I bring my attention back to my breath but this doesn't always stop the experience. Some memories are neutral, but often what bubbles up has some energy and emotion connected to it: a wave of grief, fear or anger will grip me for a little time. If I am able to be spacious, non-grasping, it will pass through. At other times, it has a power and energy that can't be ignored and the feeling stays with me for hours or days. Anyone who has been doing meditation practice for a period of time will probably recognize similar experiences.

Metta, or loving kindness meditation, seems to evoke these interruptions. It somehow "hones in" on the experiences from the past where I've closed off or shut down from life in response to some pain or fear. It's as if the softness of loving kindness will bump up against the ways I've hardened myself. And, like water around a stone, gently soften and dissolve a numbness and hardness I have carried, a numbness associated with some past experience of confusion, self-loathing or fear that I had no capacity to handle when it originally occurred. It takes patience to sit with boredom or itches or grocery lists that arise in meditation. It takes courage to sit with pain that arises out of the blue, out of the "doing-nothing-going-nowhere" space of meditation. Yet compassion has a way of finding what I don't want to feel, what I naturally resist, what hurts.

One of the themes that seems to return again and again in Metta, appears in the form of fragments from the past, snapshots of confusion and shame about growing up gay. In one memory I'm a 10-year-old on a camping trip with cousins and brothers—joking, laughing, feeling at ease. My uncle appears in his bathrobe, open in the front. For the first time in my life I notice his chest—broad, matted with dark hair—and I'm transfixed, fascinated. He notices me noticing him. All of a sudden it seems that everyone is very uncomfortable; the sense of ease, fun and unselfconsciousness of moments before is gone and is replaced by a quiet awkwardness and my embarrassment. My uncle clears his throat loudly about fishing tomorrow. One of my cousins answers and then the circle of talk, of laughter and activity continues again. But now, I am outside of that circle, separate. I no longer feel like part of it. I feel confused and alone.

Another memory—beginning seventh grade, coming back to school after summer. Everything has changed. Making friends, especially guy friends, which used to be easy is now difficult. Harassment seems to be everyone's favorite activity. I'm now an outsider. I walk too slow, talk too low and won't participate in the male-bonding rituals of one-upsmanship and attacking the vulnerable. "Fag" is everyone's favorite epithet. Now there is a wall around me keeping everyone out. Inside that wall, I'm at war with myself: I know what I am, but I'm unwilling to accept that this could be true.

In Metta, breathing, practicing compassion for myself and all sentient beings, I encounter these memories and I want to pull away, to shut down. When I am able to not resist it, to just let it pass through—I am almost always grateful. I feel more whole. It helps me to know that the alienation, fear, confusion, and loneliness are in no way unique, not personally mine. Variations of these stories are a universal part of the gay experience. Only the details vary. In Metta, images and emotions that arise are sometimes not from my own past, but are about a friend, a client, or even someone that I have never met, but I feel like I know, like Matthew Shepard. From the perspective of compassion it is the same suffering, the same pain.

I wonder if it's like peeling away layers of an onion which are really layers of suffering, layers of the hardening and contraction that this suffering has created. In meditation, when memories arise spontaneously they find an atmosphere of compassion and acceptance that was entirely missing when the original event occurred. In that moment there was no safe place to express or even recognize the fear or bewilderment or grief. That is why there is the numbness, the hardness, the coldness. In Metta, I visualize the warmth and acceptance of Buddha nature, reaching out to the bewildered gay kids, of the past and present, who are just trying to survive. Alienation, self-loathing, loneliness, threats to safety . . . gay and lesbian people all over the world experience this. In reciting the Metta Sutta, compassion is extended to the suffering of all gay people. "So with a boundless heart, should one cherish all living beings . . . radiating kindness over the entire world . . . outwards and unbounded . . . freed from hatred and ill will."

One of the subtle gifts of meditation practice in general, and Metta in particular, is that I find in myself a greater acceptance, a reclaiming of lost parts of my own history and a greater sense of wholeness.

This is especially important because one of the most harming aspects of homophobia is how it can make us not only strangers to others but to ourselves. A painful self-consciousness, a distrust of one's own natural instincts, can evolve as the result of experiences that teach over and over again that what comes naturally is not understood or welcomed. What is most true about who we are can not only alienate us from those we depend on, but also endanger our safety. Then, to adapt, we learn to suppress our natural way of being and become separated, alienated from it. Here society's good-bad duality that targets homosexuality and all its qualities as *bad* has penetrated our internal experience and made us divided inside also. Metta, or loving kindness, slowly heals this fissure, slowly closes this divide in myself.

As this hardness I bump up against softens and opens in the warmth of compassion, the pain of estrangement slowly dissolves and I slowly find my way back to the good gay heart.

Meditation Practice is one way of addressing the harm of dualism and specifically the harm done to gay people. Even with the gift of practice, I confess I really don't comprehend the hatred against sexual minorities. I don't understand how the gentle, soft-spoken nature of most gay boys and girls can inspire so much resistance and revulsion in this world. I know there are many theories and explanations about this. But none of it adds up to the loathing and aversion that gays and lesbians are subject to.

What is it about us that scares them so much? Looking at the question from a spiritual, Buddhist, rather than a political/social/psychological perspective, it seems to come back to nonduality, and the suffering that a dualistic worldview engenders. Gay identity flies challenges at the dearly held convictions of a dualistic culture. Our androgyny undermines the masculine versus feminine duality, our open and ecstatic approach to sexuality challenges the body versus soul duality, and our curiosity to explore the edge of conformity challenges the light versus dark, good versus bad duality.

In a culture that clings to a dualistic worldview as what is right and true, gays and lesbians are perceived as a threat.

What a bittersweet paradox: that a group so villainized by dualistic perception, so individually and collectively damaged and alienated from themselves as a result of this dualism and villainizing can, at the same time embody and carry the truth of nonduality in their very being. A truth that not only can heal the damage of homophobia within ourselves and our community, but also embody a healing of the fragmentation and duality of the entire society. Homosexuality is nonduality embodied. Here we find the essence of the good gay heart.

In my experience, gay people have a natural affinity for many of the central teachings explained in Buddhism: non-separateness, equanimity, impermanence and nonduality. I don't know all of why this is true. Perhaps being outsiders, even within our own birth families, denies us the luxury of complacency and thrusts us face to face with a particular kind of loneliness. This separateness causes us to examine ourselves, our relationship to the world, and examine the assumptions that those around us seem to take for granted.

Perhaps being subjects of so much irrational hatred, of bigotry that can threaten a sense of safety as well as eat away at self worth—requires, in order to endure, finding an inner resource of strength that is spiritual in nature whether we call it that or not. But nonduality seems to be a particularly powerful quality of gay identity. It may remain mostly hidden and unacknowledged in most gay men and most aspects of gay culture; the damage of alienation and disenfranchisement is simply too great. Nonetheless, it is part of all of us, a kind of spiritual heritage, a birthright that largely remains undiscovered—the affinity for the sacred.

There are clues and fragments that point us toward this aptitude in ourselves, even if we've lost touch with it all together. Like a lost city discovered buried under centuries of rubble, we can excavate the good gay heart.

The first clue is to notice the many indigenous cultures around the world for whom spirituality is an alive and vital part of personal experience and community life. In these cultures, the sacred quality of life is not exiled to some "Heaven" in the sky. Not split off from the present, to some future reward after we die. Instead, this sacredness is connected to the earth, to the cycles of nature and is available each day of living in the present.

We know little about these cultures and what we do know is fractured through the dualistic lens of the Western anthropologist or archeologist. But we do know that in some of these cultures the view of homosexuality and gay people is quite different.

In some Native American tribes we have records of the *Berdache* or more accurately translated "two-spirits, one-body" understanding of homosexuality. Here, gay people are not only an acceptable and desirable part of village life, but also have an essential place in the spiritual traditions. Clyde Hall, the gay Native American activist of Shoshone-Metis descent, describes how gay people, from his tribal culture's perspective, play an important mediating role in the world. "Gay men and women, two-spirited native people, we have a very important part to play in the restoring of balance. I can't emphasize that enough. . . . If you look at any so-called primitive or indigenous peoples—and this goes for ancient Europeans like Druids, the Celts as well—their shamans were usually two-spirited people. American Indian societies are no exception." The "two-spirits, one-body" give the gay person an aptitude, wisdom and affinity for the sacred.

Further, in the *Dagara* tribe of West Africa, gay people have a place in the culture as the "gatekeepers." The gatekeepers are sought out for the ability to make contact with the spiritual when any tribe member is seeking wisdom, spiritual insight, or transcendent experience. Gatekeepers among the Dagara are the guides between the ordinary and the sacred, honored for an ability to be in touch with and navigate through both the mundane and spiritual worlds.

What is interesting about both of these examples of gay people in other cultures is that they are not only accepted but honored for embodying or penetrating through to apparent opposites: the "two-spirits, one-body" of masculine/feminine and the gatekeeper of the spiritual versus mundane world.

In other words, as embodying or perceiving experiences that are apparently separate and divided—gay people are seen as being able to transcend dualism: masculine/feminine, spiritual/mundane, etc. Poet James Broughton recognizes this spiritual lineage linked to gay people: "It is the secret portrayed in Shiva, Kali, and Hermaphrodites. It is the concept of wholeness, a guide to experiencing the full range of yang and yin. It is the mystery of the total self."

Author and mystic, Andrew Harvey, says "God is both male and female and beyond both. In a sacred world, a gay being would be seen as the living presence of that nondual male-female character of the divine and revered as such." But we live in a modern society cut off from this sacredness. Where can we find the evidence for the link between nonduality and homosexuality in modern life? The spiritual role of gay people in modern American culture has always been vital even if it has been mostly invisible and denied. In a secular society, such as modern America, it is only through the arts (music, theater, painting, sculpture, dance, etc.) that people can seek out and discover the transcendent experience—the experience of glimpsing themselves and the world in a new and different way that refreshes and revitalizes them. Who has not experienced a film, play, song that hasn't touched them so deeply that self was forgotten? Where the separation between you and the music or the audience and the performer dissolved? These experiences exhilarate or deeply move us, sometimes change us all together. Most of us already know that gay people populate the arts field in such great numbers (even if they are often invisible, behind-the-scenes, or closeted) that it is not an understatement to say that without our presence most of these fields would stagnate if not disappear all together.

Even the ongoing wound of AIDS points to nonduality. At this current point of limited medical breakthroughs bringing a reprieve from relentless loss, no one wants to talk about the early days of the epidemic, primarily because it touches that exhausted pain of loss. But what I remember about those days is the remarkable way our loosely knit and primarily hedonistic community pulled together with a compassion and fierceness that still leaves me in awe. Men took care of lovers and friends through the hell of progressive terminal illness with extraordinary tenderness and strength and then, often they did it again and again.

People with HIV and AIDS became warriors creating a collective strength. Even as their bodies became more fragile, they took on the medical industry's apathy and greed and won decisive battles. Love and survival became a focal point for our entire community, no matter what anyone's individual HIV status might be. Everyone was awash in ongoing loss and unbearable grief and yet, instead of hardening and pulling away—there was a softening, opening to the individual and collective broken heart as expressed in the AIDS memorial quilt. During this time the central Buddhist concepts of compassion, non-separateness, and non-duality were as visible and vibrant at 18th and Castro as in any monastery.

Another place where gay people seem to be on the forefront of transcending dualism is in the relationship of body and soul. One of the foundations of Western philosophy, psychology, and religion is a separation of body and soul. Here, the soul contains all transcendent "good" qualities while the body represents all mundane, corruptible, "bad" qualities. In fact, the body and its impulses are a constant threat to the soul's salvation. Again Xin Xin Ming wrote:

> If you would walk the highest Way,
> do not reject the sense domain.
> For as it is, whole and complete,
> this sense world is enlightenment.

Much has been written about the dire consequences of this dualistic splitting of soul and body—it is inherent in individual neurosis and in the collective destruction of the planet. With all that has been examined about the need for healing of this false mind-soul separation, little has been discussed about gay people's role in this healing.

Oscar Wilde said, "Those who see any difference between the soul and the body have neither." Walt Whitman sang to the body electric as a love song to the body as living and breathing embodiment of soul. Rumi spoke of viewing the body as soul work when he said, "Conventional knowledge is death to our souls. Live where you fear to live, destroy your reputation, be notorious." James Broughton gets even more specific saying, "The genitals, the anus, and the perineum are the holy trinity at the root of your torso's experience. The penis is the exposed tip of the heart and the wand of the soul. The perineum animates all the chakras. The anus is the transforming and recycling volcano that fertilizes new growth. The proper activity in the temple is worship. Open your temple to love.''

These gay authors seem to be imagining a world where gay sexuality is recognized as a gift, not a detriment, to greater culture. These poets seem to be pointing toward physicality, not as an impediment but a path toward awakening. And universally they are celebrating a connectiveness of body and soul—how body can energize and illuminate the soul's journey. The Buddha cautioned against becoming too ensnared in attachment and desire to anything, including the body and sexuality. But his middle way equally cautions against aversion or rejection of anything, which includes the experience of the body and sexuality. The body is a practice and as much a vehicle for awakening as the mind. In *Queer Dharma* Volume One, poet Christian Huygen describes the Yabyum practice of Tibet:

> Literally "father/mother," Yabyum refers to any pair of male and female archetype deities and sexual union as visualized by Tibetan Buddhist practitioners. At advanced stages of practice, the yogen visualizes himself or herself arising in the form of both deities together, thereby generating a direct, emphatic and non-conceptual experience of the blissful and passionate union of wisdom and compassion, form and emptiness.

Here we see nonduality embodied in a soul-nourishing physical, sexual form. In a nondualistic world, the Dharma finds you in the most unlikely places. The gay experience in the world brings with it this capacity to embody and express a truth that transcends duality. It is a capacity that can help us heal ourselves of the alienation that comes with growing up in a homophobic, dualistic world. And it perhaps can fill the unrecognized, but missing, role in current western culture of the mediator, the balance, the embodiment and expression of nonduality. In this way, the entire society can be helped to recover a sense of unity, a wholeness that transcends dualism, the "us versus them" animosity, that can ultimately destroy the planet.

Meditation practice, contemplation, and welcoming homosexuality as an integral of the spiritual journey can deepen the recognition of nondualism and encourage the awakening of the good gay heart.

* * *

California poet and author, Trebor, conveys this journey, beautifully, in his poem. He writes:

IMAGINE

Imagine
if you could fold the sky into the earth
the past into the future
hate into love
If you've been up where the rain makes the rivers,
the snow melts,
and stones, like moons, float through the sky
Then you know two men making love
are re-creation
and forming in their humble way
the world whole and one again
Imagine that

Clint Seiter, San Francisco

Finding Sangha: A Gay Perspective

Clint Seiter

I remember a few years ago reading an article about Mother Teresa when she was still alive, describing her efforts to open missions in the United States in response to the poverty that she had seen in this country. When the reporter expressed surprise at this remark, Mother Teresa replied that she was not talking about material poverty, but the poverty of loneliness. In her eyes, the American culture suffered more from that than any other nation on the planet.

Underlying that observation was a serious indictment, and it would benefit Americans to think about the implications of it. A very interesting book, *The Healing Web*, discusses at length the results of studies on the effects of loneliness, how it cripples the body as well as the psyche. It shares clinical evidence that lonely people are less resistant to diseases and die earlier, that they are more inclined to suffer from a wide range of pathologies from tuberculosis to depression, heart disease, schizophrenia and other mental illnesses. Lonely people are more prone to suicide, accidents, and alcoholism.

The core mythology from which the American culture has evolved is filled with images of "the rugged individualist," the independent man (and sometimes woman) struggling against impossible odds and prevailing alone. Whether it's the pioneer who carves a home out of the wilderness, the cowboy who rides off alone into the sunset, or the Horatio Alger who rises "from rags to riches," these stories are the mother's milk that nearly every American child feeds on and is nurtured by. These are myths of hyper-individualism: if the hero perseveres long and hard enough by stint of his own efforts, he *will* get the fame or fortune or love he seeks.

It doesn't seem like much attention is being given to the dark side of these myths, to the *isolation* they seem to embody (and ennoble). Usually, the hero's quest is a profoundly lonely one. Rarely does he accredit his final success to the support or nurturance of a surrounding community of family and friends. The stories are rarely about how a

CLINT SEITER (San Francisco) was born in 1949. He is an active member of Gay Buddhist Fellowship and heads its "Feed the Homeless" project. He makes his living as an environmentalist and is a practicing Buddhist, but not within any particular tradition. His spiritual path is also strongly influenced by the writings of the transpersonal philosopher, Ken Wilber.

community prevails, how a *community* overcomes obstacles, how any victory achieved is through a shared effort.

Of course, the alienation that can be found in the mainstream American culture is heightened many times over in the fringe subcultures, where an additional type of isolation is encountered: the isolation of the disenfranchised. Sociologist Erving Goffman talks about this when he says: "In an important sense there is only one completely unblushing male in America: a young, married, white, urban, northern, heterosexual Protestant father, of college education, fully employed, of good complexion, weight and height, and with a recent record in sports." Those of us who fall outside of this "accepted norm" must struggle against the pressure put upon us to feel somehow that we are "second-class," that we cannot conform to the standards that determine what it takes to be a valued member of our culture. The further we deviate from these standards, the greater the consequent alienation.

Along this line, I was talking to a friend the other day about "connection" and the odds gay men in San Francisco face to make it happen: we live in a country whose culture prides itself on its individuality, we belong to the gender that favors competitiveness over relationship, most of us are transplanted from other parts of the country, with our biological families left behind, and we are members of a minority that is marginalized at best and despised at worst.

Those gay men and lesbians who don't uproot themselves and migrate to the major cities struggle with a different (and, I think, more toxic) form of isolation, where their very physical survival often depends upon a closeted and lonely existence. The murders of Matthew Shepard and Billy Jack Gaither illustrate only too well the consequences that some small-town gays suffer for not maintaining this code of silence well enough. The deaths of these two men were extreme, but the isolation of their lives before they were murdered was probably little different from those of countless other gay men and lesbians in towns and cities throughout this country.

The particular form and flavor discrimination takes varies from one disenfranchised minority to another; every disadvantaged group has its own special problems. For gays and lesbians, I think loneliness is particularly telling. No matter how virulently racist a culture may be, a black child usually is raised by a black family and grows up in a black neighborhood. That neighborhood may be rooted in poverty, but the child at least is surrounded by family, friends, and neighbors who think like he does and who share his minority status. Our gayness alienates us from those most important to us, and upon whom, at least initially, our survival depends, the communities that most heterosexuals take for granted: families, neighbors, churches and synagogues, scouts, schools, social organizations. The media minimizes us, politicians deny us basic civil rights, religious leaders revile us.

However, as toxic as this pariah status can be, it can also afford us certain advantages, if we have the determination and opportunity to explore them. If we are not allowed to be initiated into the communities around us, then neither are we as likely to be straight-jacketed by them. We don't have the luxury of absorbing unquestioningly the values of the mainstream, because many of those values are lethal to us in their homophobia. For those of us who finally realize this (and the tragedy is that some of us never do), we can look around us with open eyes, questioning everything, and create communities that are tailored to our own truths and our own needs. We don't have to accept anything at face value. Joanna Macy puts it well when she says: "So long as we see ourselves as essentially separate, competitive and ego identified beings, it is difficult to respect the validity of our social despair, deriving as it does from interconnectedness. Both our capacity to grieve for others and our power to cope with this grief spring from the great matrix of relationships in which we take our being."

What I'm talking about is essentially a spiritual journey as represented through sangha. Like all spiritual journeys, this would involve "the heavy questions": How can we as gay men find meaning and purpose in life? How can we connect in love with others? How can we feel whole and integrated within ourselves? How can we move away from pettiness and negativity and shame and into a greater intimacy with everything around us? These questions are valid for everyone, but gay men and lesbians must ask them within the context of their own unique situation in this culture. Those who follow a Buddhist path still must recast the Dharma in terms that are pertinent to the lives of gay men and lesbians. It can be an exciting opportunity, with both Buddhism and the gay culture benefitting from this interaction. Gay men and lesbians can be exposed to the wisdom of the Dharma and incorporate it into their lives accordingly. But, just as importantly, gay men and lesbians can leave their own special imprint on the Buddhist Dharma as it adapts to American culture. We can have a place at the spiritual table where we can share our unique perspectives with other Buddhists and exert our own influence on the great experiment that American Buddhism is today.

This is the special role that a sangha can serve. As one of the three jewels of Buddhism, along with Buddha and the Dharma, Sangha is essential in the individual's quest toward integration and spiritual evolution. Those of us who wish to take on this quest need to address the issue of sangha: where can the sangha be found that most suits the needs of the particular individual? what are the qualities of such a sangha? what is the individual's role within a sangha? what is the difference between a healthy and an unhealthy sangha? in what ways does a sangha aid in its members' spiritual development? Finally, for gay men, we need to find sanghas that affirm our gayness, and let us define ourselves in a spirituality that also embraces with joy our sexuality.

There is a wonderful passage in Jack Kornfield's *A Path with Heart* describing his vision of the spirit of sangha: "There is an immense joy that arises in a community when together we give of ourselves. To give of our own spirit, to serve, is a wonderful and fulfilling part of joining a spiritual community. This giving and receiving heart, this honoring of the sacred, creates the spirit of sangha or satsang that characterizes those who are gathered together in the name of that which is holy. The community is created, not when people come together in the name of religion, but when they come together bringing honesty, respect, and kindness to support an awakening of the sacred. This sense of spiritual community is a wondrous part of what heals and transforms us on our path."

My own search for a spiritual community has cut a broad swath: various Christian sects, New Age groups, men's movement gatherings, ecopaganism, mainstream Buddhist groups, and my current sangha of choice for the past eight years: the Gay Buddhist Fellowship (GBF). All of these communities have given me different things to value. Even those that have ultimately disappointed and frustrated me have at least shown me by process of elimination areas in which to redirect my search. I don't claim to be an authority in the subject of what makes for a successful sangha, but I have made some observations based upon my own search that might prove of some value. With that hope, I'd like to propose the following criteria, by no means an exhaustive list, for evaluating whether or not a sangha is a right fit for the spiritual seeker.

—A similarity of vision

There must be a sense within a community that its members share similar values and goals. This is not a call for a "cookie-cutter" mentality within a sangha. However, a community whose members have radically different visions about what directions it should follow will be hard put to avoid being dragged down into bickering and conflict. I've been involved in communities of well-meaning people that have been devastated by this. So much energy is wasted when there are internal struggles to define the community in different ways, rather than in moving in unison towards a common goal. As Lama Surya Das says in *Awakening the Buddha Within*: "Taking refuge in the Sangha represents our commitment to living harmoniously with others and working to bring all sentient beings further along on the path to enlightenment."

—*The need for challenge*

Conversely, a sangha can be too much in agreement. If the members of a sangha don't at regular intervals challenge each other, questioning and reassessing the directions the sangha is taking, then the sangha runs a risk of sinking into complacency, even "culthood." Like individuals, a sangha can become too comfortable with comfort. A sangha must be open to challenge, its vision must be dusted off and examined regularly to see that it still applies to the needs of the sangha as they exist in the moment, and if the sangha's present actions reflect its original vision. In particular, the sangha must avoid clinging to empty rites and rituals. Lama Surya Das states: "Nothing in pure Buddhism encourages blind faith or cultlike environments. People cling to tired dogma all the time, but that is not the Dharma. The Buddha wisely challenged his followers to open their minds and think for themselves, rather than believing in anything just because it had been said by authorities, including himself, or written down in books." The sangha needs to steer a middle course between excessive divisiveness and an excessive need for uniformity.

—*Honesty*

A successful sangha cannot operate on a hidden agenda. If the members, particularly the sangha leaders, espouse one set of beliefs but operate on another, the sangha cannot survive. There should be room to listen to and weigh criticism levied at it without responding in an attack mode. Without the opportunity presented for a clear voice to always demand an honest accounting of oneself, a community can slip into dysfunction and ignorance. As Kornfield states in *A Path with Heart*: "To tell the truth in a community is to make the community itself conscious. In these situations, it becomes a great practice to name the demons and to speak out loud with both compassion and clarity. We must be willing to ask our community, 'How are we lost, attached, and addicted, and how are we benefitting, awakening, and opening?' Speaking openly and honestly with the well-being of the community in our heart is extraordinarily beneficial. Naming the demons with honesty and kindness has the power to dispel illusion.''

—Participation

Every spiritual community, no matter how simple, requires some level of organization, some effort involving planning, time, forethought, and work. This may not always be apparent to sangha members who enjoy the benefits of the community without working behind the scenes. Questions ranging from what the purpose and goals of the sangha are to such basics as the logistics of where and when to meet, require people devoting their energies and time (and sometimes money). Are these tasks distributed fairly among the members of the sangha, or does it seem that a handful of people always wind up taking on most of the chores? Who is benefitting from the sangha and who is responsible for the sangha's survival?

The saying ''you get what you give'' is never more apt than in a spiritual community. For a number of years I meditated regularly at Green Gulch Farm, a Zen Buddhist community about a half hour north of San Francisco. After the Sunday meditation and dharma talk, there was a social period where the practitioners would meet and talk over tea and freshly baked muffins. Typically, I would eat the muffin with not that much attention directed towards it. Some time later I volunteered to work on ''the muffin crew,'' and I did so for over six years. This involved getting up at five in the morning every Sunday, driving to the Green Gulch Farm, and working with others to bake sixteen dozen muffins. Now, when I ate my muffin later in the morning, I knew what went into it: the picking of the recipe, the measuring and blending together of the ingredients, the mad scramble the crew would sometimes go through to substitute a key missing ingredient, the crisis when a batch of muffins was burnt or stuck to the pans, the glow we felt when a tricky new recipe came out well. I enjoyed my muffins immeasurably more after I volunteered to work on the crew, because I had a heightened awareness of just what went into their creation, all the human interactions and efforts that were needed to get the muffins onto the platter so that I could eat one after meditation. It was a small but effective dharma lesson for me: the awareness we can achieve through direct participation in events rather than just enjoying the aftermath. A sangha's ability to survive and remain relevant hinges on the willingness of its members to share the responsibilities involved in the running of the sangha, and each member's own growth quickens with the level of his or her participation.

—*Balance*

I believe that a successful sangha provides a balance of the inner work found in contemplation, meditation, and study of the Dharma, and the outer work of engaged Buddhism, between the solitude of the individual and the interaction of the sangha's members. Both sides are necessary. Action without the foundation of inner work can be misdirected and ill-advised. Exclusive withdrawal inside without applying the Dharma to the world outside can take on overtones of self-absorption. *Balance* is an essential concept in Buddhism, the play of opposites, the transcendence of duality. It has been a wonderful opportunity for me to experience this in my sangha of choice, San Francisco's Gay Buddhist Fellowship (GBF). Meditation is a cornerstone of GBF: the sangha offers opportunities for its members to meditate regularly on different days of the week, as well as sponsoring retreats for more intensive practice. Yet the sangha is also active in projects of engaged Buddhism: once a month members of GBF get together and prepare a dinner for a local shelter for homeless families. The GBF volunteers plan the menus, buy the food, do the cooking and baking in the shelter kitchen, serve the residents, and then sit down and share the meals with them. These dinner preparations are full of joyous energy and have provided a means for members of the GBF sangha to develop a closeness with one another that would not have been possible with the inward direction of meditation practice alone.

—*Compassion*

It's been my observation that most gay men have suffered terribly from the harsh judgments we encounter on a daily basis in the world at large. Even the healthiest and strongest of us carry the scars from wounds inflicted on us when we were too young to defend ourselves. What is even sadder is how often we perpetuate this legacy within our own community, creating nearly impossible standards (beauty, youth, material possessions) by which to judge and exclude other gay men, to belittle and dismiss them. The challenge we face is finding ways of undoing this legacy we've inherited from a homophobic main culture instead of assuming the role of tormentor in absentia for the bullies and bigots that may no longer be in our immediate presence. Again, in *Awakening the Buddha Within*, Lama Surya Das states: "The Sangha represents the positive energy and support we all need. Sangha friends can help you get through the hard patches of your path, when you feel discouraged and depleted." A sangha should be a haven for us, a place where we can draw strength from the love and support of others as we deal with the challenges that life directs our way.

However, acting in compassion does *not* mean condoning actions that are self-destructive or that may ultimately threaten the survival of the sangha itself (Chogyam Trumpa Rinpoche calls this kind of condoning "idiot compassion"). Sangha members who are acting out destructively, whether it be hurtful actions or speech, inappropriate sexual behavior, substance addiction, dishonesty, to mention a few ways, need to be confronted and guided into taking responsibility for their actions.

An essential question a person can ask himself or herself is what is the "feel" of the sangha. In *A Path with Heart*, Kornfield provides a checklist of sorts that a member can apply to his or her sangha in trying to determine its overall health: "In the spiritual community, are you asked to violate your own sense of ethical conduct or integrity? Is there a dual standard for the community versus the guru and a few people around him? Are there secrets, rumors of difficulty? Do key members misuse sexuality, money, or power? Is the practice humorless? Does the community have a heaviness and an antilife feeling about it? Is there something powerful going on that may not really be loving? Is there more focus on the institution and membership than on practices that lead to liberation? Is there a sense of intolerance? When you look at the oldest and most senior students, are they happy and mature? Look to see if the community is based on sectarianism or separation or has a fundamentalist quality to it. The vehemence with which students proclaim the 'one true way' is usually a sign of the unacknowledged insecurity there is of the great unconscious or hidden fear or doubt that underlies it."

As a gay man, I would add to this list of questions: Is the sangha gay-friendly? Has the guru or teacher come out with statements supportive of homosexuality? Are there gay members within the sangha? If so, are they treated as equals with the other members? Can sangha members inquire openly and without shame about how to apply the dharma skillfully to their sexuality? Does the teacher provide answers that are well thought out and relative to the individual's needs and circumstances, or are they just rote responses?

—Shared experiences

I have been involved in various sanghas filled with good people who were heterosexual and essentially clueless as to what it meant to be gay. I participated in those sanghas operating on the assumption that our basic humanity would transcend such differences as sexual orientation. On one level, I still believe that's possible, though frankly without as much conviction as I had before. While I like to think that my participation in these sanghas "humanized" the issue of homosexuality to the members, and maybe challenged misconceptions they carried, after a while being the token gay wore thin. As people talked about their wives or husbands, and children, and the related spiritual issues they were struggling with, I sometimes sensed their uneasiness when I tried to include my own experiences as a gay man in the discussions. I was always treated politely, but in more cases than I like to remember, no more than that.

There is much to be said about the closeness that shared experiences can bring. I have found that particularly in my current involvement in GBF. Like most groups, the personalities (and backgrounds) of the GBF members vary widely, but all of us share the common experience of being gay men in this culture, and that is a powerful emotional glue. When I talk about the struggles I have integrating my sexuality with my spiritual practice, I'm no longer met with embarrassed silences and pained expressions, but instead with an openness and recognition (and often humor) that is truly healing.

Once again, of course, the issue of balance comes into play in this matter: in this case the balance between identity and differences. I find it a wonderful thing to meditate, work and socialize in GBF with other gay men who are Buddhist. This gives me a sense of belonging and authenticity to a degree that I haven't achieved in any other sangha I've been involved with. However, I also believe that there's a hidden danger in seeking out one's own kind that we in GBF need to be aware of: the risk of insularity. The overwhelming majority of members in GBF are middle-class white men. Men from other cultures and races are welcome, but for whatever reasons (reasons, I believe, that go well beyond GBF, and include the observation that Buddhism in America is itself primarily a white middle-class phenomenon), the racial ratios in GBF have remained the same over the years. Another, recurring issue in GBF is the exclusion of women as members. There are lesbian Buddhist sanghas in the Bay Area, sanghas that GBF has ties to, but periodically the question comes up within GBF concerning what's gained and what's lost by being a sangha of men alone.

In conclusion, I believe that our fiercely individualistic, often homo-phobic culture makes it particularly necessary for gay men and lesbians to find and grow into a healthy, supportive spiritual sangha. As the transpersonal philosopher Ken Wilber says: "We are all members of the Community of Spirit. All sentient beings contain Buddha-nature—contain depth, consciousness, intrinsic value, Spirit—and thus we are all members of the council of all beings, the mystical church, the ulti-mate We." We need sangha to nurture us, affirm our humanity, be a mirror unto us and a guide for us to deeper truths and wisdoms. It's a worthy goal to find a sangha that feels right for us in our quest for wholeness, connection and the recognition of the Buddha nature that is in all of us.

San Francisco's Gay Buddhist Fellowship can be accessed online at: http://www.gaybuddhist.org/Main.html

---

Seated Buddha, bronze, Java, Indonesia, 9th cent. C.E.
Gift of the LEF Foundation
Courtesy: Asian Art Museum of San Francisco, Avery Brundage Collection, 1988.21

The Buddha is seated with legs in European pose, like the famous image from Candi Mendut (dating to 800) in Central Java. Also like the Mendut sculpture, his hands are in *dharmachakra* mudra. This iconography is common in Central Javanese Buddhas. The bodhisattvas Avalokiteshvara and Vajrapani, accompany-ing the Candi Mendut Buddha, suggest an identification of this iconographic form of the Buddha as Vairochana—an important figure in ninth-century Javanese Buddhism.

Stylistically, this piece relates to other ninth-century Javanese sculptures. The pleasing proportions of the body, the drapery rippling between the legs, and the treatment of the base and aureole support a ninth-century date. The stippling found on both the throne back and the lotus footrest are reminiscent of this motif on both the clothing and thrones of other Central Javanese bronzes.

The portability of these bronzes makes it difficult to associate them with specific regions, while the lack of inscriptions leaves us with little hope of associating works with patrons. We do know that it was common throughout the Buddhist world for both lay and religious worshipers to commission images. Through the commission of a sculpture, temple, votive tablet, or painting, people acquired religious merit for themselves and their families.—N.H.

from *Looking at Patronage: Recent Acquisitions of Asian Art*,
Asian Art Museum Publications [San Francisco], 1989, p. 40

Jim Wilson, California

Practicing Buddhism As a Gay Man

Jim Wilson

As Buddhism takes root in the west it has met with and adapted to the interests of the participants in this new culture. This repeats the pattern of the spread of Buddhism to new cultures that Buddhism has exhibited throughout its history. One of the adaptations currently in progress is the merging of cultural analyses with Buddhist analyses of the human condition. For a number of years now there have existed Buddhist Women's groups that have brought a feminist analysis to Buddhism and have in turn altered their own feminist analysis in the light of the Buddhist tradition. Black participants in western Buddhism, for example Bell Hooks, have engaged in a similar merging of understandings from their own historical perspective.

There has also arisen on the fringes of the western Buddhist community gay and lesbian Buddhist groups. In what follows I will narrowly focus on my understanding of what it means to practice Buddhism in the west as a gay man, based on my own experience and my involvement, over the past ten years, with one of the gay Buddhist groups, the Gay Buddhist Fellowship, which meets regularly in San Francisco. While focusing on this I will also make use of observations from other sources, particularly from the above mentioned western feminist analysis/synthesis of Buddhism.

From a certain perspective the question of what it means to practice Buddhism as a gay man makes no sense. The question lacks coherence because the teaching of the Buddha is rooted in observations that apply universally to all people; indeed they apply to all sentient beings in all universes. For example, the first noble truth of the Buddha states that all people are suffering, that all people experience suffering, anxiety, dread and that life is laced with that range of experiences. This condition of suffering is experienced by all people, the Buddha would assert, because of a habit of mind, the habit of clinging and craving. Because the suffering to which the Buddha referred to arises due to a habit of mind, this suffering does not depend upon the particulars of an individual's history. Rather, this suffering to which the Buddha

JIM WILSON (Sonoma, CA) was born in Chicago, 1949. He studied Zen Buddhism in the Chogye, Suke and Soto traditions and is the former abbot of the Chogye Zen Center in New York City. He teaches in the Sonoma county area and has been active in San Francisco's Gay Buddhist Fellowship for ten years.

referred, happens, is caused by, the craving and clinging mind. The mind which causes suffering is the same mind for all people.

The universality of this state of mind which gives rise to suffering is illustrated in countless stories in the Buddhist canon. One of the most famous is the story of Kisagotami. Kisagotami wanted to have a child more than anything. But many years passed and she and her husband remained childless. Finally, she gave birth to a son and she felt over-joyed. Sadly, her son lived only a little over a year and then died. Kisagotami was bereft, no one could console her. She refused to believe that her son had actually died and sought some kind of medicine or magic which would revive her son. One day she heard that the Buddha had come to a nearby town, perhaps he would know how to revive her son. Presenting the corpse of her son to the Buddha, she begged the Buddha for some medicine which would revive her son. The Buddha said that he could easily revive her son provided that Kisagotami bring him the key ingredient: some mustard seeds from a home where no one had died. Elated, Kisagotami went into the village looking for the mustard seed. She went from house to house and all of them had mustard seeds; but then she would ask them if anyone in their house had died. Of course, they would say. Kisagotami would then go to the next house and find out the same truth. Finally, it dawned on her that all people die, that what she was experiencing was not unique. She let go of her son, buried him, and eventually became a famous nun in the Buddha's order.

This story beautifully illustrates the process whereby we can put an end to suffering. For this is the other side of the Buddha's teaching; that even though human life is laced with suffering, anxiety, dread and despair, it is possible to bring an end to this suffering. Since suffering arises due to clinging and craving, the antidote to suffering is to cease clinging and craving. We cease to cling when we comprehend the universality of our situation. Notice that Kisagotami thought of her suffering as unique, as a private possession. She literally clung to her suffering, or rather her suffering was her clinging to her situation. When she realized the universality of impermanence, she no longer thought of her situation as a personal situation, something that had happened specifically to her and no one else. This allowed Kisagotami to let go, to cease to cling and to attain a measure of serenity and peace. Liber-ation means, at least in part, shifting our awareness from our own per-sonal situation to that which is universal, applies to all people, to all sentient existence.

So from the perspective of the Buddha's analysis of the human sit-uation and condition, the question of how this analysis applies to a particular group of people does not arise. It does not arise because the analysis applies unreservedly to all people. The suffering experienced by a gay man does not differ from the suffering of anyone else. The antidotes to suffering, the practices that bring about a cessation of suffering, also apply to all people. The Buddhist practices of meditation, precepts and ethics, right livelihood, etc., all designed to lead one to a state free from suffering, anxiety and dread, apply to all people. Precisely this universality of practice is what has made Buddhism such an attractive religion to so many for so many centuries. Just as people in the past have engaged in practices which will bring an end to suffering and sorrow, I too can engage in these practices and walk this path which leads to the cessation of suffering; not only for me, but for all sentient existence.

It might seem at first that this is the end of the discussion. However, the situation in Buddhism is more complex than at first it might appear. Because, although the analysis of the human condition, that all of us experience suffering, applies universally, and although the practices which grant access to the cessation of suffering apply universally, manifestation of the state of liberation does not apply universally. From very early in the history of Buddhism there arose the idea that liberation, nirvana, was available only to certain human practitioners. In this sense, Buddhism privileged certain practitioners above others. Because Buddhism takes reincarnation for granted and as a basic truth, the privileging of certain kinds of people over others was not understood as absolute. Rather, in a Buddhist context, the privilege was asserted in the following manner; some people could achieve liberation in this life, while others would have to wait to achieve liberation in subsequent lifetimes. This idea played itself out in a two-fold division of the Buddhist community into lay versus monastic and male versus female practitioners. From this perspective, the male monastic was the only person privileged to be able to attain liberation in this life. From the relevant texts, male monastic in this context means heterosexual male monastic.

It is important at once to state that this idea seems to have been controversial within Buddhism from the start. The assertion of privileged access to liberation for a particular group of people, based on their sexuality and lifestyle, did not go unchallenged. Nevertheless, this idea of privileged access did have a strong and widespread influence. Strong enough so that those Buddhist teachers who disagreed with this idea would have to make explicit statements distancing themselves from this conception.

For gay men this idea of privileged access to enlightenment and/or liberation means that, depending on how a particular school of Buddhism responds to this issue, a gay man may not be perceived as falling within this privileged class. The issue here is subtle and may not be immediately apparent to a gay man beginning to practice Buddhism. This happens because, once again, the analysis of the human condition from which Buddhism starts is considered equally applicable to all people, regardless of their background, nationality, race, or orientation. Similarly, the practices constituting the core of Buddhism, which range from worship to meditation to study, remain accessible to all people. It is only in terms of realization, liberation, and enlightenment, the complete manifesting of the teaching, that the idea of a privileged status for certain people based on their sexuality and lifestyle comes into play. Because of this, the effects of this privileging may seem remote, or only theoretical, but they do have effects.

Take the first division, that between monastic and lay practitioners. It is widely understood and believed in Buddhism that the monastic vocation is necessary for realization/enlightenment. From this perspective, the monastic vocation is privileged over the lay life. The monastic vocation grants access to enlightenment and nirvana in a way that the lay life does not. What is the basis for this belief? Simply put, the monastic life is seen as granting the time and leisure necessary for the serious pursuit of such disciplines as study and meditation. The lay life, in contrast, is understood as too busy and too fragmented for that kind of sustained pursuit of Buddhist practice. In its extreme form the purpose of lay life in Buddhism is reduced to supporting the monastics in the hope that such activity will allow them to attain an auspicious rebirth and that in some future life they may then become a monastic and in that future life enter into the full practice of the Buddha's teaching.

This privileging of the monk's status seems to have been controversial from a very early period in Buddhism. Some historians suggest that the issue of the status of lay people was a cause for early schisms in the Buddhist community. In addition, there exist texts in the Buddhist canon which directly contradict and critique the idea of monastic privilege. Particularly relevant here is the *Vimalakirti Sutra*.

Vimalakirti was a lay follower of the Buddha. The Sutra opens with the Buddha requesting that his followers go and visit Vimalakirti because the Buddha has heard that Vimalakirti is sick, and the Buddha wishes to send his regards. One by one the Buddha's disciples, all male monastics, decline the Buddha's request. One by one they explain to the Buddha that they do not wish to visit Vimalakirti because the last time they encountered Vimalakirti he embarrassed them by correcting their understanding of the Buddha's teaching. The Buddha then asks various Bodhisattvas to visit Vimalakirti, and the Buddha receives the same kind of reply from them. Until finally the Bodhisattva Manjushri agrees to visit Vimalakirti. The rest of the Sutra is devoted to subtle explanations of the Buddha's teaching by Vimalakirti.

The polemical import is clear; Vimalakirti, a lay person, surpasses in understanding and in realization all the other disciples of the Buddha and even surpasses the understanding of celestial manifestations such as Bodhisattvas. Other Sutras also have importance in this arena, such as *The Lion's Roar of Queen Shrimala*, wherein a princess exhibits profound, even unsurpassed, comprehension of the Buddha's teaching.

What lies behind this division within Buddhism? I would suggest that behind the controversy over the status of lay people lie different understandings of the meaning of enlightenment, or more precisely, different understandings of how enlightenment happens. I would like to suggest two models of enlightenment to help clarify this issue: the purification model and the awakening model. The first model, the purification model, understands the process of enlightenment, or the path to enlightenment, as a process of purification. One of the central manuals of monastic practice is, in fact, called *The Path of Purification* by Buddhaghosha. The basic strategy in this view is to gradually purify one's mind, purify one's body, purify one's consciousness, purify one's desires, etc. The practices are seen as cooling the fire of desire and clinging. Gradually in this context means over many lifetimes, even over many eons. When purification is complete, liberation emerges and one enters nirvana. An operative metaphor for this process is a pond. When the water of a pond is agitated the water becomes cloudy with mud and debris. As the agitation subsides the mud settles, the water gradually becomes clear. After a long time the water becomes so clear you hardly notice its presence.

The second model, the awakening model, views the process of attaining enlightenment differently. From this perspective the basic obstacle to enlightenment is understood as ignorance, ignorance of our actual situation. We cling to things because we do not understand impermanence. We desire things because we do not understand that they will not bring us happiness. How do we overcome this ignorance? By waking up. From this perspective the purpose of Buddhist practice is to jar us out of our habits of clinging so that we can awaken to existence in its actuality. In this sense, clinging is a kind of sleep. Think of lying in bed and dreaming. While dreaming we do not realize the actuality of our situation. When we wake from our dream we understand that actually we are lying in a bed in a room in a town. Or refer back to the story of Kisagotami. She did not understand that what had happened to her happens to all people. All people at some time in their lives experience separation from those they love; this is a function of impermanence. When Kisagotami awoke from her ignorance, when she realized the universality of her condition, she was able to let go, to cease to cling.

Both of these models are operative in Buddhism from the earliest times down to the present day (there also exist other models, but for the purpose of simplicity I won't discuss them here). The purification model serves to privilege monasticism while the awakening model grants access to ultimacy to lay people as well as monastics. Recall that the Buddha understood that the root of suffering lay in the craving and clinging states of mind; the purification model tends to focus on craving while the awakening model tends to focus on clinging.

The purification model presents several obstacles to gay men and to the extent that a particular school operates from the assumptions of this model, a gay male practitioner will sooner or later have to deal with them. The purification model comprehends monasticism as a means for extinguishing craving and particularly extinguishing desire. The Buddhist monastic institution is celibate and unisexual. Interaction between monks and nuns is carefully proscribed by numerous rules as well as interaction between a monastic and lay people of the opposite sex. The purpose of all these regulations is to create an environment that does not stimulate sexual desire (what a contrast to contemporary culture!). Because craving is understood as the obstacle to enlightenment, the removal of the causes of sexual stimulation follows logically.

Consider, however, the gay man who wishes to follow this monastic path of purification. The sexually exclusive monastic community not only does not remove the cause of sexual craving, but actually places the gay man in a sexually stimulating environment. The monastic community assumes heterosexual desire and the structure of that community emerges from that assumption. The irony here is that a gay man who wishes to follow the path of purification may actually find in lay life a context more conducive to the reduction of sexual craving than the unisexual monastic community.

Lest the reader think this a completely abstract consideration, I wish to relate the story of a gay male Buddhist I know who I will refer to as Paul. Paul studied Buddhism in a Mahayana tradition for about five years and was deeply devoted to his teacher and the community of fellow practitioners. Paul is an openly gay man and this seemed to have no impact on either his teacher or those he associated with. Paul's teacher encouraged his students to consider the monastic vocation, explaining that the monastic vocation created the only firm foundation for liberation. Paul considered this vocation for a long time and finally decided he wanted to become a monk. He informed his teacher. Paul's teacher rejected Paul's vocation, explaining to Paul that, because of Paul's gayness, the teacher could not accept him into the monastic community. Paul was deeply shocked and told his teacher that he was ready to make a commitment to celibacy, as required of Buddhist monks. That did not sway Paul's teacher who explained to Paul, that for Paul, the monastic community would not be conducive to extinguishing desire. One of the ironies in this story is that if Paul had kept his sexual identity hidden, he probably would have been allowed to become a monk. It was precisely Paul's honesty which created the barrier to accessing the monastic vocation (I will have more to say about the importance of honesty).

In an odd way I can actually sympathize with Paul's teacher. On the other hand, one could hope for a more creative response to the situation. For example, a more hermit like style of living might be appropriate for a gay male monastic, or perhaps gay male monastics might find a home among Buddhist nuns. But such creative solutions are not part of the Buddhist tradition and those Buddhist teachers raised within that tradition would find it difficult to think along these lines.

But there exists another, more central, obstacle for a gay man wishing to engage in the path of purification. It is the common gay male experience that acting on his desire represents a profoundly liberative experience. This directly clashes with the basis for the monastic community, which exists to extinguish desire through the process of purification. Gay men have a commonly shared experience of attempting to ignore and/or repress their sexual desire and a deep understanding of how this negatively affects their lives. For many gay men, the acceptance of desire, and the consequent acting upon that desire, constitutes a pivotal and positive experience in their lives.

To the extent that a Buddhist teaching has absorbed the purification model of liberation, and to the extent that a Buddhist teaching expresses that purification model, a gay man will find such a teaching often in conflict with his own experience. How to reconcile the teaching with his own experience then becomes a central task.

The reconciliation can occur within the context of the awakening model of the path to enlightenment. Just as Kisagotami did not have to get a divorce or become a nun in order to gain insight into the cause of her suffering, so also awakening to the realm of reality does not depend upon the elimination of desire. Rather, it depends upon seeing through the idea of the solidity of desire, the idea that anything, that any desire, has a substantial or abiding nature.

Desires occur within the human psycho-physical organism just as thoughts appear in the mind, just as clouds appear in the sky. Just as clouds do not disturb the sky, so also desires do not disturb our true nature. Rather, clinging to our desires and trying to turn them into something solid and substantial gives rise to suffering. Desire in and of itself is neither good nor bad. For example, the desire to attain liberation, the desire to live a more compassionate life, the desire to save all sentient existence from suffering, the passionate desire to comprehend transcendent wisdom; all of these desires guide us on the path and propel us toward liberation and nirvana. So the problem is not desire in and of itself, rather it is how we use the energy generated by desire; whether we use desire to generate suffering for ourselves and others, or whether we use that energy to propel us along the path to ultimate and unsurpassed liberation. It is precisely the insight into the liberative potential of desire which a gay man can use to comprehend the possibility of transforming desire into liberation and attaining the unsurpassed enlightenment for the benefit of all sentient existence.

In addition to the division between lay and monastic manifestations of Buddhism which have often privileged male and heterosexual monastics, there exists a division in many traditions of Buddhism based on sex. Typically, this has expressed itself by denigrating women and privileging (heterosexual) males. This expression usually manifests as caustic comments about the impurity of women and the impossibility of women attaining full enlightenment.

Every morning I read a Sutra as part of my practice and devotion. The Buddhist Sutras are sublime and very often I have found the wisdom and poetry of the Sutras nourishment for my life. Sometimes, however, I will run into a passage which expresses a kind of cantankerous narrowness, a cramped spirit. Almost always this has to do with denigrating women. Sometimes this is just a passing comment, such as when a Sutra will describe the beauties of a pure land and then casually add that in this pure land there are no women, implying that the presence of women would make a pure land impure.

This hostile view towards women expresses itself in a theory often referred to in Buddhist texts called "The 32 Marks of Enlightenment." The 32 marks refer to physical features of an enlightened person, implying that one can spot an enlightened person by their physical appearance. For example, the reason statues of the Buddha, or of other enlightened Buddhist personages, have very long earlobes is that one of the 32 marks of enlightenment is having long earlobes. Some of these 32 marks refer to specifically male anatomical features, thus implying the necessity of a male body in order to manifest complete enlightenment. This is probably the extreme to which Buddhist theory extends male privilege.

As in the division between the monastic and lay communities, so also there exist texts that counter this strong tendency to privilege male status in Buddhism. Evidently, as in the controversy over the status of lay people, the status of women within the Buddhist community proved controversial from a very early time. The Perfection of Wisdom Sutras, for example, specifically reject the idea of the presence of physical marks indicating enlightenment. (Incidentally, there exists a truly playful antidote to this idea in the Taoist text, *Chuang Tzu*. In this Taoist work, the author Chuang Tzu has a host of fables in which grotesquely deformed people, or people completely missing limbs of various sorts, nevertheless display their vast comprehension of the Tao. Clearly, Chuang Tzu does not consider physical appearance as in any way relevant to spiritual realization.)

It is not surprising that the Perfection of Wisdom Sutras would take this stance toward such a doctrine as the 32 marks. For the personification of the Perfection of Wisdom is a Bodhisattva by the name of Prajna Paramita and this Bodhisattva is female. Not only is the Perfection of Wisdom iconographically displayed as female, but also she is explicitly referred to in the Perfection of Wisdom Sutras as the "Mother of all Buddhas." This expression means that transcendental wisdom gives birth to all the fully realized and awakened Buddhas.

The traditions of Buddhism based on the Sutras written in Pali do not accept the Perfection of Wisdom Sutras as part of their corpus. But even within the Pali Sutras there exist examples of the fact that women can achieve supreme enlightenment as females. In the Middle Length Discourses, for example, there is recorded a discourse by the nun Dhammadinna who beautifully summarizes all the central teachings of the Buddha. Interestingly enough, she is shown teaching a lay male disciple. At the end of this Sutra the Buddha briefly comments on the discourse, stating that he completely approves of it and that Dhammadinna understands his teaching fully.

In addition, one of the central Sutras for the practice of Metta (Loving Kindness) and Karuna (Compassion) is the Metta Sutra. In this Sutra the Buddha instructs his disciples to develop a mind like that of a woman who cares for her only child, and that one should develop this mind so that one can have that same mind for all people, and for all of sentient existence. In other words, we should strive to treat all people as if they were our only child and as if we were their mother, whether we are male or female. The Sutra explicitly states that this practice will lead us to the ultimate peace of nirvana. In other words, the development of a specifically feminine wisdom, by both men and women, is the royal road to enlightenment.

Finally, there exist female images of enlightenment, Bodhisattvas, who play a very prominent role in Buddhist cultures. In the Chinese cultural area the Bodhisattva Kwan Yin is by far the most widely worshipped and loved of all Buddhist manifestations. She has an interesting history; originally she came to China as Avalokiteshvara, a male Bodhisattva. Over a period of about 300 years she was transformed into a female Bodhisattva. Today she is unmistakably female. (June Campbell, in her book *Traveler in Space* suggests that originally Avalokiteshvara was female and that under the male dominated Buddhist political structure of India and Tibet she was changed to male. This would suggest that the Chinese preserved the original female form of Avalokiteshvara, and that the male manifestation of Avalokiteshvara was a kind of emanation of the female form. In either case, Avalokiteshvara/Kwan Yin may be the first trans-sexual deity.)

In the Tibetan cultural sphere there exists the Bodhisattva Tara who plays a prominent role in Tibetan Buddhism. Tara has vowed to always manifest in a female form and to achieve ultimate enlightenment in a female body. So with Tara we come full circle, in direct contrast to the doctrine of the 32 marks, Tara assumes the mission of enlightenment in a female form.

Western feminist analysis of Buddhism has pointed out that in spite of these positive female presences within the Buddhist tradition, the tendency has been overwhelmingly to privilege males. This tendency has been so strong that many Buddhist women have, down through the centuries, internalized the idea that a woman can not become enlightened, that she will have to take rebirth in a male body in order to become enlightened. One can observe this in a touching dialogue of Zen Master Bankei who responds to the question of whether or not women can become enlightened by declaring in most emphatic terms that there does not exist any difference between the Buddha Nature of a man or a woman. But it is the women who ask Bankei this question, and it is the women Bankei has to convince.

Once again we can perceive in this division the two models of awakening referred to above as operating to produce this basic difference within the Buddhist tradition. The purification model lends itself to the materialist interpretation which eventually manifests in the idea that a Buddha will possess certain specific and observable physical characteristics. The awakening model of enlightenment does not depend for its efficacy on such an interpretation, and in fact specifically denies any such causal connection.

It may seem at first that the male privilege so prominent in Buddhism would work in favor of gay men, who, after all are males. I would argue against this interpretation, however. Part of the understanding of male privilege is that all Buddhas have been heterosexual males. The male body of a Buddha is a male heterosexual. To emphasize this point, consider that all the biographies of the Buddhas of past eras follow the pattern of the Buddha, Shakyamuni Buddha, of our own time. All of them get married to a woman early in their life before leaving the home life and eventually becoming enlightened. In no case that I have read does there exist a Buddha-to-be who falls in love with another man.

Western feminist analysis of Buddhism is complex and this is not the place to touch on all the issues raised. To simplify matters, I think of feminist analysis of Buddhism as falling into three broad categories: Image, Story and Body.

In terms of image, feminist analysis points out that though there exist female images of enlightenment in such figures as Tara and Kwan Yin, there exist very few images of enlightened Buddhist female teachers. All of the female manifestations are celestial. One has to do a good deal of searching to find material and images of female teachers. Feminism pays attention to image because of its understanding that our concepts are grounded in and emerge from an image layer of consciousness and that this image layer of consciousness has great power to shape our conceptual understanding and in turn shape our beliefs in what is possible. To take an ordinary example, when hearing the word "Doctor" almost everyone thinks of a male doctor. This is a very strong image in our culture's consciousness. To take a more abstract example, if I were to paint a picture of an eagle in flight and then title the picture "Freedom" I would not have to explain the picture to people because such an image fits in with our culture's image of that concept. If, however, I painted a picture of a frog on a rock in a pond and titled it "Freedom," such a picture would not resonate with most people. I suspect that many people would want me to explain what I meant. The image context of freedom, generally speaking, does not include a frog on a rock. Thus the image context we have of a concept constricts our ability to present alternate manifestations of the same reality or truth.

Understanding this we can comprehend that in the case of gay men, the situation is more troublesome than that of women in general. For though women can refer to celestial female images of enlightenment, and also to an occasional female teaching presence, the explicit depiction of a gay male presence in a Buddhist context simply does not exist. To make this clear we should turn to those schools of Buddhism which explicitly display sexuality, to Buddhist tantra. In the tantric schools of Buddhism the explicit depiction of sexual embrace is meant to symbolize the union of wisdom and compassion. Such a union is felt as ecstatic and the ecstasy such a union produces is most clearly symbolized by the sexual act. All such images are images of heterosexual embrace. I know of no images of homoerotic sexual union in a tantric context.

Let me be explicit. Imagine a Buddhist painting of two male Bodhisattvas, Avalokiteshvara, symbolizing compassion, and Manjushri, symbolizing wisdom, in naked sexual embrace. This embrace could also symbolize the ecstatic union of wisdom and compassion and for a gay man would be much more meaningful and more powerful than other images of such a union. I believe, however, that the Buddhist community would find such an image profoundly shocking.* The shock would come from the image that most people hold in their minds of what it means to behave sexually. Just as people might find it mildly disturbing to have a painting of a frog on a rock called "Freedom," so also they would find it much more disturbing to behold a picture of male sexual embrace and then be told that this symbolizes ultimacy, the union of wisdom and compassion. Yet there is no *a priori* reason to favor one image over the other, just as there is no *a priori* reason to favor an image of a male doctor over a female doctor.

On the level of Story, feminist analysis tends to focus on the fact that almost all the stories circulating within the Buddhist tradition are about men. This is not entirely true; there exist many stories in the Buddhist canon about women, such as Kisagotami, who found the Buddhist path profoundly nourishing and liberating. Still, feminist analysis has a point. The tradition preserves literally countless stories of men who have attained great levels of understanding within the Buddhist tradition, while the stories of women are scattered far and wide, tend to be less detailed, and often are overlooked within the tradition. Feminist analysis focuses on Story because we learn primarily through story telling. For example, the story of the Buddha himself is used, and endlessly retold, to illustrate how we also can in our own lives abandon pointless material goals in life, and devote ourselves to liberation and enlightenment. Everyone likes a good story because we can identify with the characters in the story and through such identification we can formulate the direction we want our own lives to take. The point of feminist analysis here is that if women do not hear stories about women, then women will find it difficult to identify with the tradition from which

---

*EDITOR'S NOTE (W.L.): Such an image, as described by the author, appeared on the back cover of *Queer Dharma vol. 1*, q.v. and did indeed shock some people, although most gay people gave favorable comments. It's the basic concept of accepting explicit homoeroticism as equal in every way to heterosexual—an idea which, despite all the advances since Stonewall, is still revolutionary for some. Internalized homophobia can take a long time to be erased.

these stories emerge. If the stories only present women in a negative context, as impure or the seducers of men, then women will find it difficult once again to comprehend the tradition as offering women the possibility of enlightenment and transcendence. If we do not hear about it, it is difficult to imagine it for ourselves.

Similarly, gay men need to hear stories that they can identify with, share with, and empathize with as gay men. If the tradition speaks only of heterosexuality or celibacy, then it is difficult for gay men to place themselves as gay men within the context of that tradition. On the other hand, the absence of stories explicitly mentioning the lives of gay men can be understood as an opportunity, for it grants a certain openness and freedom to gay men to create their own stories and their own context within that tradition, provided that the tradition has enough openness to allow for such new input. I sometimes think that the time has come to collect the stories of gay male practitioners, such as the story of Issan Dorsey and other openly gay male Dharma teachers. In a sense, gay men committed to Buddhist practice have an opportunity at this time, rare in the history of spiritual traditions, to create a legacy for future gay men who also wish to enter this path of wisdom, compassion and enlightenment. What stories will we choose?

I have already discussed the perspective of the Body at some length above, but I want to come at it from a different perspective at this point. In the Buddhist tradition there exists the idea of an "auspicious birth." And auspicious birth in a Buddhist context means, first, a birth in a body able to encounter the Dharma, the teachings of the Buddha. Next, an auspicious birth means a birth in a body able to comprehend the Dharma. Since the teachings of the Buddha contain many subtleties, this means a body mentally sound. Finally, an auspicious birth means taking birth in a body capable of fully manifesting the wisdom and compassion of a Buddha. As we have seen, on this last point, the Buddhist tradition has various interpretations as to what kind of body constitutes an auspicious birth. For myself, I take a very broad view. I have no doubt that women have the capacity for fully manifesting unlimited and universal compassion and wisdom and that therefore the body of a woman constitutes an auspicious rebirth. I also have no doubt that gay men have the capacity for fully manifesting unlimited and universal compassion and wisdom and that therefore the body of a gay man constitutes an auspicious rebirth. I also have no doubt that non-gay men have the capacity for fully manifesting unlimited and universal compassion and wisdom and that therefore the body of a non-gay man constitutes an auspicious rebirth.

Comprehending this great task, and realizing this great undertaking, how might the presence of gay men in the Buddhist community serve to further the enlightenment of all sentient existence? Asking the question in this way serves to turn the presence of gay men in the Buddhist community from a problem to be solved, to an opportunity for transformation, not just for gay men, but for the Buddhist community as a whole.

First, the presence of gay men in the Buddhist community serves as a simple example of honesty and truthfulness. Roshi Robert Aitken once spoke to a predominantly gay audience and is quoted as saying, "If you're in the closet you're not practicing Zen." I believe this comment emerges from Roshi's profound understanding of the importance of the precepts in our lives. One of the first five precepts in Buddhism says simply, "Do not lie." Applying this precept to the lives of gay men means simply living one's life in the open as a gay man. Not in an overbearing way, but with directness and sincerity remaining present as a gay man. This represents a gift that gay men can bring to the Buddhist community for it will expand the ethical dimension of Buddhism, making Buddhism more inclusive, broader and in that process the heart of compassion which is the central teaching of the Buddha will continue to blossom.

There is another, more subtle, gift that the presence of gay men brings to the Buddhist community. On the night the Buddha awakened he gained direct insight into suffering, the cause of suffering, and the path that leads to the cessation of suffering, dread, anxiety and fear. The Buddha saw that suffering arises from clinging. One of the central mechanisms whereby humans cling is dualistic consciousness. Dualistic consciousness means setting up mutually exclusive categories. Dualistic consciousness structures existence in a way that asserts that if one thing exists then another thing can not exist. Dualistic consciousness also structures existence into mutually exclusive and exhaustive categories, that things must be either one way or another way, but there can be no middle or third category.

Let me illustrate dualistic consciousness by a simple example. For many years the world maintained a border between East and West Germany. An enormous amount of energy was expended maintaining this division. Great armies were ready to destroy each other to maintain that separation. Then conditions changed and the border disappeared. Where did that border come from? From the mind. Where did it go to? The border vanished into the emptiness from which it came.

All separations between people resemble this example. They come from the mind alone. They have no reality other than that dependent upon the mind. The central insight of the Buddha, the insight that transformed him into the Awakened One, was the interdependence of all things, that nothing in existence exists separately. As the Buddha says in the Lankavatara Sutra to the Bodhisattva Mahamati, "Mahamati, nothing in existence has a mutually exclusive character." All opposites mutually generate each other and depend upon each other for their mutual existence.

The ability of the mind to project dualisms onto existence is very powerful, as the example of East and West Germany show. One of the most powerful of these projections is the dualism of male and female, which, just like a border between countries, has no ultimate basis but arises simply from the mind. Because gay men, and other sexual minorities, do not fall within the categories of how the mind has structured male and female, the presence of gay men, simply by that presence, calls into question the dualistic consciousness upon which that division rests. I believe this goes a long way towards explaining why the presence of gay men provokes strong hostility from many people. Just as an individual's attempt to ignore a border between countries will bring down upon that individual a strong and violent reaction from those invested in maintaining that border, so also those who by their mere presence call into question a strongly held sense of a basic division in humanity based on sexual behavior can provoke hostility in those who cling to such a division as real. This happens because humans tend to crystallize their sense of self, of a separately existing self, around the ideas that they hold. Their ideas constitute who they are. For this reason perceived threats to core ideas will be taken very personally because such threats seem to threaten their very sense of existing as an individual. This is why discussion among humans of political, philosophical and religious ideas often degenerate. We have all had the experience of inadvertently stepping on someone's highly cherished view of existence. Sometimes this happens because we make a joke about something that someone holds very dear and takes very seriously. The response is one of great bristliness and can often provoke great hostility.

But the division between humans based on borders between countries has no ultimate basis. And the idea that there exists two separately existing categories based on sex has no ultimate basis. There exist many sexualities and all of them co-create each other, mutually give rise to each other, depend upon each other in the shimmering web of existence. The presence of gay men in the Buddhist community gives all of us the opportunity to let go of a conceptual construct that divides people, but has no ultimate basis. In this way the presence of gay men can function as a tremendous gift.

There is no essential difference between East and West Germans. No essential difference between Serbs and Croats, between Chinese and Japanese, between races, between genders, between sexualities. When dualistic consciousness falls away we perceive the reality which transcends all of these divisions. When dualistic consciousness falls away our heart becomes as vast as the sky, capable of embracing all people, even all sentient existence in all realms and all times. This vastness of heart means the presence of the body of love, a non-exclusive love that compassionately embraces the suffering of all. It is the vastness of this heart which is the ultimate promise of the Buddha, the promise that all of us can awaken this heart for this vast heart constitutes our actual and ultimate reality.

And so ultimately the practice of a gay man does not differ from the practice of anyone else. For ultimately to practice means to cultivate the boundless presence of the compassionate heart and this boundless compassionate heart does not differ from the boundless heart of anyone else, for it is the same boundless heart and compassionate presence which permeates all of existence and manifests as all of existence.

Throughout the centuries Buddhists have been inspired by the Buddha's insight that it is possible to bring an end to sorrow, that it is possible to live a life free from suffering, anxiety, fear and dread. Different schools of Buddhism have interpreted this truth of the cessation of suffering differently. In this essay I have used two core models which interpret the means whereby one can bring about the cessation of suffering; the model of purification and the model of awakening. But there exist other models as well, such as the model of transformation so prominent in Tantric Buddhism, the model of gratitude which permeates the teachings of Pure Land Buddhism, and the model of clarity which plays such a prominent role in Buddhist philosophy and analysis, etc. Down through the centuries Buddhism has continually renewed itself through this process of continually reinterpreting and thereby renewing our understanding of the process whereby we bring about the cessation of suffering and sorrow, not only for ourselves, but also for all sentient existence. I sense at this time a nascent, not fully formed, new model of this process of cessation. I sense this model emerging at the confluence of the universal insights into the human condition that emerged from and constituted the Buddha's enlightenment, and the western liberal tradition which understood all people as worthy and laid a foundation for the elimination of slavery, the expansion of women's rights, equality before the law, and yes, the various movements for sexual equality. Buddhism can enrich this liberal tradition by providing it with the insights necessary for comprehending how the mind creates divisions between people and that ultimately one must transform the mind in order for hostility between people to cease. On the other hand, the liberal tradition can enrich the Buddhist understanding with its experience in applying this universal insight into the human condition to specific social contexts, something that Buddhists have tended to ignore.

This new model is not yet clearly articulated but I believe it has great potential. It has great potential because it arises from and has its foundation on the transcendentally real, meaning the vast heart which constitutes our actual condition.

May we all soon awaken to the presence of infinite compassion.
May we all cultivate the boundless heart.
May all people live in peace.
May all people live in kindness and caring.
May we all soon attain complete, perfect and unsurpassed
enlightenment and save all sentient existence from suffering.

Myo Denis Lahey, San Francisco

Reflections in the Mirror of Practice

Myo Denis Lahey

One way to understand being born in this human body is as an invitation to discover who we really are. This is merely an extension of the infant's marvelous interest in its own little form, its amazement over its toes, its limbs, its mysterious orifices. To take the spirit of this visceral self-examination and carry it forward into adult life, there to apply it to the fundamental mystery of our own being, is a brave and powerful *auto da fé*, an act of faith, over and against what may at first appear to be the limitations of our senses.

For lesbians and gay men, it is possible to say that finding out who we are has a special urgency; indeed, our survival as whole individuals can depend upon it. Many of us grew up in a culture where our way of loving, which runs bone-deep in us and cannot be taken from us without doing terrible violence to our integrity, was ignored, denied or denigrated. In the face of such toxicity, coming to understand ourselves as fully human beings with beautiful hearts can be the work of decades. The Buddha Way can enable us to see our wholeness and the kinship of all beings, a kinship that can finally be expressed when we answer the question, "Who are you?"

Perhaps one day the movement of clouds across the sky, a snatch of birdsong, or the rattling passage of a streetcar ineluctably affects our habitual way of looking, such that, for a moment, we cease our restless scanning of the passers-by, the street, the horizon for some haven, some resting-place, our harbor of true belonging. Instead, our gaze turns inward, in the momentous gesture that the 13th century Zen Master Dogen called "turning the light around." We needn't close our eyes or run off to a monastery to do this, though that may help temporarily. There is a way of looking at passers-by while simultaneously turning the light around. Doing this reveals that the passers-by are trooping from the recesses of our own hearts, into the light of day, and on into mystery, in a pilgrimage of unguessable duration where each step brings the pilgrim to the place of respite and solace that he seeks, and the whole is as if circled round by an enormous pair of sheltering hands. To come to know these hands requires standing up in the midst of the universe and saying unflinchingly who we are. Once the great Zen

MYO DENIS LAHEY (San Francisco) was born in 1951. He is an ordained priest in the Sōtō Zen lineage of Shunryu Suzuki-roshi.

Master Kuei-shan Ling-you was standing by the gate between the monastery and the vegetable fields. He saw his student, Yang-shan Hui-chi, coming back from work carrying his tools. As Yang-shan came up, Kuei-shan asked him, "Where are you coming from?" Yang-shan said, "From the fields." Kuei-shan asked, "How many people are down there?" Yang-shan then took his hoe, stuck it in the earth, clasped his hands together, and stood there silently. Kuei-shan said, "On South Mountain, there are lots of people cutting thatch." Yang-shan took up his tools and left without another word. If you understand the significance of Yang-shan's sticking the hoe into the ground, then you are one who can say who he is whenever he is asked. Even if Kuei-shan himself asks you to explain, you will plant your feet where you stand, and at your shoulder will be all beings. Kuei-shan might then say to you, "You know, there are a lot of people busily working on their attainment; how about you?" and with the disarming vulnerability of the true adept, you will silence him forever.

In virtually every tradition that has not lost touch with its mystical roots, there is at least an implicit command to know oneself. Socrates, Augustine, the Sufis, the Vedantists, all ask the question, "Who are you?" and declare that our happiness, our growth, our humanity hang upon the answer. How will you respond if the question is asked of you, even in your last moment? "Well, I'm a human being," you might say, or "I'm a father," or "I'm a man who loves other men." Each of these may be true, or they might all be true together, but the point might nonetheless be missed if one isn't thorough-going. In what is sometimes known as the Zen school, we say that Buddhist practice is about learning what it means to stick the hoe into the earth, and to answer, to speak the truth from the depths of one's own life. We shall go on to look at how such a thing might be learned, beginning with what Buddhists might call the Path of Preparation.

There are many ways of preparing to go on a journey. Even a simple trip to the market requires that one get organized. There might be the grocery list to find, the car keys to locate, money for purchases, and so on. But what if the journey were such that it needed virtually to be identified with one's life? How could one ever prepare for such a thing? Well, a first principle might be not to allow oneself to be paralyzed by the vastness of it all. If we juxtapose our habitual view of our life, which we have inherited from many generations of Western thinkers, with the stunning enormity of a Buddha's work as the Mahayanists see it, we might sink into despair. A more useful meditation could be a simple analog of preparing for the shopping trip: One would just ask, "All right, what things do I need now in order to get ready for my journey?"

First and foremost, one needs a body-mind. Our common English usage might bid us say, "a body and a mind," but speaking in that fashion simply encourages us to indulge in the splintering taxonomy of the western world's dominant religion, which is to say scientism. It is splintering because it allows us to divide our world into ontologically isolated parts. Once divided in this fashion, there the parts remain, in a disconnected jumble like bric-a-brac on a shelf. Buddhism teaches that things aren't really like that, and that while we can, and indeed, must compartmentalize our lives in various ways for the sake of sheer practicality, we mustn't forget that diversity is inextricably linked with unity, and that as Yang-shan's hoe strikes the earth it demolishes all categories, high and low, light and dark, wise and foolish, gay and straight. It does this because it acknowledges the fundamental, which can't be defiled by vantage points like "one" or "many." Zen Master Dogen might remind us that the whole body is like this; hence, the body-mind is basic equipment for the liberating action of saying who you are.

It doesn't matter whether our particular body-mind inspires others' approval or disapproval. What matters is that it be relatively intact and possess a modicum of strength, and that the sensorium function well enough to convey what anthropologist Gregory Bateson called "News of a difference that makes a difference"; that is, there must be dependable and informationally rich interaction between the body-mind and the world of which it is an integral part. Of course, once the basic integrity of the body-mind is established, adequate shelter and sustenance will be necessary to maintain it.

In dependence upon the body-mind, there will arise causal currents in the sea of being that is all around us. In fact, these currents give rise to the body-mind in the first place, and the relatively enduring nature of the body-mind is testimony to the continuing propulsion of *karma*, which is the traces left upon our inner and outer worlds by the exercise of the will, traces which shape the later unfolding of cause and effect in our human life.

You might ask why you should care about the workings of this *karma*. It's important because it can have a strong impact on the body-mind, and thus affect your progress as you pursue your own path to Buddhahood, which is, in fact, what we are talking about here. When someone asks you "Who are you?" and you answer in complete truth, it is Buddha who is speaking. And if your body-mind is assaulted by confusion, your ability to answer will likely be compromised. Therefore, the Buddhas devised various ways to help us attenuate the confused echoes in our body-minds. One category of these ways has to do with our conduct.

Perhaps you sometimes have days when you seem to rush madly from one engagement to the next, constantly trying to catch up with where you think you should be on your to-do list but never quite getting there. Morning passes into afternoon and afternoon into evening, and still there remain many things unaccomplished. At the inevitable end of such a day, you may marvel at how scattered and drained you feel: Your energies are depleted, your nerves on edge, and your sense of humor practically absent. By contrast, you may at times summon the determination to set aside for yourself what the Christians call a "day in the desert." On such a day you leave your to-do list in the drawer, you severely limit phone calls if not eliminate them entirely, you avoid public media like newspapers and television, and spend your time entirely alone in recollected quiet. You might use some of the day for special reading of a "spiritual" nature that you've been wanting to do. You might go for a solitary walk, or you might spend intervals just sitting in awed attendance upon whatever is emerging instant after instant. At the end of a day of that sort, you are likely to feel rested, refreshed, and profoundly grateful. This is a simple illustration of the easily observable fact that it makes a difference how we conduct our lives. When we live in a fashion that is driven, indulgent and careless, most of us will feel weak, distracted, alternately fearful and aggressive, and it may not be possible for others to rely on us in a meaningful way. But when we live such that what is at the heart of life is acknowledged, we can find balance, resilience and generosity of spirit, and in that very finding, the vitality and meaning of our life burst upon us. What, you may ask, is at the heart of life? "Who are you?" is at the heart of life. It is a mystery which seems simultaneously to enfold all beings, and to reveal an empty vastness that both terrifies us and thrills us beyond anything words can express.

You may need to subject your own conduct to careful study in order to determine what changes could be of benefit to you. This is no small matter, and it is not necessarily a study which can be accomplished once and for all and then set aside. We tell the story of Shakyamuni Buddha's beloved disciple Ananda. His mastery of the content of Buddha's teaching could not be matched by anyone, yet Buddha transmitted the Dharma robe of the teaching lineage to another great disciple, Mahakashyapa. And though Ananda had studied with Shakyamuni for many years, he went on to study another twenty years with Mahakashyapa before he was ready to inherit the teaching lineage himself. During that time the story says he was studying Mahakashyapa's *conduct*, trying thereby to determine if, in addition to the Dharma robe, Shakyamuni had transmitted something else to him. Eventually he got his answer, and that answer sprang from the loamy soil of Ananda's body-and-mind study of the Way, to use Dogen's phrase. In the *Diamond Sutra*, the arhat Subhuti asks Buddha to explain how a *Bodhisattva* sits, and stands, and progresses, and Buddha does so. This is nothing less than the exhaustive study of conduct.

It will help you to focus your study if you involve other people in a constructive fashion. Having what we call a *sangha*, or a community of fellow practitioners, can be of enormous benefit, as they can bear witness to, encourage, and challenge our efforts to negotiate the Way. An event of great significance in this process is the public ritual known as Receiving the Precepts (*Ju-kai*). In brief, in the company of our sisters and brothers we make sixteen vows concerning how we intend to live our lives. We first align our compass, so to speak, by declaring that Buddha, his Teaching, and the Community will be our refuge. By refuge we mean that these three "jewels" will be the touchstone to which we return again and again, our reference point for all acts of body, speech and mind. Then, we make a breathtaking commitment of our life energy by promising to refrain from all that is unwholesome and deleterious, to undertake all that is good and beneficial, and to save all beings without exception. We then announce ten types of damaging behaviors in which we will not indulge: Harming life, taking what hasn't been given to us, misusing our sexuality, speaking falsely, intoxicating ourselves or others, slandering others, inflating ourselves by diminishing others, acquisitiveness, harboring ill-will, and abusing Buddha, Dharma, or Sangha. Publicly making these promises exposes the tender and secret core of what we think of as our "personal" life, that patch of territory over which our small self stands in militant surveillance. We allow our fellow beings the opportunity to hear how we will negotiate the Way, and to talk to us about what they see of our behavior. It is exhilarating and very intimidating, and it illustrates how the beautiful drama of interdependence is enacted in the life of the *sangha*-jewel.

Of the Ten Prohibitory Precepts mentioned above, number four tells us that a disciple of Buddha does not speak falsely. You will find with this Precept, as with the others, that there is no path to its permanently successful implementation. Rather, it is a matter of exposing our life to the influences generated by having made these promises. When I have declared to the Universe that "I will not speak falsely," the Universe is apt to confront me with my departures from that declaration. There is a special challenge here for any of us who are members of a maligned minority. Those in a position of social dominance often develop the habit of oppression, and when we're asked who we are, the dominant ones may overtly or covertly try to get us to reply with something that

is not the truth. What shall we do then? Does our fear cause us to dis-
simulate and to try to pass for blameless members of society? Or do we
answer in complete truth, and possibly risk our own safety or that of
those we love? Here is the general challenge of coming out as gay, and
the particular challenge for someone who is both queer, and thus anath-
ema to vested social interests, and a Dharma practitioner, determined
to discover What is Buddha? moment by moment. Do not allow anyone to attempt to make the decision for you whether to step forth from
the closet-prison or wait awhile longer. Each sovereign gay being must
make that choice for himself. But you may discover that there somehow is a connection between getting your house in order, preparing for
our journey, and saying, if only to yourself, "I'm a man, and I love
other men."

As we continue making ready and gathering our equipment about us,
we might become tempted to revel in our own virtue, and to feel extremely pleased with ourselves for engaging in this noble undertaking,
namely, setting forth on the Buddha Way, the Way of "Who are you?"
This kind of pride can be a serious stumbling block to us if we're not
careful. Optimally, we'll notice our tendency to accumulate proud feelings about our practice and subject them to thorough scrutiny. This will
deflate them and allow them to melt away like other interior phenomena. Sangha will also provide a stern corrective, in the form of the
feedback we get from our fellow practitioners. If our practice community is a healthy one, our brothers and sisters will provide many occasions where we will be reminded that we are ordinary humans, who need
to practice humility in order to maintain a pliant and balanced outlook
in our endeavor of the Way. Even in the healthiest community, however, people may at times forget to examine carefully their own motivations and feelings before offering feedback to someone else. Thus,
anger, irritation, grief, depression and so on can lurk behind what is
presented as an unbiased observation about our conduct. When this
happens, we may ourselves find that we become angry or otherwise upset with the person, who may insist that s/he is "just trying to help."
Whenever we feel compelled to give feedback to someone else, therefore, it is wise for us to add the practices of gentleness and respect to
the attitude of humility mentioned above. This is not to suggest that we
should adopt an hypocritical posture, and simply pretend to respect
someone whom we secretly condemn. Rather, we need to look deeply
into our own hearts to spy out our subtlest feelings, and having done
so, deliberately and skillfully give rise to an instant of consciousness
where humility, gentleness and respect are in fact present. And having
produced one such instant, to produce another, and another, until, like

a musician learning her instrument, we can carry the tune.

Let's assume again that we are going on a long trip, a trip, indeed from which we might never return. In addition to gathering what we will take with us, we might want to ask ourselves some questions: Are my debts taken care of? Have I left instructions concerning the disposition of my effects, should I not come back? Have I tried honestly to lay to rest any hurts, grudges, or misunderstandings which it remains in my power to affect? It would be well to be able to answer these questions in the affirmative. If we leave much unsettled business behind us, it can haunt us indefinitely and disturb our recollection, because some part of us knows that our effort wasn't quite thorough-going. What of injured lovers we have left in our heedless wake? What of relatives or friends who were bewildered or frightened when it came time for us to announce our queerness? Bearing in mind that we cannot do their work for them, did we do what we could to meet them on ground where they could at least attempt to stand? If we are ill-at-ease when we contemplate issues of this kind, it may mean that more remains for us to do before we can with confidence close the door of our cozy home behind us and set out on the Path.

Now let us pause a moment and take stock: We are assembling what we need for our journey, and we have found that we need our body-mind, and that it must be functional, reasonably healthy, and acquainted with the peacefulness fostered by wise conduct. It has also been suggested that declaring who we are can include being forthright about aspects of ourselves of which others may disapprove, such as our sexuality, and that we will have to determine how best to come to terms with this fact. And we know that we must make a good-faith effort to take care of both the practical and emotional business of everyday life and tie up loose ends before we can really settle in with our momentous inquiry into who we are. There remains, however, a further element of preparation to examine, one of very great importance: Our intention.

If someone asks us, "My dear brother or sister, what is it you seek? how will we answer? It would be good to be both gentle and firm with ourselves when we look at this question. Our motivations are generally complex, and can shift about like light on water. Can we be really sure that there is not a subtle yet pernicious layer of self-interest in what we believe to be our desire to seek the deepest truth of life? The answer, of course, is that we can't be entirely sure about the all-but-invisible roots of what we desire to be so, however noble it may appear to be. That is simply the way things are with us humans. However, we can be more confident in what we *intend* to be so. That is, I may periodically discover in myself the wish that all beings be happy, live in safety, and be free from suffering. That in itself is excellent, but I can also manifest the *intention* that all beings achieve liberation and escape the bonds of sorrow, that they come to know the Way with their whole body-and-mind. Not just, "I wish it to be so," but "I intend that it *shall* be so." This is even more powerful than recognizing the desire for others' well-being, and it is related to an idea that is so important in Buddhism that millenia ago it was given a special name: *bodhicitta*. This Sanskrit term literally means the thought or notion (*citta*) of awakening (*bodhi*). It is often applied to the moment when one first gives rise to the idea that there is something remarkable called enlightenment, that it is the greatest treasure of our human life, and that it is attainable. But its most powerful development comes when we visualize it as possible for *all* beings, and we intend that they achieve it and that we shall help them to do so. This is how *bodhicitta* is the engine driving the vow of the *Bodhisattva*, the being who has determined to forsake the utter peace of final *nirvana* until every single other being has first passed into that peace. Contemplation of *bodhicitta* is worthwhile for Dharma practitioners of every level, and if we make it the centerpiece of our intention to cultivate the Buddha Way, that intention will be shaped and guided powerfully and accurately.

A certain preface to the study of who we are can be based on the examination of who we are *not*. Each of us bristles with functioning selves, which emerge and execute their behavioral repertoires in dependence upon prevailing conditions. This is nothing so dramatic as that controversial affliction known as Multiple Personality Disorder. Rather, it simply is a way of looking at how what we call "self" is co-created in the interactional vitality of beings and their karmic inheritances. For instance, let's say I have what is commonly called a brother. When my brother and I are together, our "brotherness" arises in dependence on our blood-relatedness, our shared history, our respective understandings of what it means to be a sibling, and so on. Ultimately, we cannot tease out something called "brother" and have it stand alone in the universe, without reference to the dense fabric of co-creation that is its matrix. Similarly, suppose I stand up and announce, "I am queer." It would be good for me, as a Buddhist queer, to meditate on the provisional designation of my queerness, on how queerness, though inalienably an aspect of the fact I present to the world, is not my "self," and on how heterosexuality depends for its existence on my queerness. This kind of meditation is wholesomely deconstructive of the web of interlocking identities, the totality of which we might call our *persona*, to borrow a term from analytical psychology. And as important as it is to know thoroughly each aspect of who we are in the world, it is even more important to see how none of our many selves can exist outside the nutrition of the one life we all share.

The reference to analytical psychology above raises the question of how we will understand the nature of the work we are undertaking, the nature of the journey to who we are. Are we striving for psychological wholeness? Quite possibly, but what is that? And is that wholeness itself the goal, or is it a by-product? Sometimes psychotherapy is seen as enabling us to live more effectively and less painfully in our human world. That sounds very attractive, but is that finally what we're after? Some of the great faiths present, by contrast, an adversarial posture to "the world," as if to say that our unhappiness is inevitable, given the nature of human existence as it is habitually conceived. In fact, Buddhism is sometimes seen in this light. Therefore, we are told, seek instead to be "liberated" from the toils of this life, to ascend to a more refined realm where the innumerable hurts that beset us are eased by the anodyne of *gnosis*, of salvific knowledge. These two stances can be contrasted as the psychological and the soteriological. The former may be said to stress an immanent and optimal functioning of the person in the context of *lieben und arbeiten*, or loving and working, in Freud's famous phrase. The latter extends the possibility of transcendence, of bursting the confines of the human sphere, and achieving transformation into something of which the human being, however evolved, is only a pale shadow. I should say that there isn't necessarily a conflict, here. But it would be as well to reflect a bit on whether, if what we seek is what is known as liberation, something is implied about the fate of the putative human individual who is to be liberated. While it is typically true that the appearance of our goals tends to change as we journey towards them, it can be useful to ask even before setting out how we will know when we've arrived.

Now let us turn our attention to what we could call the Path of Undertaking, or Endeavor. This begins when somewhere in our body-mind we find the need to cease studying our lists of desirable qualities and factors and *do something*. What will that be? The Buddha Way comes equipped with an enormous number of practices, ways of actually engaging the body-mind in cultivation of the Path. You may have heard of the practice of mindfulness, or recollection. This simply means developing the difficult discipline of *watching*, of studying the ceaseless pulse of life as it manifests moment by moment as tangible objects, sensations, conceptual thinking, dispositional tendencies, and consciousness. This discipline can theoretically be carried on in any posture, under any circumstance. Still, for thousands of years people have found it helpful to prop up their study using yogically potent arrangements of the body, and attention to bodily processes like breathing. Our attention gradually becomes more and more refined as we follow this discipline, until the most subtle fluctuations of the stuff of life reveal themselves to our inspection. From this, insight springs up as a necessary concomitant, as we will discuss, below. A large number of Buddhist practices can be grouped under this heading, including what is commonly called *Vipassana* (a Pali word meaning "insight"), a style of practice which has wide currency in America today.

You might feel drawn to what can be called a more active approach to spirituality, such as that of works of kindness and compassion, sometimes called *karma-yoga*. Here we make ourselves attentive to the constant stream of cries for help that are all around us, from strangers, family, friends and lovers, and we make it our practice to be available to those whose cries we hear. These cries can be extremely subtle, as instanced in a fleeting look of unhappiness on our lover's face, or they can be as deafening as those of an accident victim in terrible pain. Being able to hear these cries is only part of the difficulty of this kind of practice; we must also develop great skill at providing help in such a way that we do not fail to notice the emergence of our self-concern or self-aggrandizement, even for a moment. The problem is not that feelings of concern for ourselves come up, because they all but certainly will. The problem is that if we fail to notice them, they can distort our effort to the point where it can actually be harmful both to us and to those whom we hoped to aid.

There is, of course, the practice of seated meditation, the mainstay of the Zen school. It is like what was alluded to above in the discussion of *Vipassana*, but we might say that the body-mind composed in stillness becomes the analog of Yang-shan's hoe stuck into the earth. We fold up the limbs, straighten the back, and settle ourselves to the work of doing nothing. We call it work because, although it is empty labor, it is not to be confused with idleness. Once the storied Ch'an teacher Shih-t'ou Hsi-ch'ien came upon his student Yao-shan Wei-yen, who was practicing *zazen*, or seated Zen meditation. He asked him, "What are you doing?" Yao-shan answered, "Nothing." Shih-t'ou asked, "So you're just idle?" Yao-shan said, "No, if I were just idle, that would be doing something." Then Shih-t'ou asked him, "Then what is this 'nothing' that you are doing?" And Yao-shan said, "Legions of ancient Buddhas don't know it." We say, though, that this *zazen* is Buddha's own practice. So how could the ancient Buddhas not know it? The answer is that when we do *zazen*, in whatever posture, Yang-shan's hoe strikes the ground like lightning, and from the quiescent body-and-mind loudly come the inquiry "Who are you?" and the reply, in the same instant. There isn't room for any knowing here, save the way the blood knows the veins through which it courses. Your *zazen* practice aligns you with all the Buddhas who have walked and who will walk the earth. Bearing witness to this with the entire body-mind is, itself, *zazen*.

There are many other flavors of seated meditation practice, from tantric visualizations to yogas aimed at the cultivation of supranormal states of mind and body. The style to which we are attracted depends largely on our karmic affinities, and as such may have deep roots which defy rationalization. Regardless of what path of training we choose, or are chosen by, it is essential to apply ourselves to it with an open and unstinting spirit, if we are truly to engage ourselves with cultivation of the Way at the deepest level.

In Zen practice there is a celebrated adjunct to seated meditation, known as *koan*-study. Technically speaking, tradition holds that a *koan* is a record of a teaching moment from the lives of the Ch'an and Zen Masters. Typically a short dialog or utterance, a *koan* is often accompanied by prose or poem commentary added by a later teacher. Teachings in this form are thought to exemplify and emphasize a particular aspect of awakened activity, and to provide the student with a focus for his* efforts to clarify his understanding. The approach to *koan*-study best known in the west is that nowadays favored by the *Rinzai* school of Japanese Zen. Its roots go back centuries to China, but its current style is said to have sprung from a reform instigated by an 18th-century Japanese Zen teacher named Hakuin. In this approach, a phrase or even a single word is taken from the *koan* of choice and intensively concentrated on by the student. At least until the first *koan* is successfully "solved," he must gather his energies and bring them to bear on this "capping phrase" so forcefully that everything extraneous to the exercise is completely excluded, and one-pointed absorption is achieved. Once body-and-mind are harmonized by this effort, any seemingly-trivial event can provide a trigger for the white-hot blaze of the student's spirit to burst forth in the experience known as *kensho* or *satori*, when the student discovers his "true nature" or "original face" to be none other than the face of the very Universe itself. Following this initial penetration, the student may work on hundreds of subsequent *koans*, which are intended to mature his understanding and to prevent clinging to supposed attainments or states of mind.

It is possible to utilize the rich teaching resource represented by *koans* without depending on the generation of psychophysical pyrotechnics.

---

*Please forgive the lazy reliance on gender-biased pronouns.

Body-and-mind study of *koans* can be like walking carefully into the running stream of the teaching, like adding flour to bread as it is being kneaded. And *koans* are not limited to the recorded sayings and doings of the ancient teachers. Dogen Zenji points out that a "teaching case" is springing up before us every instant of our lives. When I held hands with my lover and incited passers-by to hostility, the body-mind poised in that awkward and frightening situation was itself the place of the "actualization of the fundamental point" (*genjo koan*), to use Dogen's phrase. If I imagine that I can turn away from that and find some better, truer place to practice, I am missing the opportunity directly ahead. "Who are you?" is not somewhere else. Buddha Dharma is as intimate as a sigh or a teardrop. It is exclusively with *living* Buddhism that we are concerned.

There is a well-known story about living Buddhism. As is typical, the interlocutors include an unnamed monk and, in this case, three celebrated Zen adepts from long ago. The monk has evidently been studying that flavor of Buddhadharma known as Madhyamika, or "the [way] of the Middle." This devastatingly thorough analysis of human life uses a powerful four-point dialectic to bring to light and then uproot the unspoken and unverifiable ontological assumptions which underlie all views that are based on the illusion of the ultimately separate existence of things. It seems to have occurred to the monk to wonder whether what he is studying so hard has anything to do with his actual life. It is as though the monk's study of Madhyamika has somehow brought him face to face with "Who are you?" This is an excellent development, of course, but perhaps the monk isn't so sure of his effort yet, so he goes looking for the teacher, who, in this case, is named Ma-tzu Tao-i, or just Master Ma. As the tradition now sketches him, Ma was a particularly imposing T'ang dynasty Ch'an (Zen) master, who was supposedly seven feet tall, which even today is somewhat remarkable. Not only was his physical stature towering, but our legends tell us that he had one-hundred thirty-nine enlightened disciples, perhaps more than any other teacher in our hagiography. Somehow we have only managed to keep track of about a dozen of them; what became of the other hundred twenty-seven, we don't know. And though each of Ma-tzu's recorded heirs was remarkable in his way, they were all men. I think it extremely likely that some of Ma's heirs were in fact women, but the tradition is patriarchal enough that their stories have been lost, to our collective shame. The "monk" in this story may have been female, or gay, or a member of one of the low-status, non-Han minority groups in China. We can't say, but as with all these stories, the tale is about "us" in the most intimate sense, whoever we happen to be.

In any case, the monk's study has brought him to a point where he must go to the teacher to ask about the teaching. This kind of face-to-face inquiry is one of the pillars of the practice of Zen. It is necessary to present oneself to the teacher in complete openness and honesty, and to state one's question or present one's understanding without dissimulation or unwarranted timidity. We need to allow the teacher to see who we really are. This can be extraordinarily liberating for gay men, because so many of us, in growing up, devised layers of "deep cover" for our protection. This is often so much the case that these layers can be very hard to shed, even when we need to do so in order to grow. We may need to be prepared to face quite a lot of fear and pain as the alarms go off, telling us we're exposing ourselves to danger. And what if the teacher we've encountered can't accept us as we are, because of his or her own limitations? That is an important issue. In Buddhism in general, and in Zen in particular, the notion of *affinity* is quite important. The idea is that our karmic inheritance will enable us to be especially in sympathy with certain teachers, and much less so with others. It is important to discern where our affinity lies before making a substantial emotional/spiritual commitment to climb into the bubbling cauldron of the student-teacher relationship. The matter of testing our affinity is tricky, but essentially involves judicious application of both common sense and deep intuition. With some teachers, our affinity or lack of it will be apparent right away, while with others a slower process will have to be allowed to unfold. If you're in doubt, talk to your Dharma friends about it. Sangha can be very helpful in this regard, as well.

Returning to our story, our unnamed monk likely has some inkling that going to ask about the teaching means joining the teacher in exposing his deep human heart, his "original face." How that is done may take an enormous variety of forms. In this case, the monk goes to Master Ma and presents his perplexity in the context of his study of the Way of the Middle. He asks, "Apart from the Four Propositions and the Hundred Negations, please explain for me the living meaning of Buddhism." In other words, "I have studied Great Teacher Nagarjuna's deep philosophy and its formal applications. But what does that have to do with this lump of red flesh (i.e. this very body-mind)?" This is also like asking, "What is Buddha," or, if you like, "Who are you?" Now the teacher, of course, should always be listening to the cries of the world, and this monk's question is one instance. And when the monk accosts Master Ma somewhere in the corridors of the monastery, the teacher could have replied any number of ways, but it seems to me that he decided to take the monk exactly at his word. So Ma-tzu looks down from his great height and says, "I'm really tired today, and I can't explain for you. Please go find Brother Ts'ang and ask him." Then the teacher just walks away. Do you see the kindness and generosity of this answer? Do you see the living meaning of Buddhism in Master Ma's words? It is doubtful that our monk friend did. Whether he did or not, he dutifully goes off in search of Brother Ts'ang who, by the way, is none other than Chih-ts'ang Hsi-t'ang, one of Ma's illustrious students and evidently another member of the community at this time. When the monk finds Ts'ang, he asks the question again: "Apart from the Four Propositions and the Hundred Negations, please explain for me the living meaning of Buddhism." Brother Ts'ang gazes benignly at him and says, "Why don't you ask the Teacher?" The monk says, "I *did* ask the Teacher; he told me to come and ask you." Brother Ts'ang sighs a deep sigh and says, "You know, my head hurts right now, and I can't explain. Could you go find Brother Hai, and ask him?" Again, our monk is handed a great gift, this time by Brother Ts'ang. Regardless, he has his instructions, so now he has to go off to look for Brother Hai. "Brother Hai" is the famous Pai-chang Huai-hai, also a disciple of Ma-tzu, who will go on to be the teacher of Huang-po Hsi-yün, who passed on the Dharma to the great Lin-chi I-hsüan, known in Japanese as Rinzai. When our monkish friend catches up with Brother Hai, he asks his question again: "I've been studying Madhyamika philosophy, with its *catuskoti*, or four-pronged dialectical argument, and it's all very interesting, as are the hundred exemplifications thereof. But I want to know about the living meaning of Buddhism!" In other words, who are you, Brother Hai? And Brother Hai blinks a couple of times and says, "You know, when I come this far, after all, I don't understand."

I think we can be sympathetic if by this time, our monk is feeling that he has had quite a full day. So perhaps he waits until the next day to return to Ma-tzu and recount these frustrating exchanges with Ts'ang and Hai, which occurred as the monk carried out Master Ma's instructions. When he does so, Ma-tzu says, "Hmm . . . Brother Ts'ang's head is light, Brother Hai's is dark." Making some allowance for the mysterious Chinese symbolism, we can note that the symbols of Light and Dark are found everywhere in Chinese representations of the world, of human life, of personhood, heaven, and earth. Light can be seen as the conscious, the deliberate, the engaged, the active, while Dark represents the still, the mysterious, the deep, the unknowable. That said, what is noteworthy is that though the monk asked his question three different times, the answer he received each time was the same. The monk, in all sincerity, asked "What is living Buddhism? Who am I?" and each time he was told, "The answer is what is right before you,

Brother. Speak your own truth!'' Do you see that? The words differ, of course. Brother Ts'ang stepped into the wind, stepped into the light of deliberate engagement, rested his arm on the monk's shoulder, and said, "My head hurts. . . . Go see our Brother Hai." Brother Hai stepped into the dark, where all the walls and towers come down instantly, and said, "I really don't know." But the answer is the same. If you're perplexed by this, it may be because you don't yet appreciate what your life is, just as it is. Nonetheless, you still may feel the hook, the little itch in the middle of your life, that these stories speak to, that these stories reach out and tickle.

You may have noticed how time can move along for us in fits and starts. One day we feel as though we are doggedly turning up the earth with the plow, the dark, fertile soil rolling back under the sky and scenting the air with its richness. Another day is like running in the woods, the path cushioned by the soft drift of leaves, our feet scarcely seeming to touch the ground. But let us assume that a day comes when what is sometimes called the "third path" unveils itself to our eyes, a day when time itself vanishes and what is left is the deafening silence of the fallen-away body-and-mind. In one flavor of traditional Buddhism, this is known as the Path of Vision, and it springs from the powerful arising of the "insight" alluded to earlier.

There is an all but irresistible temptation here to think that we have finally "arrived," that this Path of Vision is what our effort has been about. There is some truth to that: Buddhadharma is definitely concerned with the correcting of views, after all. It is necessary for us to find out about new ways of seeing the world, a world that ineluctably includes us, but that eludes us as soon as we try to make it hold still and conform to our wishes. The Path of Vision is about these new ways. It is important to remember, however, not to pitch a tent at a spot where you particularly like the view, no matter how sublime you think that view is. Because if you take up residence there, you will quite soon become "a ghost clinging to trees and boulders," as the old stories put it, just as you were before.

What, then, does one see, on the Path of Vision? Traditional formulations are many, and bear the stamp of the particular Dharma tradition from which they have emerged. One whose "third eye" is unimpeded is said to behold the functioning of dependent co-arising in all its inexorable majesty, or the eschatological necessity of the Four Noble Truths, or the cutting of the Ten Fetters and the end of the *asravas*, or karmically polluted psychic "outflows." In the Zen school, as noted, one is said to have achieved *kensho*, or seeing one's "true nature." Practically all these descriptions of the process of insight admit varying degrees thereof, but the notion is present that a crucial step has been taken. In the older south Asian strata of Buddhism, the term *srotapatti* is often used, or "entering the stream." The stream is the confluence of karmic currents which, beginning as a tiny trickle that will swell to a rushing torrent, eventually leads to full Buddhahood and traceless *nirvana.*

Now let me ask, from where you are at this moment, what can you see? You may say, "Nothing!" or "This book," or "What a stupid question." But please do not sell yourself short. What you can behold right now is what Buddha beholds, namely, the upwelling of life. You may think there is some knack to the kind of contemplation which produces insight, and perhaps there is, to a degree. But how much of a knack is there to taking hold of a hoe and planting it upon the earth in a way that brooks no equivocation? Exactly none, and that, for many of us, is the difficulty. We are so accustomed to "working the angles" of every situation in which we find ourselves, that often we can't precisely recognize when we are doing so, let alone stop, even when we want to. There are, finally, no angles at all, no reprieve or escape from who we are. Yang-shan's planting the hoe acknowledges this, as does a sunrise, or a great shout, or the last breaths of a dying friend, lover or stranger. Sometimes a gay man or lesbian will come out of the closet as a result of inklings of this encircling, inarguable truth, the truth of this body-mind. Once, as the legendary teacher Lin-chi I-hsuan lay dying, he addressed his disciple San-sheng Hui-jan, "After I'm gone, don't destroy my treasury of the eye of the true Teaching." San-sheng said, "How would I dare do such a thing?" After a moment's pause, when the only sound was the teacher's labored breathing, Lin-chi asked, "If someone should suddenly ask you about my teaching, how will you respond?" San-sheng instantly shouted. As the old commentators might say, this shout stops the mouths of everyone on earth and empties the universe from end to end. Acknowledging this, Lin-chi paid him a typically back-handed Zen compliment: "Who would have guessed that my treasury of the eye of the true Teaching would perish in this blind donkey?" A blind donkey, you see, has lost his "life," his life of pretensions to substance, of achievement, of status, of treasured past and longed-for future. There is nothing left but the hoe striking the ground, and even that is swept away in the vast, seething current that we are, that belongs to no one. At the same time, Lin-chi's remark punctures the pretensions of the shout itself. This is supremely skillful teaching, from a master on his deathbed.

So this Path of Vision is about waking up, but we need to be cautious lest we try to make awakening into a trophy-case stocked with shiny awards. In this regard, things just aren't that simple. Zen Master Dogen reminds us of this in his remarkable essay, "The Actualization of the Fundamental Point": "Do not suppose that what you realize becomes your knowledge and is grasped by your consciousness. Although actualized immediately, the inconceivable may not be apparent. Its appearance is beyond your knowledge."* Did you think you would have something to show for all your heroic labor? If you do have, your labor will have been in vain. Waking up is not about adding to the store of knowledge you have acquired in your life, so that you can then wear a realization merit-badge on your shirt.

As a further illustration, let us look at the tale of T'ou-tzu I-ch'ing and Fu-jung Tao-k'ai, two masters in the Ts'ao-tung (Soto) Zen lineage during the Sung dynasty in China. The story goes that Fu-jung studied with his teacher T'ou-tzu for a long while, trying to penetrate the mystery of the Way. He was an able and experienced student, and one day he decided to approach T'ou-tzu with a perceptive question about how Buddhas behave in the world. "Teacher," he asked, "the sayings and doings of the Buddhas and Ancestors just seem like everyday affairs to me. Was there some other way that they helped people?" In other words, when Fu-jung examined the actions of the ancestral teachers, he saw them eating and sleeping, visiting with their students, sitting *zazen* and so on. Even in the mysterious recorded dialogs, the topics more often than not were the stuff of human life at its most undramatic.

So, where can one see the magical activity of Buddhas fostering the maturation of other beings? T'ou-tzu responded: "When the Emperor is in his own realm, do his commands depend for their authority on the monarchs of bygone eras, or not? You tell me." Fu-jung opened his mouth to reply, but just then T'ou-tzu struck him in the face with his horsehair flywhisk and said sternly, "Before you ever left home, you deserved a beating!" In that instant, Fu-jung's delusions were shattered, and he awoke from his ages-long sleep. After a moment's pregnant silence, Fu-jung arose from his seat and prostrated himself to T'ou-tzu. Then he turned to leave, and T'ou-tzu said, "Hang on, what have you seen, that you bowed to me?" Fu-jung simply kept walking. As he neared the door, T'ou-tzu called to him, "Have you reached the realm where there is no doubt?" Fu-jung covered his ears with his hands, and left the room.

This is an extraordinarily beautiful demonstration of the unfolding

---

*In *Moon in a Dewdrop: Writings of Zen Master Dogen*. San Francisco: North Point Press, 1985.

of the Path of Vision. In essence, the Teacher told Fu-jung, "What do ancient Buddhas have to do with it? Who are *you*?" T'ou-tzu's blow with the flywhisk shocked Fu-jung's automatic dialog into silence. And in the ensuing vacancy, Fu-jung noticed that the Emperor was at home, had in fact never left home, and that Buddha's activity is unlimited and utterly beyond ownership. At that moment, there was nothing more that could possibly be said, so having bowed deeply, he walked away from his teacher and out into the vast Universe, without looking back. The Path of Vision can be like this, but it can also be quite different. Its unfolding is based on the operation of cause and effect, but it is as unpredictable as the twisting, diving flight of the lark. Permit me to ask: Who is at home, where *you* are? My queer brothers and sisters, it's time to answer.

Now then, we have already, in theory at least, come a long way on our journey. We left behind what we imagined was the safe haven of our old home and, guided by Bodhisattva conduct and the power of Buddha, Dharma and Sangha, set forth without exactly knowing where we were headed. In the last resolve, we had only ourselves to rely on, and Buddha's teaching, which is about nothing other than ourselves. We learned much, and perhaps had the disorientating experience of seeing what we thought was the goal shift and dance like a mirage, just when we thought we had it clearly fixed. Finally, Buddha's voice came clearly and recognizably to us, if only briefly, and our long effort was confirmed and steadied. When someone asks us who we are, we can take whatever is at hand in the moment, and stand as Yang-shan stands, no matter whether we look great as we do so, or not. Do you think that you can't do that yet? Perhaps you are mistaken. Perhaps you have ingested too much poison in your life, too many harsh lessons that left you battered, subdued and frightened. If so, please do not heed the command that you blame yourself. That command comes from other injured hearts, who, it is to be hoped, will one day join us in doing the work of shedding the outworn and confining learnings which have caged us. In the meantime, we need to remember that Buddha's Way is the path of compassion for ourselves and all beings, as we say in our ceremonies of initiation.

So, is there something more for us to do, something beyond the Path of Vision? In this formulation I have been presenting, loosely based on a fifth century Sanskrit compendium of Buddhist scholasticism known as the Abhidharma-kosha, there is. What follows next can be called the Path of Cultivation.

The Path of Cultivation pertains to those who have begun to witness the truth of Buddha's enlightened vision in their own lives, which is, of course, the point. On this Path the teachings are now our own, that is, they can be studied and verified from within our respective experience, rather than being sought for outside ourselves. The Four Noble Truths are materially demonstrated in the unfolding of our life and practice, instead of at some much-sought-after *terminus ad quem* of all our effort. Further, our experience on the Path of Vision changed our relationship to the processes of *karma*. The possibility of ceasing to create more *karma* is always present, in that we can potentially always experience things just as they are without exercising our volition to modify, magnify or eliminate them. The Path of Vision, however, increases our ability to catch ourselves in the midst of manufacturing the distorted ways of relating to the stuff of our life, ways that are based on the habitual belief in self, other, and the opportunities to manipulate them. Thus, on the subsequent Path of Cultivation, we witness both a widening of the horizons of practice, and a refining of our sense of how to balance the elements of spiritual life amid the demands and stresses of day-to-day existence.

What, then, becomes of the question, "Who are you?" The experienced practitioner knows that there is no final answer, no last word. Instead, the familiar question must be embraced afresh each time it presents itself to our consciousness. If someone asks us who we are, all the long labor of inquiry coalesces into that moment and manifests in the response: "Where are you coming from?" "From the fields." "How many people are working down there?" (Yang-shan plants the hoe and stands in silence.) In the next moment life may hand us the question anew, but in different garb: "What is the living meaning of Buddhism?" Or, "Can you help me? I've hurt myself . . ." Whether beyond the Path of Seeing or not, answering these pointed questions with the vitality and truth of our whole life is, itself, cultivation.

According to our ancestral tales, Yao-shan Wei-yen was a great-grandson-in-Dharma of the Sixth Ancestor, Ta-chien Hui-neng. Among Yao-shan's ablest students were Yün-yen T'an-sheng, and his older Dharma-brother, Tao-wu Yüan-chih. One day after the two of them had been practicing together under Yao-shan's guidance for a long while, Yün-yen asked Tao-wu, "What does the Bodhisattva of Compassion (Kuan-yin, or Avalokiteshvara) use all those hands and eyes for?" Tao-wu told him, "It's like reaching back for your pillow in the middle of the night." Yün-yen was silent a moment, and then said, "Oh, I get it." Tao-wu asked, "Oh? What do you get?" Yün-yen: "All over the body are eyes and hands." Tao-wu: "Well, that's not bad, but it's only about eighty percent." Yün-yen: "Well, how would you put it, Elder Brother?" Tao-wu answered, "*Throughout* the body are eyes and hands.'' These two are discussing the practice of the adept's Path of Cultivation and exhibiting it at the same time. In Buddhist iconography, Avalokiteshvara the Bodhisattva of Compassion is sometimes depicted as manifesting a halo of extended arms, with each hand having an open eye in the middle of the palm. This represents not merely hands extended to help, but hands which are guided by the eye of wisdom, so that they can truly be beneficial. Yün-yen is all but asking, "How does one manifest awakened compassionate activity?" His elder brother answers him, "It's like reaching for your pillow at night. Do you need special instructions for that?" What needs doing is always right before us, and the appropriate response can come from the body-mind the way the clapper of a bell sounds a note. Yün-yen appreciates this, and says so, but Tao-wu is concerned that they be thorough: The eyes and hands of compassion are not merely all over the body, but within, and around, and above, and below. In fact, the true body is itself as vast as the Universe, and brims with eyes and hands beyond counting. The paintings of Avalokiteshvara inspire the inexperienced practitioner at the same time they remind the adept how s/he must meet the responsibilities of practice: skillfully, the way our hand finds the pillow in the dark, without artifice, pretense or vainglory.

You might have had occasion to wonder whether an adept at this stage of practice will encounter marvelous phenomena, such as the development of legendary abilities like telekinesis, clairvoyance, clairaudience and the like. The stories of such things have probably been with us humans for nearly as long as we have roamed the planet, and Buddhists have told their share over the millenia since Buddha's time. Although psychic powers (Sanskrit *rddhi*) of one kind or another are listed in the traditional Indian formulations of the fruits of the spiritual life, their development has been seen as, at best, a by-product of the crucial business of attaining awakening, and at worst a dangerous distraction. The Zen school is even less interested in such things. Zen Master Dogen presents a scornful view of psychic powers in his essay, "Reading Others' Minds," from his monumental collection *The Treasury of the True Dharma Eye*. He tells the well-known story of the T'ang dynasty encounter between an Indian master of the *Tripitaka*, or the collected teachings of Buddha, and the enigmatic figure of the National Teacher Nan-yang Hui-chung, a disciple of the Sixth Ancestor. That the Indian master appears in the story with the Chinese name Ta-erh, or "Big Ears," suggests that the Zen redactors of this tale may have had a less than generous view of Indian pandits in general, but in any case, Ta-erh's fame as a mind-reader had preceded him when he arrived in the capital one day, and the National Teacher was summoned by Emperor Tai-tsung to examine the *Tripitaka* Master's powers. Their dialog ran as follows:*

> As soon as the Tripitaka Master saw the Teacher, he bowed and stood [respectfully] off to his right side.
> The Teacher asked him, "You have the penetration of others' minds?"
> "It's nothing much," he answered.
> "Tell me," said the Teacher, "where is this old monk right now?"
> The Tripitaka Master said, "Reverend Preceptor, you are the teacher to a nation; how could you go off to Hsi-ch'uan to watch the boat races?"
> The Teacher asked again, "Tell me, where is this old monk right now?"
> The Tripitaka Master said, "Reverend Preceptor, you are the teacher to a nation; how could you be on the T'ien-chin bridge watching the playing monkeys?"
> The Teacher asked a third time, "Tell me, where is this old monk right now?"
> The Tripitaka Master said nothing for awhile, not knowing where the Teacher had gone.
> The Teacher said, "This fox spirit! Where's his penetration of others' minds?"
> The Tripitaka Master had nothing to say.

Dogen follows this recounting by quoting several teachers from the T'ang and Sung dynasties who themselves commented on this story. He points out that each of the later commentators seemed to assume that "Big Ears" had, in fact, penetrated the National Teacher's mind the first two times the Teacher had queried the Tripitaka Master. Dogen suggests, however, that this is not clear since the National Teacher did not even acknowledge the accuracy of what the Tripitaka Master said. At most, says Dogen, the Tripitaka Master might have penetrated the Teacher's *thoughts*. In fact, the Teacher's *mind* could never have been located. The Teacher was simply standing before him in trackless *zazen*, completely at home, utterly himself; he had not "gone" anywhere, and thus the Tripitaka Master was defeated in his efforts to find him. The National Teacher brands him a "fox spirit," or a dangerous impostor. Here again is the Zen school's emphasis on the supreme practice of the Buddhas, namely, the adamantine contemplation of things as they are. Besides this, the reading of thoughts is nothing but a vulgar parlor trick.

Now then, dear reader, how are you doing? Are you weary of our journey, and longing to return to the familiar home you left? No one

---

*Translation by Carl Bielefeldt, in "Reading Others' Minds," *The Ten Directions*, pp. 26–34, Spring/Summer 1992.

could blame you if you are. The path to Buddhahood seems immensely long when you unfurl it like a gas station map and try to trace the route with your finger. So let's rest here a bit and enjoy the peaceful scenery. You might just lean back and let your eyes drift shut, even lean against my shoulder, if you like. You're quite safe, my brother. And while we take our ease, I'll go on talking a little longer, if it won't disturb you too much. You see, there is one final Path I need to tell you about.

When you feel up to it, just turn and look back the way we have come, all right? Oh, I see you're startled. It's as though we've ascended an enormous mountain, and from the vantage point of one of its crags we're looking down on our climb. And we can't see a thing except, as Dogen might have said, "drifting white clouds for ten thousand miles." No, I'm afraid you can't see your beloved house from here any more. Oh but come, you're weeping. Here, let me put my arm around you, as a brother might, for suddenly I notice that you shiver. There now, dear friend, look again: Is it not exquisitely beautiful, up here? What? Well, no, I'm afraid we can't just retrace our steps now. No, there is no way back at all, for this is the Path of No Further Study.

On this Path, we simply go on with our life and our practice, forever. Formal study is over. The Teaching is wholly our treasure and our responsibility. The Universe extends around us, completely transformed yet achingly familiar. At every step, the traces marking the way by which we've come vanish. Do you know the Ten Ox-herding Pictures? In the last picture, a jovial old fellow is seen descending from the mountains, making for the nearest town. There he will do nothing more elaborate than be himself, for the benefit of all whom he meets. What this might look like, no one can say. It might even look just like you, living your life with care, awareness and respect, with unselfconscious pride reaching out for your lover in the dark, your lover whose gender reflects your own as in a shining mirror. The person of the Way carries no guidebook but the Dharma of thusness, of things as they are, and no compass but his own vulnerable heart. If you meet him, you might not notice anything unusual about him at all, but after you've left, that very fact might bring you up short. His great secret is that there are eyes beneath his eyebrows, as the old stories put it. Doesn't sound like much, does it? And what would he make of our Five Paths, that we've just spent perhaps too long examining? Well, he knows a great secret: There aren't any Five Paths, you see. That was just a tale told to get us up out of our nests, to rise with the morning under our wings and span the sky with song. There isn't even one path, or perhaps there is an infinity of them, which amounts to the same thing.

But what to make of such a nonsensical pronouncement? If there are no paths, then what is there? Have we not just reduced our epochal spiritual struggle for enlightenment to an empty knot of words, a buzzing nest of ultimately meaningless concepts? The truth of emptiness is the one true universal solvent, unraveling all its touches including, finally, itself. But what of the important parameters of our life, like our sexual identity, for instance? Well, as practically every Teacher who has walked the earth has said in one way or another, all must finally be discarded, if we are to be able to face into the bracing wind of freedom. However, it is risky indeed to attempt to discard what we do not know. I cannot unmask the so-called false self until I can know it through and through. This is why, if I am a gay man, I must first find some way to understand what that means, right here in the ceaseless unfolding of "me." The *karma* of circumstance will reveal whether that understanding is to come through interaction with lovers, friends and family, or whether it will have to be only in the quiet of my own heart.

So what will you do now, my friend? I must leave you here, and let you make your own way, as you always knew you must. If you hurry along to the marketplace, you might catch up with Yang-shan, hoe upon his shoulder, leading a blind donkey by a tether. And there might be a question for you, waiting in his sweet brown eyes.

Kobai Scott Whitney, Honolulu, HI

Right Speech in the Gay Sangha

Kobai Scott Whitney

I once went to lunch with a friend who is a Benedictine monk. He brought along another American monk who is abbot in an overseas monastery. Both men are gay, but because of their church positions, they have chosen to remain closeted. The abbot spent much time quizzing me about Buddhist beliefs and practices, then he asked me why I had left Catholic religious life many decades ago.

I began expressing my feelings about the Church's hypocrisy, and about its poor treatment of women and gay people. As I talked, I began to get more and more worked up, more intense and condemnatory. Negative feelings I had not given word to for many years began to pour out. When I stopped long enough to notice the two men across the table from me, I could see that they were a bit taken aback by my outpouring—which had finally drifted into a hymn in praise of Buddhism.

I caught myself and realized I had been violating the Buddhist precept of right speech—one of the ten vows I had taken in my *jukai*, or refuge ceremony. Yet I had not lied; nothing I said to the two astonished monks was untrue. I felt I had truth and political correctness on my side. (And there is no more frequent excuse for assaultive speech than the conviction that truth is on one's side.)

I say that my speech violated Buddhist ethics, not because I was lying, but for several other reasons. For instance, I had been harsh and condemnatory. I had been firmly attached to my own opinions about what was right. I had also implicitly condemned the two men for their own life decisions. (Had they ever publicly declared their sexual orientation, they would be asked to leave a profession to which both were deeply committed.) I had implicitly been promoting myself—and my own life decisions—and disparaging them, their church and their own choices in life. I was also covertly promoting Buddhism while criticizing Catholicism.

Had they been nastier, or more knowledgeable, they might have pointed out to me that Buddhism itself has not always been kind to

KOBAI SCOTT WHITNEY (Hawai'i) was born in San Jose, CA in 1946. He is a writer, magazine editor and a longtime member of Honolulu Diamond Sangha, a Zen Buddhist group in Hawai'i founded by Robert Aitken Roshi. He started his practice and study of Buddhism at Zen Center San Francisco in the mid-1970s and was one of the original members of Maitri, which eventually became known as the Gay Buddhist Fellowship.

women or to gay people. As I stopped my lunch-time diatribe, I mumbled something about being sorry "for going on like that," yet the incident still embarrasses me when I think about it.

As a Buddhist practitioner I have found that cultivating right speech has been my biggest challenge—on or off the meditation cushion—since the mind is often filled with internal speech during a session of meditation. For me, getting through a day without violating right speech is a greater challenge—and more arduous—than doing a one-day sitting in the zendo. Why is right speech so difficult? And do gay people have a harder time with it than others?

Barbed Words

To the last question I would answer "yes" for a variety of reasons. A psychiatrist once said to me, "You have replaced physical male dominance with verbal dominance." I thought him overly glib, yet there was an element of truth in what he said. I have often noticed how verbally clever and skillful many gay people are—even those with poor formal educations. I notice this especially when I spend time in gay districts like the Village in New York or the Castro in San Francisco. Every waiter, every bookstore clerk seems out to prove how clever and campy he can be. Like local pidgin in Hawai'i, "gay speech" is a marker that indicates membership in our subculture. One of the first things young gay men learn in their coming-out process is how to be as campy and witty as possible. Sadly, gay society often teaches them how to "dish the dirt," how to "snap" and how to "talk trash." (In Hawaiian pidgin, gossiping is known as "talking stink," a phrase I have always enjoyed.)

So, as gay people, we have learned to defend ourselves with barbed words—words that might condemn straight people as "breeders" or bigots. But we probably just as often put ourselves down and, in doing so, we often disparage women by our identification with stereotypes of femininity. Negative words about women, like "whore" or "slut" or "bitch," are a frequent ingredient in gay male speech. Sometimes the use of feminine references seems innocently fun and campy, but there are negativities hidden just below such language. Fads come and go about female pronouns. In the late 1970s, when every gay man wore a mustache, jeans and a flannel shirt, female jargon was out—as were drag queens—who were banished from the gay tent as an embarrassment to the tribe. In years since, drag has come back and "Miss names" have re-emerged as politically okay, if not correct. I remember giving a friend of mine, who managed a retail store, the name Miss Management. In turn, he used to call me Miss DaBoat. Both names had elements of truth to them, so they were clever, and a bit hurtful, at the same time.

Do gay men gossip more than other people? I don't know. From observing workplace interactions for many years, it seems to me that men gossip just as much as women. So perhaps it would be giving in to stereotype to accuse ourselves of being more gossipy than others. Yet I do see a lot of negative speech in the gay community, in the gay sangha and in myself. Robert Aitken Roshi, whose son is gay, and who first gave encouragement to the precursor of the Gay Buddhist Fellowship in San Francisco, *does* see speech as a practice issue in the gay community. He notes that "Gay people are often the victims of wrong speech, but then in turn, they sometimes descend into a kind of reverse cattyness—making fun of straight people and so forth."

I also know that disputes in the Gay Buddhist Fellowship and at Hartford Street Zen Center, for instance, have sometimes resulted in harsh, judgmental speech that has polarized these small sanghas. Efforts to practice gentle, compassionate and mindful speech can only help us as individuals, and as sanghas, to keep harmony with each other and with the wider world of gay and straight, me and them, form and emptiness.

The Enlightenment Myth

For gay people, one of the nicest things about Buddhism is that it gives us very little to believe, and a lot to do. Those of us who took up Buddhism in the sixties and seventies—especially in its Zen or "Crazy Wisdom" Tibetan forms—were focused almost entirely on the enlightenment experience. And the thing we had to do to get there was to meditate. Everything else, we thought, would follow nicely from our meditation and consequent breakthrough into the Oz of enlightenment. We thought there would be no rules in the Emerald City and that all we had to do was click our heels and count our exhales.

Events in the 1980s disillusioned many of us, as supposedly enlightened teachers—both gay and straight—were shown to have abused their roles by manipulating students for their own financial and sexual needs. All of a sudden it became obvious that just meditating was no longer sufficient. As the philosophers say, it was necessary but not sufficient.

What our teachers had failed to mention was that the historical Buddha never described enlightenment as some elusive mystical, and mystifying, personal experience available only to the chosen few. This stereotype was developed centuries later, especially in the Zen Mahayana movements in China, Vietnam, Korea and Japan. Prince Siddhartha merely said that there was a way to find release from suffering, and that the Way had eight parts to it.

Meditation and mindfulness were only two of the elements in his Eightfold Path. There were six other "rights" in the path, and right speech was one of them. (The use of the word "right" in the Eightfold Path, by the way, does not mean only "correct" or "proper." It more nearly means "as things are," or even "as things should be." So right speech means that we commit ourselves to speak in accord with suchness, using language that is as wide, compassionate and flexible as possible.)

The following simple outline represents the framework that the historical Buddha discovered, and it became the program that he used to train (or re-train) his followers. It is also a list of a few of the things often forgotten when many of us first started sitting on cushions to wait for enlightenment.

The Four Ennobling Truths

In order to live as a Buddhist, the sutras tell us, we need to experience:

The Four Ennobling Truths
I.   That suffering exists.
II. That there is an origin of suffering.
III. That there can be an end to suffering.
IV. And that the way to stop suffering is by taking up:

> The Noble Eightfold Path
> 1. Right View
> 2. Right Intention
> 3. Right Speech
> 4. Right Action
> 5. Right Livelihood
> 6. Right Effort
> 7. Right Mindfulness
> 8. Right Concentration

Obviously, whole books have been written to explain this simple outline. For our purposes here, however, I will just mention Stephen Batchelor's fine book called *Buddhism without Beliefs*. In it, the writer makes clear that the four truths are not just noble, but they are "ennobling" to those who experience them. He also insists that the Four

Noble Truths are not a four-part doctrine to be believed, but are statements of realities to be experienced. In other words, we let ourselves experience the fact that life is anguish (Batchelor's replacement for the word "suffering"), and we personally discover its origin in craving, which is often translated from the Pali (*tanha*) as "clinging."

In a way analogous to the use of the 12-Steps in recovery programs, serious Buddhists attempt to practice these eight active principles of the Buddhist path in their daily lives. It is in this practice of the Noble Eightfold Path that we begin to experience the cessation, the disappearance —only momentary at first—of anguish, ignorance, and craving.

Not Just Lying

I would like to explore the origins of the Buddhist teachings about speech, then I will move on to see some practical ways that right speech can be cultivated and encouraged in our gay sangha.

In the ethical tradition of the three great monotheisms—Judaism, Islam and Christianity—there are two types of speech that are prohibited: swearing (taking the name of God in vain) and lying. For some reason, Buddhism took things much further than this, elaborating the ethics of speech into a very subtle teaching about how words have consequences. When we are at our best, words can become a part of the practice of not-harming and, ultimately, the practice of active compassion.

Aitken Roshi, who was one of the first Western Zen teachers to emphasize the precepts, says that speech was already a concern in the ethical environment into which the historical Buddha was born. "The ideal of gentle speech is one that is grounded in Hinduism and Zoroastrianism, which preceded the historical Buddha," he says.

Looking at references to speech in the middle-length Pali sutras, we can see that, *musavada*, or false speech, is the first thing prohibited. But in addition to falsity, the Buddha also instructs his monks to avoid speech that is malicious, harsh, idle, unbeneficial or gossipy. Often he warns against speech that is "sharp," or that "praises the self and disparages others." At this early stage of Buddhism, the five *panca shila* were given as guidance for all sangha members. They were: not to kill, steal, lie, abuse intoxicants or abuse sex. These five precepts are still accepted by nuns, monks and lay people in all schools of Buddhism. According to Aitken, "the Buddha and his early successors understood the importance of right speech very well. With the development of the Mahayana, five additional precepts were added: not to speak of the faults of others, not to praise the self while abusing others, not to spare the Dharma assets, not to indulge in anger, and not to defame the Three Treasures—the Buddha, Dharma and sangha. The total roster in the Mahayana is called the Bodhisattva Precepts, or the Ten Grave Precepts.''

Asked why later Buddhist tradition expanded the lay precepts to ten, Aitken says he thinks it was the diffusion of Islamic learning after the eighth century C.E., which introduced both the zero and the ten-centered decimal system to the East. "People wanted a round number and they liked the idea of ten," Aitken says. "The ten were derived from those named by the Buddha in the *Brahma Net Discourse*. With the rise of the Mahayana and the development of Chinese Buddhism, the original Pali discourse and its commentaries were replaced by a new *Brahma Net Sutra* that sets forth the ten as we have them today." Directly or indirectly, five of these ten precepts involve speech.

Creating the Other

Right speech is just as important as right mindfulness or right concentration (meditation). Yet mindfulness and meditation are the two things that excited most of us when we first explored Buddhism. The other six "rights" seemed either obvious or unimportant.

The injunction to right speech means not lying, of course, but it means much more than that. Buddhist ethical thought has always separated human activity into three parts: thought, behavior and speech. Speech is the bridge between thought and behavior—and is itself a behavior based on thoughts. Buddhism has always viewed speech as an activity that has consequences, a behavior that can harm or heal others.

More subtly, we know that speech can be used to distance ourselves from others, as when we judge them harshly or when we create words to make them Other. When we talk about "them" or "those people" or "you people," we are subtly making another group into the Other. The next step in this process is to make them Enemy—straight people, fundamentalist Christians, Serbians. We use speech to make ourselves right and the Other wrong. I'm reminded of an example of this from the life of Issan Dorsey Roshi, founder of Hartford Street Zen Center.

Before there was even any clear name or understanding of the disease we now call AIDS, Issan regularly visited a young gay man in San Francisco General Hospital who had the then-mysterious disease. Taking Issan aside after one of his visits, a stern and disapproving head nurse commented to him that this particular patient had probably had more than 400 sex partners. Miffed at the woman's moralistic and condemnatory tone, Issan terminated the conversation: "Only 400 partners!" he said loudly, as if on stage. "Is that *all*?"

Like many of us in the gay community, the nurse was making a harsh judgment about someone she saw as Other than herself. Just as we currently condemn and distance ourselves from those in our own community who have unsafe sex, or who still use drugs or smoke cigarettes. We think nothing of condemning our opponents on the same-sex marriage issue or on the ordination of gay men and lesbian women. There is a lot of smug political correctness in the gay community that lets us justify the automatic condemnation of the Other. What if people on both sides of the so-called culture wars would listen to each other? Deeply.

The abortion issue for instance, has good ethical arguments on both its sides. Yet opponents would hardly even concede that point—or keep their mouths shut long enough to listen to an alternate view. Few of the great religions train their people to listen. Religious professionals are trained to preach or give dharma talks, to proselytize and to convert; but how many opportunities for learning and growing have we missed by all this impassioned and persuasive talking?

The Dalai Lama talks about the practice of "enemy yoga." It is the ability to listen deeply to, and to learn from, someone we think we should hate. We use speech to defend our egos or attack others who we see as a threat. We want to be right and we want others to know that we are right. But what if we could entertain the idea that the Other might have something worthwhile to say? Enemy yoga means actually listening to, and practicing acceptance of, those we like to call our enemies.

Like my own example at the beginning of this piece, we often use speech to hint or declare to Christians or Jews that Buddhism is a better religion than theirs. Yet Buddhist ethics teach us to respect the spirituality of others and to refrain from creating propaganda for our own beliefs. Thich Nhat Hanh has mentioned this especially in regard to the indoctrination of children into our religion—or any other.

Sometimes we play subtle games of one-upmanship with speech. In disputes, we often maneuver to have the last word—a behavior that arguing couples often perfect to a fine art. Or we want to name-drop to prove how important we are: "As I was saying to the Dalai Lama . . ." or "when I was studying at Daitoku-ji." I have often noticed in sangha meetings how often some people like to make their own status clear to the rest of the group. I see this especially with people who are psychotherapists. They don't seem to be able to get through a meeting without reminding everyone who they are. Lawyers and physicians are sometimes guilty of this one-upmanship too.

Dishing the Dirt

Right speech also means not participating in gossip. In some precept instructions, gossip is defined as "repeating what I do not know to be true about others." But even negative statements about another person that are *true* can have damaging consequences. So the twin yardsticks of maliciousness and idleness can be applied here. If the sharing of negative information is done to help someone understand the other person, then that information may not be gossip. But if bad news about another—even though true—is shared just for entertainment, titillation or ill will, then it certainly violates right speech.

Personally, I find gossip one of the hardest negative behaviors to rid myself of. There seems to be something exhilarating about sharing the misfortunes and faults of others. I'm not sure why it is so attractive, but it is. Perhaps it is the natural curiosity people have about others; perhaps it is the same impulse that keeps millions of people around the world watching soap operas or trash-talk programs that dramatize the sleazy misfortunes of others. Perhaps that is it: Gossip makes us feel more fortunate, and more virtuous, than those we talk about.

But gossip destroys harmony in small communities and makes some members isolated or demonized by the self-righteous judgments of others. Aitken Roshi says that "Gossip puts people in a box: 'so-and-so is like this.' It means we disregard the possibility that the person may be, at that very moment, correcting themselves." Gossip freezes people into a pre-judged, always negative role.

One of our Honolulu Diamond Sangha members once told Aitken Roshi that his schedule did not allow him much time for zazen, so he decided to commit himself to right speech in his workplace—a busy urban newsroom that was rife with back-biting and verbal nastiness. As he started this practice, he made sure not to condemn others for their uncharitable speech. He simply refrained from participating. He no longer listened to or passed on gossip. He tried not to say anything spiteful about others. After a year of this, he evaluated his progress and found that his office had become a much kinder place—and that his own example had started to change the behavior of others. This was right speech in action.

Aitken Roshi notes another precept that is very related to speech. "In his comment on the Eighth Precept, 'Not Indulging in Anger,' Dogen Zenji says, 'There is an ocean of bright clouds; there is an ocean of solemn clouds.' Sometimes a sunny response is appropriate, sometimes a solemn one. But not a harsh one. Harsh language pollutes the Dharma." Anger and speech are not a good combination.

Thich Nhat Hanh advises his students to withdraw from situations when their anger is too strong for them to speak without harm. At meetings within our local sangha, we use another of Thich Nhat Hanh's methods. Someone is charged with keeping a small bell, which they ring anytime during the meeting that they feel appropriate. When the bell sounds, talking stops and the room goes silent as we count our breaths up to ten. This "mindfulness bell" is a way of reminding everyone of the emptiness and silence behind the sound and fury of speech. It also reminds us to listen to others and to keep our own speech as ego-free and generous as possible.

Which reminds me. Listening is the flip side of speech. Some teachers, like Joan Halifax and Thich Nhat Hanh, have adapted the phrase "deep listening," from the counseling literature. The idea here is to recognize the speech of others as equally important as our own. It means that we try to listen to others with as much care and mindfulness as we bring to our meditation time. We try to hear others with a mind emptied of any pre-judgments or biases against the speaker. It means we do not think of other things while someone is talking to us. We listen as if we had all the time in the world. We don't cut them off by looking at our watch or making excuses to rush away. Giving people our time is as generous an act as giving money, food or shelter. This is especially true when that person is less good-looking, less clever or less socially poised than others in the community. Listening can be the act of a Bodhisattva.

Another important part of listening is the ability to keep a confidence. There is no greater asset in any small community than the person who can listen and keep their mouth shut. Someone once said, "If you feel you have to swear someone to secrecy, then you probably shouldn't trust them with anything important." People need to be able to talk to someone they know will not betray their confidence.

Aitken Roshi comments that in Chinese and Japanese thought, being able to keep a confidence means "you actually accumulate *toku*— the power or authority that one acquires through virtuous action and speech. It's an important kind of authority that you find in many primitive societies. You will hear it mentioned often in Japan. Someone might say: 'I have not *toku*.' If you are known as a gossip, you will not have *toku*—and you will be feared."

Again, keeping quiet can sometimes be the highest form of right speech.

Meditation and Right Speech

Speech always starts as thought, and our thoughts are mostly composed of words—thought sounds and images also play a role in mental life. It is in the practice of meditation that we may first start seeing how chatty (and catty) our minds are. Noticing is a big part of the meditative act, and it is also the first step in any process of change. So first of all, meditation helps us to notice how we mentally talk to ourselves.

How often have I spent a whole period of zazen rehearsing an embittered speech to my boss? Or how often have I spent time on the cushion inventing a clever comeback to what someone said to me last night? Very often.

Issan Dorsey said that in zazen we "just sit down and see what happens." Often what happens is mental speech. In some traditions, meditation instructors tell us to notice this yakking and then turn back to the object of concentration—the breath, the koan, the visualization. We notice, then we return. Notice and return. Meditation is the art of return. This practice of noticing and returning lays the groundwork for the practice of right speech—where our first task is to notice how we are speaking, whether in our thoughts or out loud. Once we notice, we can begin to change those habits of speech that are less than our Buddhist ideals.

So the process can start on the meditation cushion, but it should not stay there. In my own practice, whenever I noticed myself having a negative thought about myself or someone else, I use an abbreviated *metta* practice adapted from the Vipassana tradition. (The Pali word *metta* means something like "boundless loving-kindness.") Whenever I notice a spiteful thought about another person, I now actively try to face the thought by meeting it head-on with a metta formula. If a negative thought about so-and-so comes up, I say to myself mentally: "May she be safe. May she be healthy. May she be happy. May she awaken." I try to carry this practice throughout the day. If I am driving and someone cuts in front of me, I will notice myself saying venomous things about the other driver. So I stop myself and say the metta formula: "May he be safe. May he be healthy. May he be happy. May he awaken." Sometimes I have to repeat the phrases several times before my anger subsides, or before I actually start believing what I am saying.

For me, this constant intervention with my negative thoughts can be annoying, especially when I am tempted to revel in my righteous anger, especially when these thoughts happen so many times during a day. Yet after doing the practice for awhile, I begin to see how often I think mean things about others. This practice also subtly counteracts my internal negativity—which is what always bursts forth into the act of ungenerous or malicious speech. On the cushion or off, this is a process of noticing myself going off track and then returning to my vow of compassionate, nonjudgmental speech.

Sometimes *not* speaking can be a negative behavior. One of my own tactics in dealing with others whom I dislike is to avoid them whenever possible. Whether in the workplace or in sangha activities, I will pointedly not speak to them when thrown into situations where I cannot avoid them. This is the famous passive-aggressive behavior that some of us are so good at. But even though "passive," it is still aggressive, still hurtful.

So here is the guideline I made up for myself: I will maintain civility. That means that if I pass them in the hall I will greet them appropriately. "Good morning," or "Hi, how are you"—whatever fits. I do not have to spend time with them, but I do have to acknowledge them respectfully. This is also a good rule in recovery from arguments. I once got into a shouting match with someone in the office. We both walked off pouting at the end of the day—each of us, no doubt, convinced of our own rightness in the dispute. But later that night I resolved that I would keep the rule of civility with him when I saw him the next day.

And I did. When I came in the next morning, I passed his desk and said good morning to him. He did not return the greeting. But I kept it up, just small civil greetings, and within a few days he was returning the greetings and within a few more days we were interacting normally again.

There are other times when not speaking is the best thing to do. I once got into an argument with the lady who lives next door to the zendo. It was about her dog, which was barking at all hours of the day and night. Soon she turned the subject away from her dog's behavior and started attacking the sangha. "He's barking because you guys have people coming at all hours of the day . . . and there's been a peeping Tom here . . . and what do you guys do up there anyway—ringing those bells? You're a cult or something!"

I was dumbfounded by her venom and stood there at the fence in our backyard thinking all kinds of things. The phrase "paranoid bitch" came to mind, and I wanted to say it out loud. But that would have been my own poison, so I just stood there, angry and silent. After the count of a few breaths I turned and walked away. I think that was the best I could have done at the time. The incident was so upsetting that I recall it almost every time her dog barks—and I have to repeat my mental metta formula over and over still: May she be safe. May she be healthy. May she be happy. May she awaken. And her stupid dog too!

So keeping the vow of right speech sometimes means keeping your-self silent and at other times, in other situations, it means you must speak.

Right Speech as Koan

Gay people have a long history of being shunned and condemned by the speech of others. As gay Buddhists we should always be learning from this sad history. And we need to notice how we have internalized these condemnations and turned them against ourselves and our brothers and sisters in the sangha—or in the larger gay community

In the Diamond Sangha tradition of koan study, the Ten Grave Precepts are given as koans once the student has passed all the other "cases" in the curriculum. But maybe the precepts should be given first. Treating "not lying," "not praising myself and disparaging others" or "not indulging in anger" as koans means that students would have to struggle, turning each of the vows over and over in their minds while on the cushion—and throughout the day. Just as "Mu" can become a constant mantra-like sound in one's mind, so too these inspiring and practical guidelines for speech should be examined and reexamined over a period of time. Koans can become like cut jewels: a treasure we carry with us all the time, turning it one way and another and seeing a new facet each time we look at it. In the same way, we can carry our com-mitment to right speech with us each day, always learning new things as we look at it from the ever-changing reality of our daily lives. This sort of practice leads to practical results. As a meditation begins to prove to us the ephemeral nature of ego, we also begin to realize there is no self to defend. We discover that all living beings are—like ourselves—just intersections on the net of Indra. So there is also no such thing as the Other, and no such thing as Enemy. When we experience this, then we begin to understand the inner logic of the precepts.

A friend of mine, who is a very politically active gay psychiatrist, told me something he said he would never say publicly. He admitted that he does not believe the gay liberation rhetoric that says that gay peo-ple are just as good, just as healthy psychologically, as straight people. What he really believes is that we have an in-built "damaged goods" aspect to our emotional lives. Perhaps because of the condemnatory speech of straight society, whose messages we have internalized since childhood, our own self concept has been damaged. Self esteem is defined by some theorists as the feeling left over after we talk about our-selves internally—as when we repeat over and over again certain negative thoughts like: "I'll never amount to anything," or "I'm such a dizzy queen." The repetition of such thoughts leaves us in a feeling state that could be described as discouragement or demoralization—and this is what constitutes low self esteem.

If my friend is right, and I believe he is, then gay people need to pay special attention to how we speak to ourselves inside our own minds. If our internal soundtrack is always calling us hurtful names, always judging and criticizing, then it is no wonder that we end up speaking similar words to those around us. When we turn such negativity toward others—gay or straight, woman or man, Buddhist or Christian—then we pass on a damaging ripple of negativity that hurts all of Indra's net.

I am not saying we should give up inventive, fun, campy speech. As a writer I am fascinated by the power and artistry of words. Like our sexual behavior, our habits of speech are part of what defines us as gay.

So we need to keep evaluating how we use our words. And this constant evaluation is very related to the practice of meditation. Over time, meditation begins to show us that there is no abiding self to esteem or to defend, no ego to aggrandize or to protect. So meditation is crucial. But we need to remind ourselves that it is only one-eighth of the Eightfold Path. The practice of meditation and the practice of mindful speech—together with the other six "rights"—can begin to release us from the suffering that led so many of us to Buddhism in the first place. Right speech can be a deep, many-faceted practice that delivers new insights each time we work on it. And it is an essential part of what Zen ancestor Dogen called the *Genjo Koan*—the essential and unavoidable puzzle of our daily lives.

James Thornton (left) and Martin Goodman, Santa Fe, NM

Presence Makes the Heart Grow Fonder: Gay Relationship As Spiritual Practice

James Thornton

The last thing I ever thought was that I would marry Martin. He wasn't my type. He didn't live in this country. And he wasn't gay.

But let me back up for awhile. It's 5:30 A.M. one morning in the Castro. I'm just moving into an apartment on Castro Street above the Anchor Oyster Bar. The apartment is in the back, quiet, and there are open boxes everywhere, my possessions slowly crawling out of them. I'm tired of unpacking, and spent the previous night in the neighborhood gay bars having a few beers and trying to connect. I came home late, tired, alone and a little tipsy.

The phone rings. I answer it, wondering through the fog in my head thicker than the fog outside, who could be calling at 5:30 A.M. It turns out to be Maezumi Roshi on the other end of the line. He's my Zen teacher, up from Los Angeles for a meeting at the San Francisco Zen Center. He wants to come over to see my new apartment. And he wants to do it *now*.

So I snap awake like a good cadet and jump out of bed, taking time on my way out the door to fish a work of his calligraphy out of a box and put it on display so that he'll see it when we return.

I pick Maezumi Roshi up and we drive back. When we get to my apartment he pulls out a cigarette, lights up rakishly and smokes. This is bad boy Roshi. I've heard about but never seen this side of Maezumi. Puffing away, he walks up to a collage I've just hung up, the work of a New York artist friend. It somewhat surreally depicts a naked young man, buttocks broad, shapely, and white below a tan line looking coyly out at the viewer over his left shoulder, his hand on the breast of a smiling, fully clothed girl from the 40's, all under the Brooklyn Bridge.

Maezumi and I have talked many times about being gay. With the curiosity of a Japanese aesthete who collects human souls, he's here in the Castro to satisfy his curiosity a little. He goes up to the collage and studies it, then says, "but his bottom is just like a woman's!"

"That's why I like it," I say.

"Ahhhh!" he says with the grumbly growl of a Japanese male seiz-

---

JAMES SOSHIN THORNTON (Santa Fe, N.M.) was born in 1954 and has practiced in the Sōtō Zen tradition for some time. He has recently completed a book on spiritual practice and the Earth: *A Field Guide to the Soul*.

ing some understanding, "so *that's* why you like it!"

"This," I thought, "is a very modern sort of dharma discussion between master and student!"

Maezumi grasped something of my experience for the first time. He was from a culture that prizes the union of opposites, displaying autumn flowers in spring and summer flowers in winter. A culture with its own long history of gayness too. He took my appreciation of the feminine quality of the young man's buttocks as a sophisticated and refined taste, and I liked that.

Maezumi's acceptance of and curiosity about the inner workings of my gayness helped me to go deeper into Zen practice, since I felt it was a safe space to discover who I really was in all my aspects, not leaving sex out of it. Here was a path that not only preached realizing who I was but actually encouraged the discovery and practice of it. And my Zen practice in turn helped me to accept being my gay self.

* * *

Which brings me back to Martin. We met in Germany, where I was on a long solo retreat. I started out doing zazen many hours a day in the little atelier room in the village hotel where I was staying. After months of this, I wanted more from my zazen. So I experimented, letting my sitting evolve in the direction it seemed to want to go. What emerged was a meditation that went on for many weeks, deepening all the time. It was essentially a view of my life passing before me, much as they say happens in an accident or a near death experience, where the whole life can flash by in a few seconds. Here, though, the life went by but took weeks in the viewing, so that I could study it thoroughly.

What I saw was hard for me to accept. I had absorbed homophobia from my culture, elaborating it and perfecting it with a subtlety and breadth that few explicit homophobes could dream of. I had acted like a member of a slave caste, taking in the views of its repressive masters and making them real in my own life. I saw that I had come to a decision in the bottom of my heart, below my vision. The decision was this: I was unworthy of love. My work and life would forever be marginal. As I looked into it more, it became clear that I had made a practice—a spiritual practice—out of reinforcing these negative judgments about myself.

I started seeing that a hundred times a day I'd reinforce these judgments. It could be as simple as seeing the cute young postman hop out of his yellow Volkswagen to deliver the mail. I'd think, "Oh, he's cute, I wonder what he does on weekends?" Then I'd find myself making an internal negative movement of the soul: "You mustn't think that way!"

Or my practice of reinforcing negative judgments about myself could be much more elaborate. I was picking men to fall in love with where the relationship was destined to fail, often before I'd even had the consolation of sex. I did this over and over with men who were young and willowy and confused. Every time the relationship failed, which I'd virtually designed it to do, I took it as proof that my judgment about myself was right: I wasn't worthy of love. Here again I'd loved someone, they'd rejected me, and I had all the proof I needed.

As the meditative view into my life deepened, I saw that I really had taken this negative mantra—I am unworthy of love—as my practice. By reinforcing negative judgments about myself, I made them true, and made my life unlivable. What was hard to admit is that I was doing it to myself. I was playing the victim, and I was also the oppressor. But the fact that I was the oppressor was mighty difficult to admit, and so I wanted to blame someone else for my misery. I spent a lot of time looking for others to blame. Candidates included the hatred in our culture and the homophobes who spread it, the immaturity or remoteness of the men I fell in love with, and lots of others.

Ultimately, though, I saw that as long as I blamed anyone else, nothing in my experience could change. Only when I took full responsibility for my feelings, thoughts, and actions could I begin to live the kind of life I wanted, in which love and creativity could flow.

Seeing how I'd trapped myself in playing out a negative drama that I was scripting, producing, and acting, I decided to try a countermeditation. Several times every day, I did a practice in which I blessed my body. I blessed everything about it and every part of it. I was ashamed of my body, the vehicle of my gayness, so I decided to be wildly positive as a kind of spell to dissolve all the negative feelings and associations I had built up about it over the years. I hoped that if I blessed my body I could begin for the first time to appreciate and love it. And I hoped that if I could love my body a little, maybe I could love myself a little, too.

The practice itself is simple, and I'd recommend it to anyone, no matter what you may think your relationship with your body is. I'd start at my toes, and work my way up, talking to my body as you'd talk to a baby, blessing it and telling it how grateful I was for all it did for me. In case you'd like to try it, the meditation goes something like this, and you must feel free to ad lib, doing it in your own way:

"I bless you my toes, for taking good care of me. . . . I bless you my legs, for walking me, for your strength and endurance that I seldom think to thank you for" . . .

And so on up to the sex, where so much emotion is attached, and therefore particular attention must be paid: "I bless you my dick and balls and asshole, you are beautiful and perfect and wonderful, and the source of sexual fun, and I am very grateful for you. Thank you for all you do for me, and I apologize if I have ever been ashamed of you or spoken badly of you, or done anything to hurt you. . . . I will take good care of you from now on, just as you have always taken good care of me, and will do everything I can to find you a good lover to play with!"

And this way of blessing continues through all the parts and all the organs of the body, up through the stomach and liver, the heart and tongue and eyes and brain, the scalp and skin, the face and ears, and every part of us.

At first, I felt silly doing this. But since my unconscious practice had been so negative, my conscious practice had to provide a remedy. Over the coming weeks it did. As I worked with the practice more, becoming more comfortable with it, I started to enjoy it. I spent more and more time doing it, letting all my feelings about the various parts of my body emerge, so that I could talk them out to my body. I began to have an intimate conversation with my body about our relationship.

As I discovered buried feelings, I'd bless and thank my body deeply and sincerely, acknowledging all the love for and care of me. All of which I had taken for granted. As I did these blessings it became clear that I could never really love another human being until I loved my body in a way that was unashamed. This practice helps to find that natural love for our own body. It is a surprisingly powerful antidote for all the negative experiences and shames, fears and dislikes we hold about our own body, which is after all the closest human being for each of us. The one we can practice taking care of, to learn how to take care of others.

After some weeks of working with the blessing of the body, I moved on to being as fully aware of my breath and my body as I could be, all day long. This practice, fundamental to all real mystical experience, went much deeper and progressed more smoothly as a result of the practice of blessing my body. When we bless the body in this way we are accepting who we are, and celebrating our life as we have been given it. This practice intimately acknowledges the miracle of life that we've been blessed with.

*   *   *

When my long retreat ended, I hoped I would be able to behave more lovingly toward myself, and thereby be more open to life and to a real relationship. A real relationship with a real man was what I wanted more than anything else in life.

I'd like now to share some aspects of my relationship with Martin, as spiritual practice. To write about all of the relationship, all the passion, trusting respect, and mutual support, would take a joint autobiography. So here are some perceptions about practice in relationship drawn from life.

All the work that I'd done releasing negative judgments about my body and my gayness was just the rehearsal for the relationship. It turned out to be particularly helpful in allowing me to give Martin space to work out his feelings about being gay as well. This was an important early stage of our life together, as he'd entered the relationship not thinking of himself as gay but as bisexual. Coming to terms with being gay was something he had to work at, and I was able to be supportive to the degree that I had released my own homophobia. It especially helped me not feel personally threatened by his process, and this in turn helped his process to flow.

This early stage in our sexual relationship was the first time I had really experienced how, when we work through our own pain, we can be more understanding of someone else's. Perhaps this is the primary value of suffering, that by working it through, we know in our own experience something about the suffering that others feel. And the more we have let go of our own suffering the more we gain the space to help someone else with theirs.

A relationship is not always easy. That's why it is good practice. Our most intimate relationships seem designed to bring up whatever is darkest, most painful, and annoying in our psyche, all the things that need to be understood and released. In a way it is a wonderful thing that these shadows emerge into the space of relationship, for it is only by getting to know them that we can release the beasts in the forests of our hearts.

A difficult issue for me in our relationship has been something that seems mundane when you talk about it: our different senses of neatness. I'm a compulsively neat person, and I saw Martin as representing a different aesthetic! This led both to calm discussions and angry sessions . . . which of course were about much more than just neatness. They were about commitment, power, trust, and other fundamental issues, all expressed through the more accessible vehicle of neatness.

I would use my root practice of offering my anger to God and the Universe, whenever neatness issues were driving me mad, and it would usually pass. One time it didn't. We were staying in our tiny house in the French Pyrenees, both writing books. One day I just found things weren't neat enough, and I exploded. I had the sense to go out for a walk, another fine remedy that usually worked. But that day I just couldn't let the anger go. Even after a vigorous hike in the hills, I was going home convinced I couldn't live with him any longer.

Just then he came around a bend and found me. Silently he came up to me carrying an apple, cut the apple in half, and offered one half to me. We sat on the bank of the river that flows below our house, watching it while munching. When we'd finished, he said, "I'd like to show you something," and took me for a half hour walk, all still silent, to show me something wondrous: a bee orchid, a kind of wild lady slipper, that I'd never seen. I was charmed, my anger disarmed.

Being a moody, irritable, and emotional person, I've been concentrating on letting the emotions, when they are strong and negative, pass through me like a thunderstorm. To do this I remember that I am the landscape not the storm. This helps to let the storms pass through. You might try remembering this when a strong negative emotion arises:

I am the landscape, not the storm. My awareness is the landscape, and it endures, the storms of emotion blow through it and go. I am the landscape, not the storm.

How we go to sleep every day is especially important. I try never to go to sleep angry with Martin. When anger is there I let it go as fully as I can. When I resist doing this most is when it is most needed. A crucial part of this practice is a goodnight kiss. No matter what you've been feeling, you can always let it go, and give a real goodnight kiss. Never go to sleep angry with your lover, and you have a wonderful way to go to sleep.

* * *

Martin and I often are both working at home. We have lived in some very small spaces. For two years while building our house in Santa Fe, we lived in a 28 by 8 foot trailer with no running water or sewage facilities. During this time we each wrote separate books, much of it done in that small space. How did we work to find space within this closeness, which otherwise might have felt like confinement?

One was to think of ourselves as always voluntarily on retreat. We worked out an ecology of time and space and duties, a simple schedule that we have stuck to ever since because it works so nicely. A main part of it goes like this: One person cooks dinner for the other and washes up. The same person keeps washing up through the following breakfast and lunch. For the next dinner the roles reverse. The person who was cooked for last night now cooks, and takes on the washing up duties for three meals. This way you always know that your turn to be cooked for will come. You will be catered for, and so you can just relax into whatever you are doing.

This practice brings a kind of certainty, peace, and equality that are good, along with some very good dinners! When we are both writing we allow either person to avoid talking about their creative process, and to veto any such discussion, through breakfast and lunch. Before dinner we declare "party time," have a drink, and catch up on everything great and small.

* * *

Sex has kept surprising us. We were surprised by becoming lovers at all. Neither of us was the other's type. Martin wasn't young and willowy. He was too big, too mature and an equal in every way. I was scared to enter into relationship with an equal, though only an equal could ever have satisfied me. But this was uncharted territory for us both. Our hearts were whispering love, but our loins weren't screaming do it.

It meant moving from lust to love. From the fire in the loins that compels sex if you can get it, to the fire in the heart that warms everything with its light, reaching down into the loins as well. It meant making love instead of having sex. That was new to me. It felt more feminine, and accepting that this is what I wanted was a new challenge, too.

To move to a relationship based on making love instead of having sex was a special kind of practice. I was used to responding automatically to someone who was slight, young, barely available. Martin was a grown up, bigger than me, and fully present. Often in relationships sex comes first and love fails to follow. I wondered: if love comes first, will sex follow?

It turned out to be a gratifying experiment. It's a revelation always to make love rather than have sex. It's a gentler experience, heart open, fully present, all of you engaged. When having sex expresses love, there is no tiring of it, only a deepening with the passing years. As the intimacy deepens, sex becomes ever more natural, expressive, fun. A bonding of the animals we are, the ultimate place of safety and reassurance in a world that's often harsh.

Mostly we all forget we are mammals. We get so enmeshed in our everyday concerns and excitements that we lose sight of the fact we're animals. Animals who are programmed to have sex and to explore relationship. While simply having sex can be a good thing, since it frees the animal side of our nature, making love allows us to be both ape and angel at once. We can express our fierceness and our sweetness, our body's and our heart's delights simultaneously.

Let me suggest a way of practice for love-making:

> *Allow yourself to become very relaxed as you lie naked together. Go into your breath, and feel your whole body, letting it relax, letting all concerns go. Then let your awareness go to your heart, and let it open. You might imagine a rose opening from a bud into full flower in the space of your heart.*
>
> *Let yourself feel your heart open, and feel love for your partner. Hold him quietly or caress him gently and let your feelings of love for him come forward and flow from your heart to his. And let yourself feel his love coming into your heart and filling you, so that there is an exchange of loving energies. You might imagine this love enfolding the two of you like a comforting cocoon of light, radiant and warm.*
>
> *Then begin to make love, slowly and gently at first, letting your physical touch convey the love in your heart, and letting the sensations of being touched convey his love to you.*
>
> *Then go on to loving experiments, building to your climaxes. Stay with your partner, focusing just on him, letting any fantasies of others go. Stay totally present, no one else. Just him, here, now.*
>
> *When you come, offer it to the Divine, as a gift.*

When you make love in this way, your orgasm is not a finale, but an exclamation of joy in a continuing conversation with your lover and the Divine. It's a strong, gentle way to connect the two of you to what's eternal. It helps to establish the feeling that for you and your partner, there is always a third party involved in your love, the Divine, real and present in every moment of your relationship. When you experience your relationship in this way, it helps to create a spaciousness in which problems can be worked at more easily. When you are in an eternal love triangle with your lover and the Divine, problems are smaller than your intimacy. Everything, even when difficult, becomes the practice that makes you more loving and more aware of the Divine presence.

It's a good practice to offer our orgasms, and so come closer to God. A good gay practice. For such a long time we've been told that our orgasms are unholy. That's a lie, of course, and this practice of offering our orgasms removes a shadow from our souls.

* * *

Being fully present with our lover when making love, and letting all fantasies go, is a profound way of practicing being in the present moment.

Being fully alive in the present moment, open to its wonders, intimate with reality as it unfolds in our arms. Letting all fantasies go brings us gently into the joint moment we make with our lover, into the reality we bring into being together. To let all fantasies go is also practicing faithfulness, trusting this relationship, opening to the possibility that this man in my arms will open too, and grow with me. Unless we ourselves open in this way, the relationship cannot continue to grow to its fullness, sinking always-deeper roots into reality, bringing forth ever more wondrous blooms.

When we let all fantasies go and open fully to the present moment, holding our lover in our arms, we deepen the experience of making love. Barriers fall and hearts open. To let all fantasies go is analogous to letting our own harsh judgments about ourselves go. When I let my harsh judgments go about myself, I am able to appreciate who I am. I am able to let the miracle of myself unfold in real time. I am able to appreciate and be grateful for this life, and to love and accept myself, perhaps for the first time.

When I let all fantasies go and make love to the man in my arms, barriers I have set up to loving him for who he really is begin to fall. When I can appreciate his skin, his smell, his affection for me, appreciate him entering me or him receiving me, when I can feel all this and not want it to be any different, then I am happy. It is a different sort of happiness from any I have known. It is a soft excitement, an unexpected joy. It is not something you can anticipate. For you do not think about it, you live it as it unfolds. This space of "not wanting it to be any different" is the unique place where we can make love. Not wanting him to be different at all, accepting the gift of being with who he is right now, that is making love.

If you enjoy this practice, there is a way of taking it deeper, too. Call it dream yoga.

We all have dreams of sex when we sleep at night. Off in a dream world, we may meet one man or many who offer sex that excites us. And we all know what it is like to have sex with a dream lover and wake up wet with come.

You can practice being faithful with your lover in your dreams. You can decide not to have sex with anyone in your dreams other than your lover. You can remember this as you fall asleep. Then when you meet some man in your dreams and start having sex with him, you can remember that you've decided not to do this for now. When you remember this in your dream, you'll find that you awaken, and then drift down into a different dream, feeling very much in control of your life.

This dream yoga of faithfulness is a powerful practice. It integrates all the levels of our psyche. It allows us to be present in an open-hearted way with our lover whether we are asleep or awake. It deepens the experience of making love, in that it is a deep choice about wanting our lover to be who he is, and not someone else, even when we are dreaming.

These ways of being fully present and giving up fantasies may seem threatening. It may seem that they are a way of giving up our freedom and our fun. But I experience them otherwise. I find that they make our real relationship with our real lover deeper and more pleasurable. And remember, when you decide to release fantasies in your waking or dream life, you retain the choice to have subsequent fantasies. If you experiment with letting fantasies go, you can always experiment with fantasies later. We retain the power to invite fantasies again, and when we do, they come at a moment's notice. So we are not giving up our freedom to let fantasies go. We retain our freedom to have them. Instead, we are experimenting with our freedom in a different way, enjoying for a while our freedom to be fully present, and to experience as much open-hearted reality as we can.

*   *   *

After Martin and I had been a couple for some time, I wanted to have a marriage ceremony, to celebrate in public the commitment we celebrated in private. For a long time, Martin wasn't keen on the idea, and I thought I'd just have to let it go.

We live in Santa Fe, and follow how state politics treats gay people. In 1996 we were following a bill in the legislature that banned same sex marriage. Same sex marriage didn't exist anyway of course, but the legislature wanted to make a point of it.

A peaceful protest was scheduled for 11 A.M. one morning in February on the steps of the state capitol building. The notion was that ministers of many denominations would marry gay couples right there on the steps, a demonstration that the human heart surmounts political repression.

At 10 o'clock that morning, Martin appeared in the kitchen where I was making tea, and announced, "Well, my dear, we are getting married this morning on the steps of the capitol. You have ten minutes to put on your best dress!"

Soon we were there, me wearing a linen jacket in fact, in a group of 40 or so other gay and lesbian couples, surrounded by a larger crowd of sympathetic folks. A lesbian Navajo priest started the ceremony by calling in all the ancestral spirits, and the spirits of the Earth, and you could feel the spirits come. A dusting of snow started, like spiritual light made visible falling down to bless us.

As the group took its vows, the NBC nightly news camera zoomed in on us, and as we sealed our vows with a kiss the camera was full on me and Martin. We had never had a kiss in public before, and celebrated our first one on the news that night. Something not many of our straight friends can say.

*   *   *

The most valuable thing we have to give is our attention. Love is attention. Where our attention goes our love goes.

But I had to learn to curb my attentions too. We entered into our relationship with different comfort levels around being physically and emotionally expressive. Martin is probably more expressive now than I am, but at first I was the more expressive one, and thought I was being loving by being physically expressive all the time. Because I thought that this was what being in love was all about, I often let myself feel hurt when Martin didn't want to share in that sort of expression when I did.

It took me a long time to see that my idea of being loving was limited. I thought it meant giving full play to my own feelings, as this was a strong emotional need of my own. I thought being romantic was letting all my feelings out whenever I felt like it. It took a long time to see that being loving meant looking beyond my own need—even when that was to express love in the way I understood it—to see what it was that Martin needed at the time. Not just what I need, what he needs too.

It's a strong practice, recognizing your own need, looking beyond it to see your partner's need, and acting in a way that tries to accommodate both needs. This has become one of the central elements in the practice of relationship for me. To follow this practice gives insight into how unloving I am. And when I find myself being unloving—being irritable, selfish, competitive, and so on—I can work on these things. Not by judging myself for being unloving in these ways. But rather by seeing my unloving feelings like a gardener sees weeds. A gardener might think, "I love this patch of earth, but there are a lot of weeds . . . If I pull them, I should have more flowers and fewer weeds next season."

So I try to weed out the unloving impulses that arise, by becoming aware and letting them go, trusting this will help the gardens of intimacy grow.

*   *   *

There's a way in which we are never alone, but exist only in relationship. We are intimately connected with all living things, with the Divine, with our loved ones, our family history, and so on, networks of connection stretching through all aspects of our lives.

Seeing relationship as practice can extend beyond our most intimate relationship to embrace all the relationships in which we find ourselves. Whatever insights into the spiritual life we have must be brought into play in our relationships, if they are to have any value. It is in our relationships with everyone we encounter that these insights must find expression if they are to do so at all. The texture of our relationships expresses our spiritual understanding. Fine words accompanied by unloving conduct mean we have more to work on than we think we do. And we all have work to go on doing always, as we begin again each day to find the loving way.

The longer I am in my relationship with Martin, the more I appreciate him, and the grace of being in relationship with him. There is some truth in the old line that distance makes the heart grow fonder—when we are apart I live in a yearning to reconnect that often compels me to poetry.

But more and more it seems to me that presence makes the heart grow fonder. When we are both present, fully present, then we are really alive, and never have a moment's doubt as to *why* we are alive.

The ultimate view of Mahayana is emptiness, but this viewpoint does not exist in the lower teachings. If you really look into your experience of existence with the eye of meditation, you begin to see everything as the play of emptiness. Phenomena [as referential co-ordinates] become exhausted and you finally arrive at their essential nature, which is emptiness. But, having said this, you might be led to say: "In that case we should not need anything." But whether you need anything or not is up to you. It simply depends on your mind! Just dryly talking of emptiness is not enough! You must actualize it and then see for yourself. If your mind is really empty of referential manipulation, then there is no hope, no fear, no negativity—your mind is free of that! It is like waving your hand in the sky! Whatever arises is completely unobstructed.

The purpose of meditation is to remain in this natural state. In that state all phenomena are directly realized in their essential emptiness. That is why we practice meditation. Meditation purifies everything into its empty nature. First we must realize that the absolute, natural state of things is empty. Then, whatever manifests is the play of the dharmakaya. Out of the empty nature of existence arise all the relative manifestations from which we fabricate samsara. You need to understand quite clearly how things *are* in reality and how they *appear* in terms of duality. It is very important to have this View, because without View your meditation becomes dull. Just simply sitting and saying: "It's all empty" is like putting a little cup upside-down! That little empty space in the cup remains a very narrow, limited emptiness. You cannot even drink tea from it!

It is essential to actually know the heart of the matter as it is. In the absolute sense there are no sentient beings who experience dissatisfaction. This dissatisfaction is as empty as the clear sky, but because of attachment to the form display of emptiness, [interdependent origination] the relative sphere of things becomes an illusory trap in which there *are* sentient beings who experience dissatisfaction. This is the meaning of samsara.

—from Dzogchen View of Tantric Ngöndro,
    A Teaching by His Holiness Dudjom Rinpoche
    (1904–1987), Supreme Head of the Nyingma School

Alzak Amlani, Mountain View, CA

From India to Africa to Buddha: Weaving a Path Home

Alzak Amlani

About five years ago I had the privilege of taking a seminar with the author Hal Zina Bennett, about creativity, spirituality, Zuni symbols, and writing as an opportunity to encounter the true self. He felt that self expression in any form dares each of us to reach in and pull out what is truly ourselves, and bring a new way of seeing into the world. He taught me that I may not be saying something that many before me haven't said, but the *way* I say it, the particular spin I put on it, colored and tempered by my unique life experience, allows another to hear it for the first time. It also allows me to hear it more fully, seeing and understanding new facets. He explained that we don't need to be experts in self-knowledge to write meaningfully. Knowing ourselves about ten percent of the time seems about as close as most of us get, and perhaps, that's enough. Bennett wrote in his book, *Write from the Heart*: "That ten percent, like the infinitesimal specks of pollen that cling to a bee's wings, can beautify and nourish the world if we dare risk it." In the East a bee is the symbol of a mind focused on truth and beauty. In that seeking from teacher to teacher in the form of practices, books, relationships, dharma talks, therapy, fulfillments, disappointments, and the silent voice within, each of us has collected our own unique blend of pollen. The writing is perhaps my ten percent, my risk, a mirror for others and myself of this inner journey within a Buddhist context.

Buddhism spoke to me in 1985, when I took a course on the psychology of death and dying. I began reading some of Stephen Levine's work, as well as the *Tibetan Book of Dying*, I practiced many of the meditations and wrote a paper on the contemplation of my own death. It was probably the most useful assignment the University of California had ever asked its undergraduate psychology students to undertake. At the same time I was also practicing Raja Yoga, which included one-pointed meditation, devotional practices, and asanas. Although all of this con-

ALZAK AMLANI, Ph.D. (Palo Alto) was born in Uganda in 1963. He is a licensed psychologist in private practice using Eastern and Western approaches in serving primarily gay individuals, couples, and families. He gives talks and conducts seminars on Queer Spirituality, Transpersonal, Cultural, and Eco-Psychology, and Nutrition and Spirituality in the SF Bay Area. He has also published articles in those areas.

centrated work was deepening me, the essential turning point and inner crucible were forged much earlier in my life.

From my personal and professional experience as a psychotherapist, it appears that most of us are called to find meaning and begin a spiritual quest after certain crucial experiences of suffering. For some, this suffering is a constant ache for something more, what is referred to as *Dukkha* in Buddhism, a sense that something is off, not quite right in life. For others this *Dukkha* is riveted by some significant death or loss. For people with a different sexual orientation than the norm, the common experience of being an outcast, as well as facing familial and cultural homophobia while coming out can surface this experience of *Dukkha* earlier in life. The AIDS epidemic has catapulted many individuals, and perhaps the gay community into the impermanence of physical life. In my work on racism and the Sangha, I've interviewed several people of color who have faced issues of oppression and can relate to experiences of shame, inferiority, anger, and fear towards the majority. These feelings parallel those experienced by gays and lesbians.

In the Fall of 1972, I was walking home from elementary school in the capital of Uganda, East Africa. Uganda is a small country, next to Kenya, then known for its richest mineral water and coffee plantations drenched with rain and an equatorial sun. It was populated by native Africans, East Indians, other Asians, and a few Europeans, mainly from Britain. It was a haven for those seeking to explore East African wildlife, begin a new life in a developing country with open opportunities, or exploit the natural resources and cheap labor abundant at the time. In the early 1900s, given the stagnant Indian economy and the stratified class structures, many Indians left Northwestern India and sailed southwest across the warm Indian Ocean to East Africa. They often docked in the small ports of Kenya and began their trek with a native African guide across the jungles. My grandfather was one of those adventurous souls who brought his family, which included my father, from India to begin a new life in East Africa.

Consequently, I was born in Uganda. I remained a Ugandan citizen until the Fall of 1972, when Idi Amin, a ruthless dictator, declared that people of all races, except the native Africans, be exiled out of the country within ninety days. From that day onwards we were stateless. Our passports were taken away; controls were put in all commerce; there was tremendous looting and the beginning of kidnapping and killing. Much of this I saw as a young boy on the streets of Kampala, the capital. A warm, peaceful town with papaya trees, mango groves, and sugar cane fields turned into a militant war zone overnight. In short, we were warned: detach or die. This was the ultimate Buddhist practice—one the Tibetans know all too well. My father, an entrepreneur, had to give away or shut down his businesses within forty days. My mother owned and successfully operated the only Montessori school in Kampala. She walked away from the realization of her calling and lifelong dream at its most successful point. Within weeks, our extended family and community would be scattered across the globe. The words of the Buddha in the *Mahaparinirvana Sutra* provide direct and searing counsel in confronting our attachments to everything we think we are and possess.

> What is born will die,
> What has been gathered will be dispersed,
> What has been accumulated will be exhausted,
> What has been built up will collapse,
> And what has been high will be brought low.

We were thrust into the common stages of death—denial, anger, bargaining, depression, and acceptance. We gave everything away, said good-bye, drove off our driveway, and flew off the continent on East African Airlines—all of this in about sixty days. After some time of living in a hostel in Naples, Italy, we found ourselves in Los Angeles, California.

My two brothers and I walked to elementary school in a rough neighborhood in Los Angeles, just a few years after the L.A. riots, to encounter threats and regular physical attacks by boys who thought we were white. Another experience of reverse discrimination—we were not welcome here either. Unlike my brothers, my quieter and more timid personality saved me from serious fights. This was one advantage of being a sissy. One day I think a higher power took over and my two brothers and I walked out of school and declared in unison to our parents, we were never going back to that school. In essence, we were on strike. Of course, they offered their usual Indian counsel about tolerance, patience, courage, and standing up for ourselves. In short, they maintained, you must go back to school. This was done in Gujrati, a Sanskrit based language known for its diplomacy and cajoling through parable and anecdote. We didn't buy it, not this time. Our decision was already made.

It must've been on this day that my parents realized we were in America and their children were going to be independent Americans. There was no going back. We had been forced out of the garden of Eden, our home, the place of familiarity and comfort. The primary, idealistic vision of life was annihilated in only a few months. By recalling the life of the Buddha, I am reminded of how when he left his father's kingdom he was cast into the real world of disease and death. His naive days under the protection of his family were over. The little comfort and safety the gay community may have enjoyed before the AIDS crisis were also shattered, practically overnight. One of the reasons I think Buddhism speaks to many of us at this time is because the Buddha's story mirrors our process of facing fragmentation of our personal and collective worlds. Carl Jung sadly stated that *fragmentation* would be the prevailing archetype of the twentieth century. As we look back on this millenium and acknowledge the current world crisis, we can easily resonate with Jung's perception.

Fragmentation often precedes wholeness. As the Buddha so poignantly described, death is followed by rebirth. A rebirth of another order. The old consciousness must die since it cannot comprehend the emerging consciousness—one that is closer to the Buddha. Honoring and becoming skillful at allowing things to crumble when it's time, and then being present for the rebirth, is a central theme in spiritual life.

Fortunately after my family survived the biggest explosion of our lives at the hands of Idi Amin, we finally moved to Santa Monica, a pleasant coastal town where other Indians were also settling. This move was a significant turning point. It felt like grace—a quiet peace after a storm. My experience is that if we can fully move through the crumbling of our lives with a certain amount of consciousness or reflective awareness, then when the resolution arrives, it is at a deeper level. A new understanding, letting go, clarity, compassion, or peace arrives. In the words of Jack Kornfield:

When we finally look at horror and joy, birth and death, gain and loss, things, with an equal heart and open mind, there arises a most beautiful and profound equanimity.

The political explosion we endured was followed by a personal explosion—learning about my gayness and coming out. Actually, I think I've been gay ever since I can remember. I would get nervous around an uncle who would come and visit from London—wondering whether he noticed and liked me. I so much wanted his attention and approval. Throughout much of my childhood, I had one close male companion to confide in. As boys we would go on bike rides, walk to the beach together, listen to music, and just picnic in the backyard and tell each other our stories. I think gay boys have a natural proclivity towards reflection and making meaning out of their experiences. This may be due to a more developed inner feminine, what Carl Jung called a man's anima—a man's feeling nature or soul. Some Jungians suggest that unlike a heterosexual, a homosexual man is less likely to project his soul image onto another, but rather relates to his inner process as a deeper aspect. The psychologist Terry Tafoya talks about this in Native American terms, naming it two-spirited. Gay boys have to begin to make some sense of their two-spiritedness—carrying the feminine in a male body. We project our persona, or developing outer masculine image, onto a person of the same sex. We fall in love with our uncles, fathers, and other boys—seeking attention, admiration, acceptance, and protection of our inner sensitive parts.

Unfortunately, these tender feelings are often not seen, misunderstood, or shamed. I remember numerous incidents where such exposing of my inner feminine and desiring closeness with another male were shamed. This is not only a shaming and rejection of erotic feelings, but also our soul nature. My love of men, beauty, and spirit are deeply connected. Shaming my eroticism shames my connection to my body, nature, the feminine, and ultimately the Divine in physical form. I believe as explained by therapist William Schindler in his article "Gay Love as a Spiritual Path," that gay men have a natural proclivity towards the path of the ecstatic rather than the ascetic. He explains:

> The ascetic approach emphasizes renunciation of sensual experience in an effort to achieve a one-pointed state of mind or a transformative insight; the ecstatic approach emphasizes engaging sensory experience with a radical shift in attitude to experience the divine essence within the forms of the phenomenal world.

Schindler explains that as gays we experience quite a different relationship to the erotic by virtue of inhabiting physical bodies that are erotically stimulating to ourselves. Some of us may not experience this if we learned at an early age to deny and censor homoerotic impulses and awareness even to ourselves. We take the object of our erotic desire with us, moving, breathing, bathing, and even sleeping with our own male body. Perhaps this is why a strictly ascetic, long-term monastic approach may not be appropriate for a gay man. Forcing an ascetic approach on a gay person creates greater neurosis, frustration, anger, depression, or spiritual pride.

When I first began meditating in the early eighties, I imposed an ascetic approach upon myself. I truly believed that the monastic life was most suited for someone seeking the quickest way to enlightenment. This was partly what I was learning in the Yoga tradition and it was also a reflection of my own lack of acceptance of my sensuality. I equated sexuality with impurity, attachment, and bondage to the physical cycles of death and rebirth. There was no beauty, love, or spirit related to it. It was the denial of an essential avenue of the senses to awaken and intensify my connection with the essence of all life. Unfortunately, some of the yoga meditation teachers that I consulted in the early eighties, felt that as a gay person, I was in a perfect position to renounce a mate, family, and the world and become a monk.

I attempted to live a celibate, ascetic life. I practiced long meditations, spent much time in silence and solitude, reading, and praying. Although this formed a fairly solid base of spiritual practice while enjoying cultivating inner states of consciousness, I was pushing away my gayness. I was working hard at attempting to transcend my sexuality and become more pure. I was still thinking about joining a monastic order. I had already been through some therapy and realized on one level that I needed to explore, understand, appreciate, and integrate my gayness. Nevertheless, the monastic pull and the fear of fully coming out and working through the wounds of being gay in my family and in a homophobic world were overwhelming. Spiritual practice helped build a ground and some equilibrium to do the psychological work that followed, but I was also using the practices to hide my essential humanness.

Jack Kornfield's thoughts point out the problems with this approach:

> We hear about transcending our ego, or seek to attain divine states and purity, beyond desire, beyond the body; we are taught that enlightenment is to be found through renunciation; we believe it is somewhere beyond or outside ourselves. The notion of attaining a pure and divine abode fits unfortunately well with whatever neurotic, fearful, or idealistic tendencies we may have. To the extent that we see ourselves to be impure, shameful, or unworthy, we may use spiritual precepts and forms, we may hope to create a pure spiritual identity. In India this is called the Golden Chain. It's not a chain of iron, but it's still a chain.

As I continued to stay in therapy I worked on re-establishing a relationship with my body. Through dialoguing between the body and mind, allowing one to speak to another, I truly heard the lack of acceptance and judgment the mind was wielding on the body. I heard the body cry out for touch and warmth. As I now work with gay men in my practice I notice how they are using sex to fulfill the need for touch, affection, acceptance, and safety. Often memories of craving affection from their fathers arises and remembering how their fathers pulled away, fearing closeness with their more effeminate or homosexual son. I recently heard Andrew Harvey, the gay mystic and author explain that the original word for God the Father was *Abba*. *Abba* translates to daddy, not father. Daddy is closer, safer, and more intimate. I think a gay child or man, often more in touch with and even identified with his feminine side, has a special desire for daddy's love. If worked with appropriately, this could be an avenue for valuable spiritual growth. When I have heard men dialogue with their image of daddy or father, both as their dad and as an archetype, they will first experience fear, shame, and even hatred. As they keep dialoguing and feeling, it will turn into sadness, longing, and desire. This can either be fulfilled in human form or can be worked with in meditation.

In my own personal work touch became a powerful way to get out of the trap of the mind with all its expectations and standards. Getting a massage or being held gave me the experience of safety and trust that the body had forgotten. It relaxed and opened me. I remember a few instances when I would look in the mirror after a couple of hours of my partner and I holding each other, and my face looked completely different. My forehead, jaw, and neck would be fully relaxed and my eyes clear and soft. My partner noticed that my skin had a soft radiance. Although meditation had offered some wonderful states, this was different. My body had been held in the arms of love and acceptance and my heart heard it. It was a fuller experience of embodying. I consider this to be one of the significant spiritual experiences I've had. Perhaps it is in moments like this where the body meets the spirit.

I am reminded of numerous studies described by Dr. Dean Ornish in his book, *Love and Survival*, about health, touch, and intimacy. He explained that no factor in medicine—not diet, exercise, smoking, drugs, surgery, genetics—no other factor has a more powerful effect on our heart, and premature death and disease, and from virtually all causes, as the healing power of love and intimacy. Touch is a direct connection with each other—the largest organ is the skin. Premature babies in one study who were given three loving massages a day, for just ten days, gained weight 47% faster, and left the hospital 6 days sooner, saving an average of $10,000, just from touch. James Lynch at the University of Maryland, measured a significant reduction in irregular heartbeat that occurred when the nurse or the doctor just took the patient's pulse. Sometimes in an intensive care unit, surrounded with all that machinery, the only contact that many patients have is that moment when they get touched by their doctor or nurse. Researchers observed couples in cafes in different parts of the world and counted how many times they touched each other, on the cheek or arm, or wherever, in one hour. In Puerto Rico, they touched 180 times an hour. In Paris they touched 110 times an hour. In the U.S. twice, whether they needed it or not, and in London they didn't touch at all.

In my travels to India and Africa I noticed that children were held most of the time by numerous members of the family. The mothering and nurturing is done by various maternal figures—aunts, uncles, grandparents, older siblings, and neighbors. It was rare to see a child in a crib, stroller, or even in a separate bedroom. The maternal matrix is more greatly intact than it is here in the West. This creates a greater sense of belongingness, acceptance, and trust that when in need others will be there. There is a deeper incorporation of the maternal and the feminine. From my observation it appears that when there are less material resources, human beings become the primary resources. This calls forth a deeper sensitivity, maturity, and ability to give of oneself to another. Selflessness and perhaps detachment to things becomes a way of life. Although in many parts of India and Africa there is much poverty, I have also noticed a greater sense of contentment and joy. I remember a friend telling me about an experience with a very poor maid in Bengal, India. He was a guest in a very small home where this maid would come and clean. She was extremely poor, away from her family and had a few belongings she kept in a small bag in the hallway where she slept. My American friend had admired a small, beautiful, metal sculpture of one of his favorite Hindu deities in her bag. At the end of his stay when the maid wished him good-bye, she gave him that statue. He witnessed that her joy in giving was equal to his in receiving. Although this may be a small object, it nevertheless speaks to the natural sensibilities of generosity of some of the poorer people living in the villages of the world.

One of my mentors and dear friend for about ten years is Robert Johnson, the Jungian analyst and author of several books including *He, She, Inner Work*, and more recently, *Balancing Heaven and Earth*. When I did my roots trip to India in 1996, I spent about ten days with Robert in Pondicherry, South India. He has been journeying through South India for about seventeen years and knows it like the back of his hand. We had ample time sitting at small Indian cafes drinking chai and sharing experiences, observations, and questions, while I was enjoying the procession of beautiful men draped in their traditional colorful shawls and flowing Indian lungis and dhotis elegantly wrapped around their waists. On one of those mornings Robert told me a beautiful story about same sex intimacy between men in India, which he also writes about. He shared:

One day I was riding my bicycle, minding my own business—though nothing is ever entirely one's own business in India—when a young fellow came along paralleling me. In good Anglo-Saxon style I moved over slightly and dutifully looked straight ahead. The young fellow remained parallel to me, so I moved over a little farther—but he was still there. Presently he reached out, took my hand and we proceeded for a block, riding together hand in hand. He turned off at the next street and I never saw him again. But feeling was engaged and a bond was made that is the genius of India.

What this made clear to me as an American is that one of the great barriers to us, with our Western mind of understanding, is that some of the forms of love which are not common to us we tend to sexualize, and we ascribe sexuality to things which aren't necessarily attached to that part of our nature. I am in no way diminishing sexuality, but it's not everything. To ride a bicycle holding hands with a stranger, this is the homoerotic world. It is affection, devotion, one of the ninety-six kinds of love described in Sanskrit which we cannot comprehend.

In South India *Skanda* is considered the God of homosexuals. The myth of Skanda describes male bonding, cohesion, community, and non-procreative sexuality. The name Skanda is associated with masculine procreative function and means "spurt of semen," being born of Siva's semen. Several other deities have homosexual, androgynous, transvestite, and bisexual attributes. Ozmo Piedmont, Ph.D., has done extensive research in this area. Although Indian mythology abounds with homosexual relations, contemporary gay India has split off homoeroticism with its spirituality. Nevertheless, there are a few individuals and groups integrating and reviving the gay culture.

In India, I would frequently see men holding hands, sitting close together in restaurants, touching, and speaking affectionately to one another. It was such a delight to experience intimacy exchanged with deep glances and open hearts. An Australian friend commented that he would like to be reborn in India just to enjoy such exchanges. I found in many men a striking comfort with feelings and relatedness as I conversed and spent time with them. They would look deeply into my eyes, hold my hand, and would delight in my enjoyment. The various defensive personality structure so common in men socialized in the West are less developed in men of Eastern and indigenous cultures. Westerners could learn from these older traditions on how to be men, without personas, games, and layers of false selves.

The cult-like vanity with its obsessive focus on looks, image, and muscles only keeps us from fully dropping below the shallow line to discover the real essence of what it is to be a gay human being. Our constant fear of growing old keeps us from growing up. Fortunately, a wide variety of social, sexual, and now spiritual subcultures have developed in the gay community. Another phenomenon has also continued over the years, almost unabated. Michelangelo Signorile in his book, *Life Outside* describes it well:

There is an overriding, mostly white, youth-focused, and often drug-fueled social and sexual gay male scene that is highly commercialized and demands conformity to a very specific body ideal. Its cultural influence and impact are significant, and it affects many—perhaps most—gay men, even if they think they are far removed from it, regardless of whether they belong to other subcultures or social groups within the gay world or not.

Signorile explains that after many years of being stigmatized as effeminate and less than manly, many white, middle-class gay men also enthusiastically conform to an idealized version of physical manhood of—"muscles, mustaches, and tight jeans." He suggests that the influence of this hypermasculine "clone" aesthetic is inebriating many levels of the gay collective. Even for those who eschew the pumped and hairless clone, and have access to a wider variety of gay men and gay subcultures, "the shaved muscle boy aesthetic and all of the baggage that comes with it is omnipresent." The traps of beauty, youth, and being thin, commonly reserved for middle- and upper-class women in the U.S. are quickly spreading to gay men. When dating and in situations where men are seeking partners, I've noticed how quickly we go down our list and either approve or disapprove a potential partner in minutes. I can recall numerous times when friends and clients after having enjoyed the company of a date, explained convincingly, "I really am not attracted to anyone who is under six feet; He's just a little too stocky for me; Everyone I've dated always had a swimmer's build." Often older men who have practiced spiritual disciplines for decades reveal being exclusively interested in athletic thirty year olds. Is it a desire they need to act on, or can it be enjoyed internally? Do same-sex relationships where there is a significant age difference work better? They also wonder if it is their attempt to regain and enjoy youth and vigor. Perhaps, in a youth focused culture, it's difficult to appreciate their own and their peers' beauty as they change and age. I've talked with healthy, conscious men aware of issues of racism and sexism who reject terrific and attractive men after just two dates because they didn't feel that intense sizzle after four hours of knowing them. If we look at these questions without blame or judgment, especially through gay Buddhist spirituality, much can be learned about ourselves. Are we living in traps that keep us from developing relationships with people who understand us, share our values, and can meet our deeper needs, even if they aren't gorgeous models, work out every day, and start looking like muscle robots? Do we now have to add looksism and body fascism to the "isms" and "obias" we've struggled with?

The gay media plays a significant role in reinforcing particular stereotypes that many of us subconsciously imitate and expect from others. These include the little publications—"bar rags"—found in every major American city, filled with images of "perfect" gay men setting the standard. Signorile notices that:

> These same images are played back to us again and again in gay porn, on safer sex posters, and in dozens of gay newspapers and several glossy national magazines that often sport pumped-up coverboys and fetching ads selling products and events, from underwear to hot parties.

Does this obsession with the hyper-masculine have anything to do with internalized homophobia? Is this obsession fueled by the fear of not living up to the heterosexual definitions of masculinity? Is it a reflection of not healing due to exclusion from the "in" crowd as teenagers? Is joining this cult of pseudo masculinity another way of never being excluded again? Are we in any way imposing the shame and lack of acceptance we experienced growing up in a straight, competitive, homophobic culture onto ourselves and each other? Have we as gay men traded in our imprisoning iron chains from the heterosexual world for golden chains of the gay world? These are questions that reflective, psychologically, and spiritually aware men in the gay community need to be asking. I think these are spiritual issues because freeing ourselves from the false self perpetuated and reinforced by cultural entrapments is a central theme in spiritual development. Moving the center of gravity from the ego to the Self, as Carl Jung said, is the work of the spiritual aspirant.

In this challenging process of undoing into no self, we seem to need teachers in numerous forms. Some of my teachers in the Buddhist tradition have been Joseph Goldstein, Stephen Levine, Arinna Weisman, Eric Kolvig, Mark Epstein, Gil Frondal, and Jack Kornfield, who provides some excellent guidelines on choosing a teacher in his book *A Path with Heart*:

> If we are seeking a new teacher, we should inquire directly about how they teach. How do they view the path of practice, and what is the goal? What form does their practice take? How do they guide students? Will we be able to spend time with this teacher? Will we actually get students through the arduous parts of the spiritual journey? What is the sense of the community around the teacher? Then we need to look at what is asked of us. Does what is asked feel healthy and appropriate? What commitments are necessary? What kind of relationship is expected? How much time is required? What does it cost?
>
> In seeking a teacher, we must listen to our heart, and we must look at our-

selves with honesty. What are we really seeking? Is this what is offered by this teacher and by this way of practice? What draws us to this teacher? Does this teacher and way of practice fit my temperament and serve me, or conversely, does it reinforce my fears and neuroses? Would it serve me to go into a large and extroverted group community when I'm a very shy person who has hidden for years, or might I get overwhelmed and stuck further in my shyness? Do I need the discipline of a strict Zen master, and the stick that is used to keep students sitting straight, or was I abused and beaten as a child, and would this only recreate and reinforce a painful and negative sense of myself? What cycle of my spiritual life is it time for—silence or service, meditation or study?

But more than teachers, especially for gays, I think we need mentors. The way of mentorship is an age-old tradition. The term "mentor" is derived from a character in *The Odyssey*, who was entrusted by Ulysses to care for and educate his son, Telemachus, for about ten years. The goddess of wisdom, Athena, disguised as Mentor, would often help guide the young Telemachus. A good mentor is a kindred spirit who sees something special in us, perhaps what we could become; psychologist Daniel Levinson describes it as "the realization of the Dream." Could this suggest that the Buddha teaches through the medium of our mentors? As I look back into my life I am aware that my sister, who was eight years older than myself, was one of my first mentors. We would go on long walks together, even when I was only seven or eight, and we'd talk and share stories. A trust and constant companionship was forming between us. She would ask me questions and help me find the answers I was looking for. She was the first person in my family to whom I came out. I remember, when I was fifteen, the two of us sitting in her little car on the seashore of Magnolia Bluffs near Seattle, WA, when I finally put words to those difficult feelings. She was extremely accepting and had no judgments on me. It was a good beginning in my coming out process. We were kindred spirits. As I matured and she faced some challenges, I also at times mentored her.

Gregg Levoy in his book *Callings*, has a passage on such relationships:

> This perception of oneself in another person is one of the cornerstones of what Carl Jung called generativity, in which elders turn around and begin helping, serving even the generation coming up behind them. It's part of the work of individuation, of people-making and culture-making. It's an essential part of growing up and old, Jung said—a station of the cross. If elders aren't encouraging younger people, a vital link in the chain is missing, a gap opens in the bucket brigade, and the water buckets are dropped onto empty ground.

Generativity, the passing of the baton from elder to younger, is *inherent* in mentoring. The original Mentor was a gift, in a sense, from father to son, from sovereign to successor. "We all need someone higher, wiser, and older," Ray Bradbury once said, "to tell us we're not crazy after all, that what we're doing is all right. All right, hell, fine!"

In graduate school one of my professors, who was an extremely bright and humble man, was a mentor to me. Not only was he a genius researcher, but also a quiet, spiritual man. He was Caucasian, yet he reminded me of a Chinese Taoist—patient, clear, and wisely accepting of even undesirable outcomes. Although he had quite a bit of power over me, he never used it to advance his agenda. He securely carried for me my own gold of talents and abilities. Through the years he has helped me reclaim my projections and cultivate those talents that I have continued to admire in him. This is the quintessential dynamic between mentors and mentees—humbly accepting the student's own higher qualities as they are put on the teacher, so that in due time, they can be returned to the student for his or her benefit. When appropriate the mentor is a guide providing a map in helping surface the mentee's inner sagacity. The teacher must also be willing to carry the student's lead and be seen as negative and unlikeable. For a gay seeker this can be a great opportunity to become aware of, and work through, negative father issues. The mentor has the opportunity to grow bigger, take a few blows, and still endeavor to remain loyal, present, and offer unconditional love. Throughout the process the mentor recognizes the mentee as one of his indirect teachers. At a later point it might also be appropriate to let the student go. Today, my advisor and I continue to meet and work together on research projects at the William James Center for Consciousness Studies in Palo Alto. Mentors come in numerous forms, change over time, and can last a day or a lifetime.

I am in the process of transitioning out of an intense ten year relationship with one of my mentors who is both a Zen monk and a psychologist. We worked through numerous aspects of our relationship: teacher and student, father and son, racial differences, sexual tension, and developing a friendship outside these roles. He has helped me honor my inner teacher and my grief, as we've moved through various phases of our relationship. At this point he is preparing for the death of his body. I hope to be a companion as he makes his transition. Recently he shared a powerful Zen story with me.

A traditional Zen master in a Japanese monastery had a dozen or so very respectful and obedient students under his guidance. The atmosphere was firm with loyalty and devotion to the master. One day a student got up, stopped his master from his instructions, and said: "You old humbug, I see through you," and walked out. The master exclaimed: "He was the best and it took him ten years to realize it."

Perhaps the last compliment you can pay your teacher is to leave.

One of the characteristics I find invaluable about the Buddhist tradition is that teachers are built in. Anyone doing serious practice seems to have a teacher who supports, models, and points out blind spots. Since growing up in a homophobic world means hiding our gayness, it often gets split off from our spirituality. Having teachers who are open to understanding what gay spirituality may look like allows us to explore archetypes within the gay psyche and find ways of expressing spirit that are congruent with our natures. Additionally, it helps dissolve the internalized homophobia many of us are plagued with. Schindler shares in his article about the gay aspect of God:

> To be able to embark upon the mystical quest with maximum confidence, enthusiasm, and energy gay people need to overcome their sense of ontological alienation from God; they need to know that God also truly is Gay, not in an exclusive sense but in the sense of "That too." God is gay because God is the source of love, all kinds of love. God is Gay because God is both male and female as well as that which is neither. To truly know that God is Gay, that their deepest self is one with the Divine Self, gay people need to learn how they can approach God with and through their gay sexuality, without having to try to leave the essential component of their being at the door, as it were. What is needed to unleash the power of gay love to propel gay persons to the threshold of mystical realization, therefore, is a living spiritual tradition with direct access to the lines of transmission of powerful, systematic spiritual technologies, coupled with rigorous elimination of intra-psychic and interpersonal homophobic processes that divide and dissipate one's psychic energies.

Because we change, sometimes our teachers change. As I have changed I have also incorporated into Buddhism various teachings from Hinduism, Sufism (which are my roots), Shamanism, transpersonal psychology, and more recently eco-spirituality. The life and message of the Persian poet and mystic Jalalud-Din Rumi have made a profound contribution to my practice in the last year. In 1998, more Americans read Rumi than any other poet. I think Rumi speaks quite deeply to a gay heart because he fell completely and fully in love with his teacher Shams of Tabriz. Rumi's poetry is an outpouring of longing for his Beloved Shams. It is said that after they first met, they were arm in arm for 40 days. No one knows exactly what transpired behind those doors, but his beautiful, brilliant, and sensuous poetry speaks of the immense love and profound wisdom that was birthed out of their relationship. Whether there was any sexual component to their union, no one will ever know, but it certainly is homoerotic. Following is one of my favorite poems that Rumi spoke after his Beloved, Shams, disappeared:

> When you feel your lips becoming infinite and sweet
> like the moon in the sky,
> When you feel that spaciousness inside
> Shams of Tabriz will be there too.
> Something opens our wings
> something makes boredom and hurt disappear.
> Someone fills the cup in front of us.
> We taste only sacredness.

Rumi is considered a non-dual mystic-poet. Non-duality is the recognition that in the absolute sense there is no I and you. Everything is the same consciousness manifesting in various forms. Ultimately there is no goal to be reached and nothing to be attained. Anytime there is a goal, there appears an I, which is rooted in duality, where the tension of opposites creates *Dukkha*, or suffering. We are the Self and exist always. This is expressed in all the great traditions. Lama Surya Das, the author of *Awakening the Buddha Within* teaches it through the Nyingma Lineage from Tibet, the *Dzogchen*, meaning the Great Perfection. In India this view is referred to as *Advaita Vedanta*, and Self-inquiry or *vichara* is the primary practice, where the seeker continually asks, "Who am I?" Through that asking one recognizes that the various "I's," thought to be oneself, are temporal and therefore bound by birth and death. Anything existing in time and space must die, and therefore will cause suffering. The Buddha said, "No bodhisattva who is a real bodhisattva cherishes the idea of an ego entity, a personality, a being, or a separated individuality."

Rather than always trying to be non-attached to experiences and results, I ask myself, who is attached? The following shortened version of a dialogue with myself ensued.

Response: In doing this, I realize the root of my attachment is fear— fear of being destroyed.
Question: Who is afraid of destruction?
R: It appears that the body is afraid. It is afraid of death and annihilation.

Q: Who is noticing this fear of the body?
R: Some presence/witness/awareness recognizes the fear of the body.
Q: Can this awareness be destroyed?
R: I don't know.
Q: Has this presence ever not been there?
R: It was there as a witness when I was a young child.
Q: Is it changed or hurt by the various experiences in life?
R: It simply notices everything.
Q: Put more of your attention on this awareness and see what happens.
R: It appears that my heart opens. All these thoughts and desire then appear.
Q: Once again turn to that awareness.
R: It's there as silence. It's very calm and very quiet. It appears that nothing exists here. Then there is joy, a release, a burst of life.
Q: Now look at the fear again.
R: It has dissipated, almost dissolved. I am reminded of Rumi's words: "There's no need to go outside. Be melting snow. Wash yourself of yourself."

I worked with my fear by turning back or returning into the no self, or Awareness. By constantly looking at the spaciousness, the ego or fear became transient. I have also worked with various clients, who have some background in meditation, in this manner quite often. Recently, I attended a training on non-dual approaches to psychotherapy by an organization called Spiritual Wisdom and Mental Health. Peter Fenner, who was a Zen Monk for ten years, worked with us in what he called "undoing the self." Western psychology is very good at building the ego, but it takes such an Eastern approach to free the ego, or more accurately, to realize its unreality. Actually there have also been Christian and Jewish Mystics who have experienced and written about the same undoing. Lama Surya Das points out that the senior Tibetan Lamas are suggesting that non-dual approaches "are the teaching of our time." The practice is applicable to any circumstance or situation, and easily integrated into modern life. It dissolves the boundary between practical and daily living and cuts through habitual stories and interpretations which limit us. This is not to suggest that our personal stories don't have meaning; they do. Even when painful, they can be quite beautiful. But there is another level of knowing and freedom that transcends the content of our lives and is unborn.

The words of the Indian Sage, Ramana Maharshi, provide a direct seeing into Truth, which is our deeper nature:

Reality is simply the loss of the ego. Destroy the ego by seeking its identity. It will automatically vanish and reality will shine forth by itself. This is the direct method. There is no greater mystery than this, that we keep seeking reality though, in fact, we are reality. We think that there is something hiding reality and that this must be destroyed before reality is gained. How ridiculous! A day will dawn when you will laugh at your past efforts. That which will be on the day you laugh is also here and now.

At present my own efforts are changing. For years I have practiced more arduous disciplines of sitting for hours, fasting, and intensely focusing on my goal. Perhaps that was the approach I needed at the time. It may have also helped me gain a sense of self-mastery and control, something I didn't feel as a child. It also provided another way to become my own person—individuating from family and culture. Currently, I am resting more, letting go. The awakening has already happened. The natural state is Buddhahood and it actually takes more effort to stay separate from Oneness than it does to recognize that. One's natural state should be effortless. When I put aside techniques and will, that which I seek through effort arises without effort. The Persian poet, Rumi says it this way: "Not only the thirsty seeks the water, but the water seeks the thirsty as well." All we really have to do is drink—let the water seek and quench us. For those of us in the West who are so conditioned to do, expend effort, and make things happen, this is an awkward proposition. The Dzogchen and Advaita teachings have helped me sit with this. Teachers in both of those traditions have asked me to do less, be quiet, rest, and just pay attention. Some of them have gone as far as saying there is nothing I can do about my realization. It's time to let grace work. This suggestion is frustrating and even scary, especially for someone who puts such great value in daily spiritual practice.

But I am learning that often it's the mind and ego, the "I" which wants realization so badly, that is actually where the problem is. The "I" can never have Buddha nature. How can something as vast and mysterious as Pure Awareness be understood by the mind? Alzak will never understand it. It's even arrogant of me to presume that I can ever get it. As this surrendering into not knowing and not being able to get "It" occurs, there is a shift. The spaciousness, love, trust, and freedom I've wanted simply appears. It just is. In most cases, I just want to be quiet, not think. Of course, my mind wants to jump in and get back to work—analyzing it, questioning it, and wanting the experience to last and remain in that form. At that point I just watch the agile mind attempting to control the situation, and usually laughter appears. It's now become funny and even entertaining to witness the futile attempts of the mind to find the secret formula for this great sweet Presence that we all want. But the mystery is that this deliciousness we are seeking is seeking us. The Sufis say that the deliciousness is seeking itself. It knows exactly what to do and how to do it. The more I can get out of the way, the more I can enjoy its genius and play in my life.

Ramana Maharshi puts it this way:

> Do not fuss or worry about what you have to do or not to do. What as work has to be done through you will be done whether you like it or not. Simply be Still, be inwardly Still.

My friend and mentor, Robert Johnson, has often said he feels best when he's nobody, a zero. When I have visited him he has sometimes said to me, "It's easy to be around you because you're a nobody." Emily Dickinson's Poem 288, composed in 1861, says it best.

> I'm Nobody! Who are you?
> Are you—Nobody—too?
> Then there's a pair of us!

I have noticed that often the greatest fulfillment in being with another has come when both of us become empty of self and let the Void fill the gap. At first there might even be discomfort, but after some of the words have decreased, a Great Silence, an Awareness, or Peace seems to pervade the space. Honoring this space and paying homage to what appears is my spiritual practice. I find this occurs even in the midst of suffering and disappointment. By fully acknowledging and surrendering into the pain, a profound connection is made. We are both in it together, and in our togetherness there is deep compassion and love.

I would like to end with the wisdom of the Dzogchen teacher in the Tibetan Nyingma tradition, Urgyen Tulku Rinpoche, author of *Repeating the Words of the Buddha*. After Dilgo Khyentse died in 1991, Urgyen Tulku, who had been a teacher to the Dalai Lama, was regarded by many as the most eminent Dzogchen teacher in the world. Arjuna Nick Ardaugh in his book, *Relaxing into Clear Seeing*, asked Urgyen Tulku in Nepal, about his fear of leaving this serene monastery and returning to his family and responsibilities of the world. Arjuna reports than the Rinpoche gestured to the view from the panoramic window, to the chaos and pollution of the Katmandu valley far below, and quietly said these words:

When the Heart is so overwhelmed with compassion, seeing the suffering of humanity, that the hairs on your arms stand on end and tears involuntarily flow down your cheeks, then you are in the natural state. And when you are so overwhelmed with devotion and love, seeing the beauty of all sentient beings, that the hairs on your arms stand on end and tears involuntarily flow down your cheeks, then you are in the natural state.

Michael P. Hyman, California. Photo by Customs Image

Doubt and Commitment in Buddhist Practice:
A Gay Perspective

Michael P. Hyman

I was born Jewish, but it didn't seem to be enough. The arrogance of such a statement, bypassing over 5000 years of tradition and countless lives of sacrifice, arrests me as I write it. As a student of the Holocaust, I recently visited Auschwitz. Wherever I go, I seem to encounter ancient Jewish cemeteries and memorials to Jewish suffering.

The sound of klezmer, the prose of Singer, and the relentless litany of Holocaust memoirs bathe me in my Jewishness. Even if I wished for it, there is no escape. But I don't wish for it—I embrace this huge part of my life. I never trusted Jung's collective unconscious until I realized that there had to be more to this enormous awareness than the tiny spark of one's solitary life.

Nevertheless, I'm one of those "Bujus." Judaism was not enough. I could blame it on my kind and loving parents, whose mundane secularism produced a "lox and bagels family." My father and I stood side by side in the tiny Bronx tenement synagogue only on High Holy Days, my mother at home, cooking. My parents sacrificed their dearly earned income and three of my five afternoons a week for five years, just so I could sing a memorized, three page haftorah for Bar Mitzvah. I could blame the American diaspora, which for my generation offered no spiritual inspiration. I could blame the Old Testament, which liberally bestows wisdom and judgment alike. I could blame God, if I had any faith in its existence.

But of course blame is a diversion, wasteful for our short lives. The entertainment of blame fails to satiate my appetite for understanding. I continue to pick up books that attempt to link Buddhism and Judaism. Or books that explore the esoteric in Judaism. The most recent hit, now a movie, is *The Jew in the Lotus*. Its author, Roger Kamenetz, begins with the earnest superiority of a spectrum of modern Jewish practitioners and theorists who journey to Dharmsala in northern India. Their mission is to convey the secrets of religious and cultural survival to the Dalai Lama and his Tibetan people. Two striking things emerge from this remarkable meeting: first, certain underlying mystical points

MICHAEL P. HYMAN (Sonoma, CA) was born in 1945 and practices at Sonoma Shambhala Center. He is currently exploring the Dzogchen tradition. Living with his partner Bill Shean (a Tibetan practitioner), Michael is a pathologist and writer. He dedicates this article to his parents.

of contact between the Jews and Tibetans (belief in angels, Unity, etc.). Then, he encounters all these Bujus and begins to inquire, why do so many Jews find Judaism insufficient and why do they drift to Buddhism?

I left Judaism as a religion before I encountered Buddhism. I left because the Judeo-Christian god means nothing to me. The conventional American Jewish ritual of the 50's and 60's transmitted its lyrical beauty only insofar as I remained ignorant of the meaning. As soon as I translated the insularity and vengeance which follow upon words of love and redemption, I could go no further. The culture of Jewish renewal and New Age demystification of the liturgy softens the punitive quality of Yahweh. In doing so, it dilutes the poetry and music. For me, whatever it has become, it is no longer Jewish.

The Jewish tradition has always been strongly intellectual. But modern American Judaism is largely cultural. Contemporary American Christian fundamentalism is avowedly anti-intellectual. Buddhism beckons to the intellect even as it requires a commitment to practice.

In *The Jew in the Lotus*, Rabbi Zalman Schachter and Jonathan Omer-Man become intrigued by Buddhism and practice the Jewish esoteric. Despite years of Buddhist practice, I am always willing to reconsider, "Is there a way back?" If I were straight, would that make a difference? No. The god of traditional Judaism calls forth a kind of devotion that I don't possess. He has no power. The rarified Jewish esoteric seems opaque, almost deliberately so, in contrast to the clarity of Buddhism.

But Kamenetz concedes that the genius of Judaism, what it really offers in contrast to Buddhism, is its roots in the exoteric, ethics, and reliance on family life, i.e., they still want to hook me up with the rabbi's daughter. I'm sure I could find some congregation that would accept me in the way that so many gays slide into Episcopalian pews: the nicely dressed token fagala confirming the standard liberalism of a suburban, hip, middle class, reform congregation. I cannot embrace this spirituality because it seems so tribal and my other tribe performs unspeakable acts that require a lot of tiptoeing by all involved.

For the gay Jewish man, maybe more than he is willing to acknowledge, the gay iceberg sinks the Jewish Titanic. There may be isolated congregations in Massachusetts or L.A. who accept my sexuality or even on occasion, an all gay/lesbian one, but Judaism by and large is practiced as a social religion where I am not welcome. As a little boy I sensed the danger of judgment among the bearded with their prayer shawls. I still do. But, these are my people. To summarize: There is a yearning to believe, but I don't. There is a yearning to fit in, but I can't. So

I may as well depart forever: impossible.

There is another book in front of me: *Kaddish* by Leon Wieseltier. It's the story of a man's re-entry into Judaism on the death of his father. I will read it. And so it goes.

*   *   *

Twenty-five years of American materialism brought mid-life crisis and the inevitable self-inquiries. First, Alan Watts, then Kapleau-Roshi's *Three Pillars of Zen*. I was on my Way. I went to Rochester, N.Y. for the necessary interviews, joined the local group in Denver, and signed up for my first sesshin. It seemed extraordinarily goal-oriented. People were encouraged to get up at night and sit. We were crammed into an urban basement on the floor. People hacked away with winter colds, climbing over one another all night. I couldn't sleep at all. Next day I heard a city bus drive by the window. I got up and left, never regretting it. I gave up zen for two or three years.

Then I read *Zen Mind, Beginner's Mind* by Suzuki Roshi, the great teacher who died in 1971. The spark re-ignited. I searched far and wide for a teacher in his lineage. I tried to find Baker-Roshi in New Mexico and later in Crestone, Colo. He was always somewhere else or not available for new students. Chino-Roshi, not exactly a "dharma heir" but in Suzuki-Roshi's lineage, was much closer to my Denver home. He answered the phone personally from his Taos, N.M. home. I remember calling him from work, dark at 5 P.M. in December, barely understanding a word of his fragmented English within a poor phone connection. But I did comprehend his imperative: "Just go sit!" Clunk.

Most books, teachers and students at that time emphasized the need for a teacher. I even visited Glassman-Roshi in Riverdale, N.Y. During a hybrid Jewish-Buddhist ceremony, there were folks dancing and singing. Murmurs of discontent in the kitchen revolved around the social-activist direction towards which Glassman was drawing them. At that time I was not interested in what later became his brilliant Greystone-Peacemaker mandala.

So I wandered further and found my teacher on the west coast: the one who was available, who welcomed me. He is deeply, indissolubly connected with Suzuki-Roshi and the Soto tradition. The Zen Center seemed a pleasant, beautiful place, a true retreat center. Sense of place and landscape are very important to me. Eleven years ago (it seems much longer), I took refuge and bodhisattva vows at that zen center and asked Roshi to be my teacher. Actually the way it goes is that he invites you to take these vows. I came out, leaving a 17 year marriage, just a few years before taking refuge.

At each place I had sniffed out but encountered no palpable gay energy. Since this search was Serious Stuff it did not occur to me to seek a gay teacher or sangha. Perhaps naively, I assumed that Buddhists meant it when they preached the inter-relatedness of all things. I hadn't heard of the Gay Buddhist Fellowship nor was I prepared to move to San Francisco. I wanted an established teacher/sangha. My reading and conversations had disclosed none with a lavender aura.

Before I joined the Soto group, Roshi and his students asked me very little about my background and I asked very little about what to expect. Six months before taking refuge and bodhisattva vows, in Dec., 1986, I attended my first full sesshin, Rohatsu. It was hell. I couldn't sit still, couldn't sleep. Most of the time I felt enormous self-consciousness and chronic anxiety. As an M.D., I did not trust the reassurances that the numbness in my legs was harmless. I felt intimidated by the authority and confidence of the senior students, however quiet and gentle they may have been. The week magnified every neurosis. All my life I have felt different, separate (surprise!). Was this sense of alienation the result of my sexuality or just more baggage associated with it? Who can tell?

Sitting next to 40 strangers mostly clothed in black, chanting Japanese syllables and eating super-fast in a ritual (oriyoki) which only I seemed not to know, catapulted me into that realm of another world where self-expectations controlled and distorted every reaction. Panic ensued when I found out that the final all-night sitting, traditional in Rohatsu, was not optional (as I thought it would be). I sat in a chair and felt guilty. In later years I sat several more Rohatsu's and they were no problem. Once in a while a sense of sourceless gratitude and devotion filled my being and enabled me to go on. I felt a resonance with the Japanese aesthetics of zen. Overall, something "good" had happened and I knew that I should continue on this path.

No one inquired about my personal story and I, mystified and a little terrified by these strange surroundings, volunteered nothing. Just before retreat or sesshin, there is an informal evening supper. One may speak but the atmosphere is that of transition into silence. Sitting in relative quiet around a table full of mostly unknown practitioners, I was not about to sing out, "I'm gay! Are you?" During sesshin there is complete silence except for emergencies, i.e., "The tofu is burning!"

Afterwards there is an informal lunch where everyone is crowded together; the energy of silence flips into the energy of chat and munch. Unless you live at the Center or in the immediate area, the opportunity for intimacy is minimal. I discovered that student turnover was quite high and most faces were new each time. Although raw with the vulnerability that accompanies these sesshins, I was also numb with exhaustion, and in no mood to disclose or discuss my personal life, including sexuality. It is very easy to "fall into the cracks," to seek a corner or a shady tree. On the other hand, I do not remember a single time when anyone from Roshi on down asked me how I was doing, how do I feel about this experience? When sesshin finally ends, everyone goes home to sleep. I fled by bus, then plane, back to Denver and work.

Upon meeting Roshi, I told him that I am gay, have a partner who is Buddhist in another tradition, have been married with children, etc. I sensed no judgment or interest on his part. Living in the east, midwest, and mountain west all of my life, I was ignorant of the omnipresence of gays on the west coast and the relative tolerance of diversity that one finds there. He was concerned mostly about my posture and tried to alleviate my worries related to my difficulties in sitting meditation.

However, I had unconsciously accepted a pattern where the teacher-student relationship seemed to skim the surface. I assumed this would evolve. I am sure it has for others. I really had no notion about what was supposed to happen. And I had immersed myself into a practice setting and style where interpersonal contact was very limited. No real risk of anyone knowing my deepest fears and feelings, including my passion for guys.

It is said, in zen, that the silence of sesshin reveals intimacy in a way that is unknown to speech. In a way, this is true. Psychologically, you get to know yourself over time, and others see your cues. But I had just emerged, only a few years before, from the closet and a long marriage. At this place I had slipped back into that world of anonymity.

Roshi asked those who lived afar but were taking vows to write weekly essays on each of the Buddhist Precepts and mail them to him. This I did (along with the woman in the Denver sitting group who was to become my best friend over the years). He never commented on them to either of us.

The ceremony was one of the happiest moments of my life. "Taking Jukai" is a formal commitment to the Buddhist teachings and practice. It also acknowledges the student-teacher relationship. My partner, Bill, who has roots both in vajrayana (Trungpa Rinpoche) and zen (Maezumi-Roshi) was there. At that point, anyone who looked could tell I was gay. I felt that if Bill's presence offended teacher or sangha, that litmus test would send me an important signal. No one cared. We were given a tent together. I realized another, more senior student was gay but he seemed aloof, interested mostly in his practice and older friendships. Then and now, this and most Buddhist sanghas I have known embodied a natural tolerance for diversity. It did not feel manufactured or plastic.

Roshi gave me (now you sew it yourself) a beautiful purple rakusu and a name, "Winter Pine." It sounded bleak, but he told me that it means "endurance, uprightness, and aloneness." Not loneliness, but aloneness. I liked that, although I was surprised and mildly disappointed that the names were in English.

Bill had other practice priorities. Despite all the silence there was plenty of flirting at Z.C. Relationships and marriages emerged and blossomed. In my early 40's, I came across as uninterested in the opposite sex. Several women probed my availability. I told them. The questions stopped.

Over the next ten years I traveled from Colorado to California about two or three times each year for sesshins. Initially I attended the shorter, 3½ day ones, thinking they might be easier. But a full day's travelling on either side, added to no break from an intense job on both ends, eventually showed me that longer sesshins were physically easier. Of course, climate, mood, sangha, Roshi, poison oak, and everything else ensured that each sesshin was unique and you never knew. . . .

Abstention from sex is one of the sesshin rules. The circumstances of rustic accommodations and a tight schedule tend to mute desire: taking a shower is a major achievement. During all those sesshins I would initially scan the group, then sink into the practice schedule, eyelids half-closed.

As I look back on those years, the astounding feature is how little I actively questioned what I was doing. I took the "Just do it!" approach and figured "they" knew what "they" were doing. "They" included Roshi, his senior students, and the whole tradition. Sesshin rules within the sangha are precise and highly structured. I just followed them.

Near the end I participated in a sesshin where I was assigned to sleep in a yurt. Yurts are large, round enclosures used by Tibetan nomads, heated by wood stoves. Two other men were there, one a psychologist whom I knew. The other was a lithe, sexy fellow, open and smiling, new to the scene. My mind and glands began to race. I broke the rule of silence (oh!). He was curious and friendly, very energetic, and lay talking parallel to me, four feet away. Clearly comfortable with his feminine side, he contrasted with most of the straight guys I'd seen who were deadpan or macho zen.

Only near the end did I discover who he was, from the numerous bumper stickers on his car, one of which abhorred the evils of male circumcision. I liked him, and something in me began to wonder if all this time facing a wall in silence is the proper approach for me. I thought of my first sesshin and the city bus outside, the wonderful smell of its exhaust and the juiciness of it all. How could I know?

This is a very important and subtle point to consider: Faith, dedication, trust, and self-discipline, and focused energy comprise what we call "commitment." Faith derives from a connection to the lineage and its teachings. Dedication includes the vow to live a compassionate life. Trust contains the sense that the prajna or wisdom of the teacher can be relied upon in difficult moments. Constant questioning of what one is doing leads to paralysis. After an intuitively satisfying search for tradition, teacher, and sangha, the energy, I think, should go into the practice.

Enlightenment was not a worry; that was never my goal. Having full faith in the truths of Buddhism, the notion of enlightenment struck me as so conjectural that thinking about it was a waste of time. I just wanted to live a decent life. Whatever else followed, in a sense, was none of my business. I once heard Joko Beck say that she had never met anyone who was "fully" enlightened. She described enlightenment as eventually growing tired of your thoughts. Not to worry.

Living far from the Center but visiting it regularly meant that I was part of the sangha but never felt close to it. People came and went on a regular basis. Roshi began to visit his affiliate centers far afield, including ours. Since our group was so small, about eight people, we got to see Roshi up close: not quite the color of his underwear, but close enough to confirm our perception of him as an "ordinary person." Not only sage and teacher, but also a man who makes mistakes and exhibits human foibles.

This is a second important but subtle point, on which anguished volumes have been written. The American koan: So your teacher sleeps with students, gets drunk all the time, spends money irresponsibly, and is never around. When is that not o.k.? Teachers are human. No one is perfect. Despite close proximity to controversies of this kind, I have not found the answer, but believe the question worth asking.

In any case, my teacher's life, to my knowledge, never seriously raised these concerns, at least not to a public level. But as I observed him at our regional center, with the microscopic attention that only Buddhist teachers and American presidents get, I could not avoid the conclusion that he had plenty of neuroses. His responses to various people and situations sometimes lacked insight or wisdom, were "off." Imagine me, a nobody-beginner, thinking this. At this point, memories of devotional students crop up, explaining that a teacher's wisdom works in mysterious and paradoxical ways which we may not comprehend, that it's not our place to judge. Crazy wisdom?

Maybe. There were numerous situations, not the demoralizing cataclysms of famous teachers with which many of us are familiar, where after years of turning the other way, rationalizing that he must know better, I finally could not ignore the feeling that he had different standards for himself and others. That with some frequency his judgments were paranoid, hurtful, and destructive. My best friend and I began to openly discuss these "foibles." Another danger point: that of projection, which reenforces your ignorance with that of others who agree with you. In Buddhist meditation we look at the nature of mind. We see that our thoughts are projections of ego, just passing scenery. When do you take your observations seriously enough to do something about them?

In my interviews with Roshi ("dokusans") I could only remember kindness, but no real introspective questioning. Certainly nothing about my life beyond the Center. He never alluded to it. The turmoils of midlife crisis, the terrors of alienated teenage children; these all seemed worlds away. This kind of self-examination was painful, long, and unavoidable. Did I really want to throw away the "priceless jewels" of a true teacher, supportive sangha, a developed center, and a genuine path of practice because I am too fucked up to realize that there is nothing wrong out there?

Finally, there was a moment of direct student-teacher contact with my best friend that struck me as clearly aggressive and wrong. There. I said it! "Wrong." I could no longer approach this teacher sincerely with devotion and trust. When I bowed to him it felt hypocritical and empty. Finally, watching and watching and watching the interplay of all the actors, I could not continue in the same smiling role. When you cannot do it, are unable to do it, it might be time to trust yourself.

I describe this story at such length because I feel it is the natural result of practice not only to doubt what you are doing but ultimately to realize that there is nothing and no one to rely on besides your own intuitive sense or feeling about these things. I still pay affiliate dues and have not formally renounced the student-teacher relationship but I have not gone back to practice at Zen Center for two years. This happened just after moving to California, ostensibly to be closer to the teacher and sangha. What happened? Had I bailed out from intimacy, or recognized a dysfunctional relationship that had run out of steam? Was this fear of commitment now that I was fully able to see eyeball-to-eyeball with my teacher, and be seen by him and the sangha? Was I heaping judgment on him purely out of insecurity? Or had I moved so close that I could no longer maintain old rationalizations of seemingly strange responses?

In the search for tradition, teacher, and sangha, we look for "the truth," for inspiration, for connection. Maybe we kind of fall in love. "Falling in love" is not the marriage. We should look closely at the forms and see if they make sense. If we're looking with unglazed eyes, we will know. But it's not always easy, and we make mistakes, and things change. I couldn't sit still for three years and then one day I could.

I think we pay far too little attention to "style of practice." I had always loved Japanese aesthetics, but perhaps too much? Had I been willing to follow forms that were unsuited to my personality so that I could enjoy the rest of the zen drama? It took me many years to realize that austere zen practice mostly fueled my self-expectations, led to arthritis and chronic insomnia (which I'd never had before). That 4:15 wake-ups followed by 108 bows now strikes me as crap. That I gag at the notion of wearing those black robes. That the air-tight schedule paradoxically allows me no room for rest or contemplation. That work in the kitchen under someone more neurotic than I becomes martial, frantic, and oppressive.

Another person in identical circumstances might find them idyllic. I know many do. I don't, and after all these years have to trust that. Someone has yet to write the book about all those people at practice centers who develop chronic fatigue syndrome, various immune and autoimmune disorders, fibromyalgia, and myriads of chronic incapacitating and frequently vague illnesses. As an M.D., I feel sure they are more common there than in the ordinary population. Why? Furthermore, I have found approximately equal craziness within and without practice centers.

During all those years no one said a word about my sexuality; I sensed no hidden allusions or homophobia. You might say that it was not an issue for them and that was good news. But having recently come out, this was an explosive issue for me. Devoting so much of my time and energy to practice kept a lid on it. But practice is not therapy and teachers are not therapists.

At some point it seemed imperative to meet with Roshi and "spill the beans." Why wasn't I showing up? This of course generated enormous anxiety but it is characteristic of Roshi that upon entering his study, my fears dissolved. And it is characteristic of me that I couldn't tell him the whole story. I told him I want to take my practice more into the "ordinary world" in the form of work, voluntary simplicity, and compassionate activism such as the county AIDS program. I didn't have the courage to risk his disappointment or anger by relating my departure to his own behavior or to the student-teacher relationship.

After leaving the Zen Center my practice energy drifted more towards the local Shambhala Center. I had taken the training program and attended Assembly several years before, when a dusty corner of my subconscious knew I was heading in another direction. Shambhala is a secular alternative or adjunct to traditional Tibetan Buddhism. Intended to foster a sane and non-aggressive society, it emphasizes sitting meditation (much less strict than zen) and the arts. Although the Sakyong (Mipham Rinpoche) is formal head or teacher, I have not made a formal commitment to him. There is an active teaching program. The local group is small and personal. We talk and argue at times. There are several openly gay men and women as well as others with families, and all seem totally comfortable with the mix of sexual energies.

Ha! Wherever you go, there you are. The smaller the pond, the bigger the koi. Unless you live and practice alone, you rub up against others, with all the attendant neurotic sparks. But if you practice only alone, is that not a betrayal of your bodhisattva vows, to help others? Shambhala centers have their share of form alien to the West. Tibetan Buddhism is rich with form, strangely reminiscent of Catholicism, replete with shrines, ritual, hierarchies, endless devotional chants and supplications in Sanskrit. Had I traded the baby for the bath water?

The county AIDS volunteer training program encompassed about ten weekends. These sessions were practical and sometimes difficult, because you were asked to reveal yourself in the process. Though crafted to enable me to help others, I found them more powerful than any introspective work I'd ever done, and very good practice. I discovered to my shock that there are large numbers of compassionate people, gay and straight, of all ages, who aren't Buddhists! A few are Southern Baptists. Many are New Age spiritualists, what Trungpa called "spiritual materialists." Some are after bliss, or running from the pain or depression in their lives. But I found that their good hearts are as warm as Buddhist good hearts.

So what does all this have to do with practice? Roshi once said, "If your practice is working, it will make you more open, a more open person." Does that sound vague? I think we all know what it means. And we and those around us know whether it's happening or not.

A devotional European zen student describes three reasons why people quit practicing: pain, disappointment in the teacher, and lack of commitment to a scheduled practice. He says that pain from sitting meditation is either exaggerated, projected, or acknowledged and worked through. Some injuries must occur but he feels that they are no more common than any other activity such as the ordinary workplace.

The autumn after my Jukai, during the three day October sesshin, it was over 100 degrees in San Francisco and much hotter in the Sonoma County, remodelled old barn of a zendo, without fan or air-conditioning. We all wore long black robes and the sweat and griminess seemed infinite during that weekend. It was after that sesshin and reinforced during each subsequent one that I developed the chronic insomnia that dominated my life for most of ten years, almost destroying my career, including the frequent use of sleeping pills to get by. Ultimately, I took early partial retirement. Now, I do not go to sesshin, my sleeping continually improves, and I forget to notice where the sleeping pills are. I regularly hear parallel stories, often orthopedic problems.

There are many who sail right on. I reiterate that we have natural styles of practice that match or conflict with various traditions, and seem appropriate for our bodies and psyches. We should pay heed to this relationship, rather than assume that if we only try hard enough, beat ourselves to a pulp, we'll fit in, fit the mold, we'll get those egos to surrender, achieve a breakthrough, become good zen students or whatever. It's easy to fall into a macho zen trip and in many places the energy seems lopsidedly male, with females in their traditional roles as servers or veggie choppers. On the other hand, if you quit whenever things become uncomfortable, don't even start.

I have heard it said, many times, that practice is a container. That the pressures of tight schedules and discomforts are consciously designed to push students to their limits, to the point where egos are transcended by a different kind of understanding, i.e., kensho, satori, whatever. I am sure this is true for some, but I urge centers, teachers and their senior students to pay attention to the needs of participants beyond smiling at tea. They should freely acknowledge and discuss that not everyone belongs in zen or the vajrayana. It seems obvious but I doubt most beginning practitioners understand this.

Many Buddhists participate in the voluntary simplicity movement ("live simply so that others may live"). This movement generates awareness/mindfulness, is compassionate in its benefits for others, and would seem to embody an entire spiritual practice in itself. However, the practice of voluntary simplicity paradoxically consumes time: walking instead of driving, one car instead of two, cooking and baking instead of dining out, growing your own food. This makes us busier, leaves less time and space for formal practice. Nevertheless, finding ways to conserve and cut the speed are for me ordinary life as practice.

My devotional zen friend emphasizes the importance of committing to a realistic sitting schedule. I agree with him. If you sit only when you have extra time, when it's convenient, or when you feel like it, you will rarely sit, and hardly ever when you most need to. The space allotted for sitting becomes just one more thing to do. We resent it. I resisted the 25 min. drive up that twisting, slippery one lane, mountain road because it occupied the only remaining time in my day. Simply to shove it in ultimately fails for most of us. We need to make that shift in our consciousness where sitting is not a luxury or entertainment, but an integral part of the day, like brushing our teeth. Something else will have to go. At first it feels that we are being cheated of time. Then the benefits of meditation feed our desire to include it in our day. But for most employed, busy people, it's more or less a struggle, because we are doing too much.

I think that formal meditation, alone or in groups, at home or at a center, is most effectively done as a primary commitment, considered as a central axis of one's life. The specifics of duration and frequency of sitting are individually determined and not so important. The schedule should be realistic but relatively inflexible or it will not endure.

There are times in our lives when for some reason, sitting meditation is not an appropriate activity. Usually temporary, these include periods of intense emotional disturbance or physical struggle, when sitting can make things worse. Examples are people in borderline states of psychosis or extreme chronic fatigue syndrome. Classic sitting must be modified or something else is needed. There is a crucial difference between effort and struggle. Practice requires effort. It aims toward the absence of struggle: relaxation.

For most of us, Buddhist practice usually offers sitting meditation as the centerpiece. As the sitter progresses his definition of practice broadens. The distinction between sitting meditation and the rest of the day's events blurs. Teachers lecture that your whole life is practice, that each moment contains the opportunity for awareness/mindfulness and compassionate living. Especially near the beginning, for many Buddhists this must sound like some worthy but esoteric goal, something you nod your head to but don't really expect to happen.

If you hang in there long enough, it does. When the time came that I no longer found it possible to practice zen in its formal, traditional way under Roshi's guidance at the Center, there was a period of grief, of true mourning. Some important part of my life was lost. I intentionally say that in the passive, past tense, "was lost," in contrast to the active form, "I gave it up."

It is my feeling, one that grows ever stronger as I age, that our lives evolve in ways that are deeply mysterious. Control is a delusion of youth. Our karmic streams are unfathomable (this is a joke on much of modern therapy). It sounds deterministic, and in a sense it is. We make choices all the time. We ascribe them to our genetics, environment, family, luck, circumstances, past lives, spontaneous insight, "free will." In the very next minute, do you really think you control what you will do or say? Gays who bristle at the moniker "preferred lifestyle" are quite familiar with this issue.

The notion of karma subsumes all of the above. It implies that the individualistic Western sense of man as a "free agent" is false. We don't know where our choices come from, really, and probably don't need to. This does not mean that we are not accountable or responsible for what we do. We are moment by moment creations of our karmic streams. To go on, we have to take responsibility. But it's an ego-joke to think that the small self generates *de novo* the actions we take, that we begin this life *tabula rasa*.

So in our practice, why shouldn't karmic associations and consequences, constantly active, exert their undefinable influence on our spiritual as well as sexual direction? To repeat, this does not imply helplessness or powerlessness in our lives. It mandates neither celibacy nor promiscuity, nor does it dump us passively in a remote ashram until "something happens" nor does it discourage this activity.

We do what we do, guided by traditions, teachers, neuroses and lucidity, and we never really know exactly why or how a choice comes about. Despite our love of knowledge, especially self-knowledge, this perspective is not bad news. Our lives, our practice lives (the same thing) evolve in some way and we could revel in the acausal synchronicities—or perhaps apparently linear path that our lives follow.

Earlier, I chronicled my practice path, beginning with formal zen for ten years (a short time with zen) then simultaneously turning away from zen towards a more secular practice based on plain sitting, Shambhala training, simplicity, community service, and a genuine attempt to apprehend practice in the substance of daily living. As I write, I am embarking on an exploration of Tibetan Dzogchen teachings in a Western context. This tradition seems vibrantly alive and direct—oddly simple but not easy.

These changes feel challenging. Though I feel a sense of loss and sometimes guilt at leaving Roshi and the Zen Center, I don't think they are a copout. Who is to say that what seems now to have been "a mistake" was indeed that? It got me "here" wherever that is. As tidy as that statement appears, I believe it is a big error to fall into a practice center assuming that since it is Buddhist (or Hindu or Christian or whatever) that you will adapt to the difficulties at hand, that it makes no difference where you go. In one sense, it is true that whatever you go through, you'll simply be at a different spot, and "good" and "bad" are merely words that we use to describe various levels of comfort/

discomfort.

But in the relative world, I think it matters a lot. I suggest to anyone who is about to explore a spiritual path that he take his time. The New Age since the 60's created a generation of spiritual shoppers who bounced from center to center, teacher to teacher, like hummingbirds sipping nectar and zooming off to the next flower. These people never landed long enough to truly savor an existing practice scene. But the opposite extreme also creates unnecessary obstacles.

If your practice is sincere, manifesting effort, endurance and a true yearning to experience the marrow of living, the ride will be bumpy no matter what you do. Personal obstacles commonly mirror practice obstacles. Wherever you go, they'll be there.

We face this dilemma: Although Buddhists acknowledge the dualistic nature of ego-mind, we have to rely on our personal experience, usually before any deep practice-related insight occurs. The challenge is to persist without stagnation, to endure without masochism, to commit with both eyes open.

While the bumpy road may produce periods of depression, anxiety, doubt—a groundlessness that does not feel good at all—ultimately over time practice should lead to some sense of joy and appreciation for being alive, of fluidity and openness in our reactions to obstacles. I can't talk about nirvana or enlightenment, but there is a shift. It may take years to notice. We may not notice it at all; others will.

Many people feel that practicing Buddhism and being gay are unrelated situations. For these people, belonging to a sangha with a gay focus is irrelevant, seems foolish to them, perhaps a distraction. They don't need "support" from their sangha for their sexuality. Others feel the opposite.

I don't see a reason for conflict on this issue. We find ourselves gay for reasons that no one really understands. Many gay practitioners have had to cope with massive experiences of suffering and death on a scale that is virtually unknown to the modern Western world; this includes the gradual disappearance of everyone they know and love. For many who have gone through this, a Buddhist sangha with no direct experience of the cataclysm is just not enough. Anger and fear are universals, but gays have had a unique time of it in this generation, and there is no reason why they should not seek the practice-company of others who deeply understand, through the bonds of common experience, what they feel.

These feelings must find their expression or projection through practice. As a gay man with mostly straight friends in a small town, I don't think they "get it." My experience with AIDS has not been as intense as many others, but if a gay sangha were nearby, led by a teacher with whom I connected, I would choose to practice there. While individual gays may or may not connect with each other, the common ground of experience is highly likely to be helpful along the path.

What are the skillful means for working with obstacles? Some centers simply count on one's "processing" them through sitting meditation. Gay men and women undergo more or less constant pressure through-out their lives, just by being around, regardless of AIDS. I cannot imagine these conflicts not affecting one's sense of path. A sangha and teacher who can respond, day to day, on this level would, I think, be highly desirable. They are rare.

My sangha was basically a WASP sangha. Although a rare member was gay or had AIDS, I do not think (through any fault or defect of theirs) that they comprehend the specifics or needs of the tragedy of AIDS. Oh, there's the "grave matter of life and death." There's genuine feeling of and lots of discussion about compassion—about the dangers of seeing oneself as fundamentally different from others. These things include all the concerns of gays, but the speakers or meditators are too often dealing with abstractions.

Even for myself, coming from a heartland city, my comprehension of the suffering is incomplete. I have lost my best friend and others to AIDS, but I cannot imagine losing 40 or 50, or everyone you know, all your close friends. Having heard these stories since moving to the coast, I can easily see why gay Buddhists might want to practice with other gay Buddhists. Having sat just once with San Francisco's Gay Buddhist Fellowship, I want to practice more with my gay brothers, to better understand and help where I can. And to laugh our own laughter. Always with one eye on the universality of the human condition.

I cannot imagine anyone taking a fixed view on this. You may want a gay Buddhist sangha or not. Or as a part of your formal practice. And this might evolve one way or the other over time. So what? Affiliation with a predominantly gay sangha is part of the "style of practice" issue which each person must decide for him/herself. Bear in mind, though, that the search for a teacher may be long and arduous. Requiring that a teacher must lead or be connected to a gay sangha narrows the long odds of finding him. On the other hand, maybe the gay sangha is the teacher. Many gays within the GBF belong to various lineages with different teachers but sit with gay men to meet just that need.

A legitimate teacher with transmission carries the blessing of his lineage. Practicing with a pluralistic group such as the GBF makes available the teachings of many teachers and traditions. An individual may choose to affiliate with one or not.

It seems so simple at first: you just sit down on a cushion. Before you have time to exhale you are embroiled in a hundred issues relating to practice, with no obvious resolution. Often I would like to return to that first moment: just sit down. But regardless of form or tradition, all practitioners encounter their abyss, in different disguises, perhaps many times.

Joseph Campbell said, "It is by going down into the abyss that we recover the treasures of life. Where you stumble, there lies your treasure. The very cave you are afraid to enter, turns out to be the source of what you are looking for. The damned thing in the cave that was so dreaded has become the center."

And this is all I suggest: that as we continue the path of practice, we ask for honesty of ourselves and others. That we commit and re-commit, or decline to commit, wholeheartedly with both eyes open and the mind of doubt. That we find the strength to trust our experience as we follow the Middle Way. "Just do it!" does not imply blind obedience.

A warm, eager heart does not oppose the mind of awareness. In an engaged, healthy practice, they are partners, not rivals. Campbell also said, "The purpose of the journey is compassion. When you have come past the pairs of opposites, you have reached compassion." The opposites are hope and fear and their variations.

Our egos create belief systems to support our illusion of solid, separate existences. Practice (spaciousness) allows the illusion to expose itself until the naked ego is seen as transparent. This is good work and supports our vision of a compassionate world. Our lives can be seen as the movement of energy within space or vastness. Our thoughts, both the disturbing and pleasant ones, are no more than that movement. We create our difficulties by impeding or obstructing that movement. If we truly relax, beliefs dissolve and our thoughts and emotions come and go. The openness created by practice reflects the spaciousness (that is always present) where thoughts are not attached or held on to. And so we might choose a practice where belief systems are "undone" as Byron Katie says—"uncreated."

Looking back in that way, I think I viscerally decided to change tradition, teacher and practice because the process described above at some point began to reverse: belief systems were being created, of course by me, but abetted, not questioned, by the structure and nature of my affiliation. On the other hand, is this not much ado about nothing? Practicing with the mind of doubt, wholeheartedly, you are guaranteed only the fullness, the appreciation of being alive.

From Shechen Gyaltsap:

Nothing to illuminate,
Nothing to eliminate,
Looking perfectly at perfection itself,
Seeing perfection, one is perfectly free.

Anthony E. Richardson

How My Teacher Taught Me Tibetan Buddhism: A Gay Practitioner Remembers

Anthony E. Richardson, M.D.

*D*riven by impulse and attachment, we reincarnate, creating the agonies of birth and death that shape our lives. We ride on the wheel of becoming, the stream of karma, cause and effect. And, with both free will and ignorance, we are blind until illuminated by the enlightenment of our teachers.

Since the eighth century, Tibetan (Vajrayana) Buddhism has thrived and grown thanks to the support of its peoples and the enlightened mind-streams who have willingly chosen to reincarnate as teachers. These men/women are called Rinpoches, "precious jewels," and are responsible for the development of a complex variety of thought patterns, writings, images, yogas, ritual practices and meditations designed to help us wake up. Waking up is something we are all involved in to some degree and is the process through which we see how we are placed in the scheme of everything.

The amount of wisdom in Tibetan Buddhism after twelve centuries of refinement is enormous. We now have access to some Rinpoches who are in the 14th or 15th reincarnation of the mind-streams that have been moulding this information and are helping us adapt it to our current culture. Many people are attracted to this body of knowledge, seeking to understand how everything works or why things are as they are, and, from that point of view, Tibetan Buddhism is a philosophy. For others of us, it offers a place to put our faith and is clearly a religion or spirituality. (When we talk about faith in Buddhism, we mean the place in which the heart's desire for meaning and support is met, unlike the current Christian sense of needing to suspend cognition and take a spiritual leap.) For still others, it is both a philosophy and spirituality.

Buddhism functions as a lens to understanding, but not as a prescribed code of action and conduct, certainly not in the way that most Christian religions do. There are forms of Buddhism that have very clear rules of behavior, but, in Tibetan Buddhism, codes of conduct can be superseded by such larger concerns as compassion. For example, there

TONY RICHARDSON was born in Australia in 1949 and is a psychiatrist, psychotherapist and somatic therapist, who practices and teaches in the San Francisco Bay Area and Sydney, Australia.

162 / Anthony E. Richardson

is a rule that says you shouldn't kill anything that's able to think, any sentient being. But it may be more compassionate to kill a being who is about to inflict death on others and thus many lifetimes of bad karma on himself. Any rule of conduct in Vajrayana Buddhism is secondary to such concerns.

We have no commandments; they're principles. We are interested in how Buddhist precepts can be used to move one toward awakening. "Awake" is the same as being enlightened. The problem with the notion of enlightenment is that it becomes a goal, something to attain. If we say "waking up" instead, you can see it more as a process. Even enlightenment, from what I understand of it, is an on-going process. It isn't like turning on a light, at least not until all the karma has ripened.

Enlightenment is attained when the ego is made sufficiently harmless to allow us to become spacious and at one with pristine awareness. Because the ego hears this as a test or marathon, holiday or escape, we are unable to hone our intention cleanly. Tibetan Buddhism has taken the serious stabilizing steps of having us dedicate the gains we make to all sentient beings and having us vow that we each will voluntarily return to a body to help others once we are enlightened. Unlike us, enlightened beings can choose whether or not to be reborn. Every time an enlightened being takes a body, it's a choice; it's not a natural thing for them to do. But they are continually choosing to be reborn in different realms of reality. Being reborn enlightened means that if an enlightened being decides to take human form, it's to help us.

The actual experience of making a body is flawed because all bodies are flawed. So the body itself is hardly ever fully enlightened. It has troubles and problems and all the things that human beings have. There is no way to be in a body which doesn't have difficulties. Also, it is said that being enlightened and in a body is very uncomfortable. Since the body is very insistent and keeps bringing us back to take notice, we are likely to pay attention to it. And that means we're going to pay attention to earthly concerns. They say that it's particularly important, when an enlightened being takes a body, for him/her to be in good company, for that seed to be worked with and cultivated. That's why other enlightened masters take enlightened children under their wings. Otherwise they tend to become somewhat special children whose stream of enlightenment is lost. They don't become unenlightened, but the intention of being helpful can be lost; they lose their reason to be here.

These potential teachers can be incarnated next in many possible realms. They may be in a bardo, the place between death and rebirth, so their mind-streams would be lost to us. They may be in the Buddha land doing whatever it is they do there. We might not see them again for several thousand years, in our time-frame. Functionally, we've lost that opportunity of having an enlightened master with us. So it is better, they say, for these children to be recognized early and to go into relationships with teachers.

Tibetan Buddhists see the universe as primordial space which is timeless, without phenomena, and everywhere. An outcropping of this is samsara, the place in which we exist. Samsara is characterized by life and death, the six realms, and the places between lives called "the bardos." There are long and complicated descriptions of samsara in Tibetan Buddhism. (Refer to *The Three Levels of Spiritual Perception*, by Deshung Rinpoche, translated by Jerod Rhoton.) These descriptions are the basis of the ethical system of the Tibetans and contain many of their rules of daily living. Primordial space is the foundation and raw source of samsara and is shapeless, but also has patterns called "the Buddha lands." Each Buddha land has slightly different flavors and currents, the currents of power and generation.

Being born in the human realm is the most precious and the best way to speed up enlightenment. You can become enlightened in the other realms, but it's much more difficult. As a human being you've got better circumstances to help you along the path toward becoming enlightened than you do anywhere else. But some births are precious human births, and others are not. The Tibetans say that if you're born to spend every bit of energy you have making sure you get enough food and water, you don't have a lot left over for anything else. This would not be a particularly precious human birth. A precious human birth is one that offers the space and the time to consider some of these things we're talking about here, and the teachers particularly revere such a birth. They would like us to revere it, too, and try, not so much to get enlightened in this lifetime, but to treasure it enough to continue on the path of rebirth back into precious humanness.

Rinpoche said that in the west we understand karma very badly. We don't understand that karma is carrying us. Most of the streams we are following are very positive. They have gotten us here. And most of the forces that are carrying us and holding us are positive, very much on our side, helping. There are some shifts that we have control over, that we have some choice about, that will help us even more. If we turn ourselves against those shifts strongly and harshly enough, which takes an enormous amount of effort, we can injure our progression and ourselves.

This all sounds as if human history should be movement in a positive direction, which is possible but not necessary because, if there are no rules and there is no judge, who says we're doing better? We will continue to harm ourselves and each other; being embodied is still a difficult experience. We like being in bodies, and other attachments and all expectations come from that bodily attachment. But at any particular time there are a number of human beings who are not activating those ego-serving parts of themselves and are close to awakening. The last part of the journey, which is thousands of lifetimes, goes a lot quicker because you're growing all in one direction. When you're at the primitive levels, it takes a lot of work to achieve a little, and later it takes a little work to achieve a lot.

Some circumstances affect that. The most famous one is when an enlightened being of great power, such as a Buddha, comes along and is able to turn the whole wheel of karma, the whole mishmash of how cause and effect works, and scrub us all clean, if you like, putting enormous positive force into all of our karmas. Each time there's an actual, historical, embodied Buddha born, one of the things he does is turn the wheel while he's here, a period called a Golden Age. During a Golden Age a lot of primitive feelings in all of us simply are not necessary. We're not living with as much deprivation, jealousy and competition because there's not so much need for all that. And, because those feelings are not engaged, they don't become important things that direct us, so we can take great jumps during those times. It's really good when a Buddha pops in to say, "How ya doin'?" and give the wheel a spin.

Tibetan Buddhism can seem a little arrogant. It tends to talk about being faster and deeper and suggests that with Vajrayana Buddhism you can attain more in fewer lifetimes. But this isn't intended arrogantly. It is true that Tibetan Buddhism is a particular and more convoluted form of Buddhism, harder and more rigorous in that it attempts to include and then dissolve to oneness all known and unknown phenomena. This approach ultimately opens up all hiding places, so you're dealing with a lot of uncomfortable stuff at the emotional and physical levels. A person chooses the form of Buddhism which bests suits his temperament or his stage of growth. And, at least in the west, there isn't a lot of argument about who has the better path. But there *is* a lot of discussion over whether to use particular Vajrayana practices.

The practice most in question is guru yoga. We are in relationship to our masters and see them as the actual embodiment of enlightenment. When our teachers start to act out in strange ways, it creates an enormous disturbance from where we sit in western culture. A teacher's acting in ways that are not culturally sanctioned may be "crazy wisdom" and an opportunity for us to bring our world view into question. However, some of the crazy wisdom stuff has been used to argue that you're better off without a guru, without a teacher, and you should somehow do it yourself. Guru practice is one of the central tenets in Tibetan Buddhism and is much misunderstood by other Buddhists.

Though Tibetan Buddhists believe in hell realms and god realms, Buddha is not god. There is no god in the western sense in Buddhism. For Buddhists, omniscience is a stream that runs through all of us. We are moving inexorably to awakening that place within us or shedding the obscurations and the blindness we have to our true natures. Gautama Buddha talked about that process of ridding himself of the obscurations to Buddhahood.

In the beginning there was the combined sentience of all of us. And one of us, all of us, a number of us, some of us—there was no "us"; you can't even talk about it. Somehow, oops, there was the formation of a thought which immediately created samsara, which is everything that we apparently experience. And then, inevitably, the sentience divided itself up into hunks and the hunks into bodies. Once you start making form, the rest is the natural course of what's going to happen. If the last hunk of sentience awoke, samsara would go away, but the Tibetans don't expect that ever to happen. They don't seem to feel that thinking this is all going to get better one day is helpful. Rinpoche talked as though this is the field in which we are working, this is just how it is now. But helping and progress are possible. Everyone is going to progress anyway, progress beyond samsara. What Tibetan Buddhists are doing is speeding the process along and trying to make it less uncomfortable.

Once you've taken a body, you're stuck with limitations. In Vajrayana Buddhism, we strive to accept that we are this way. How to deal with our attachments, expectations, and lack of compassion are the main foci of Vajrayana Buddhism. There are things you can do to help yourself, given that being embodied means you will have preferences and desires, that your body requires things to be one way rather than another—some people like noise, some people don't like noise, some people like cold, some people like hot. That doesn't feel like a choice, but it's a preference of the organism, and some people, when their preferences aren't met, have many difficulties and obsessions, obstacles that arise and take up a lot of their energies, don't allow them to be available, at least consciously, to the process of awakening. They experience too much involvement with their feelings that their house is wrong or the temperature is wrong or noise is intrusive. You can name thousands and thousands of such preferences.

And we function as though there are limitations on how kind we can be to ourselves and to each other. Our unkindness is generated by the sense of self preservation that comes with the body, so being bad to each other is a direct result of fear. We don't want to accept that, but accepting it is part of waking up.

The ultimate cure for this is enlightenment. Until we attain that, intermediary aids make up a large part of the Buddhist knowledge base, but are secondary to the real goal of awakening. Tibetan Buddhism talks about techniques one can use to include these difficulties and not say that you should just get over it, really: don't activate it, don't give any energy to it, don't spend time with it. Tibetan Buddhists understand that really the issue is to *do something*: without taking any interest in your own jealousies or needs or wants, practice kindness.

Once you include things like emotional states, attachment states, energetic states, and body needs, Buddhism makes it easier for you at first, but, if you formulate an enlightenment intention coupled with the intention to be helpful to others, it becomes harder again: no hiding places. And the real work begins.

So what do we focus on? The two pillars of Vajrayana Buddhism are compassion and wisdom. We're working towards enlightenment and awakening, but we're doing it by practicing being compassionate and learning wisdom. In Tibet a lot of Buddhism was about teaching people how the world worked. They put together a whole pantheon of studies about deities, energies, colors and sounds to try to make the population think more, not just in their heads, but within the whole of their organisms. The students began to embody states which were larger than their previous experience, possibly generating wisdom. It was like our going to university and reading the great authors. For most Tibetans, the ritual practice stimulated the ability to imagine and encouraged empathetic identification.

In the west the Tibetans have been much more interested in our learning to be kind to each other. They see us as beings who have quite a capacity to imagine things beyond our own experience and to relate to psychological and energetic experiences which are not just about us. That is, we can read novels and identify with the characters, the situations they're in, the forces acting on them. Those of us who are educated are no longer concretely bound by the places we came from as a sheep herder might be. We have developed the ability to experience things vicariously. When we read a book we're able to put ourselves in it. The average Tibetan yak herder tells stories about his teachers and is likely to spend time at his monastery practicing to be a deity—not a god, but an energy distribution. It's a culturally adapted way of learning.

The teachers are willing to share this Tibetan way with us, but they're also interested in our learning kindness. They see that westerners don't seem to want to be kind to each other. "Kindness" is another word for "compassion." It requires the wisdom to recognize that we are all different. Even in our differences, we are struggling as best we can to move forward in some way, and compassion is only possible when we recognize that—even though we may not agree with the ways other people are doing it, we may not support them in those ways, and we may think what they're doing is harmful—we still care about these people. Not necessarily their personalities, their present structures, or their current ways of getting on, but as human beings we care for them.

Buddhism can look passive, and it is true that often the best thing is to do nothing (though usually we are incapable of that). But there can be an act of compassion directed by wisdom that pulls back the curtain. It may involve loving a person, having sex with him, smiling at him—any one of innumerable possibilities. Action is best if it arises from the place where wisdom and compassion meet. Once you have experience of the meeting of compassion and wisdom, it's important to value yourself as the knowledge and experience you have, value the effects the teachers are having on you, take it all seriously and support the realness of all of it. Let it be real in your love life, real in your neighborhood life, real in your internal life. Otherwise, you make a coat out of it to wear at convenient times.

It may seem that I'm using "wisdom" and "knowledge" interchangeably, but I don't mean conceptual knowledge. This form of knowledge, the ability to be able to put yourself into a great writer's novel—into the complexity of a character or a situation which causes you to be subsumed into the whole experience in the book—is one of the things that you would experience if you were doing a particular practice, say, of a deity like Green Tara or Avalokiteshvara or Manjusri. Practicing energy distributions by doing deity visualizations or yoga exercises allows you to know how your body feels, how your mind thinks, and gives you the possibility of watching how you function. This stabilizing so that your opinions and emotional states do not subsume you is prerequisite to the development of wisdom. When you know yourself well enough to notice at what point you lose the spaciousness inherent in the practices, you begin to have a method with which to foster wisdom. It's very difficult to tell the difference at first, and we assume we are bad at it and almost give up. So we use mantra, song, sounds, mandalas, pictures, or acts of devotion to help us. Telling stories of historical Buddhas and of our experiences with our masters are also helpful (thus this article).

You get so used to the feelings, the sensations, the state of wisdom and compassion, that, when you act, you've got that as company, as stronger company. This is hardly ever clearly distinct from the ego's need to do it the way you want to do it. The wisdom is to be able to hold that all at the same time. Remember it is always a new situation because nothing occurs twice, so there is different wisdom for each situation. It takes many years to learn which one fits where. But, generally speaking, in Tibetan Buddhism if you ain't got compassion, you ain't there. Once you ask the question, "How is this of benefit to all beings?" then everything involves compassion. Everything involves caring, and wisdom will arise pretty well spontaneously.

In Tibetan Buddhism expression of ritual is how you get to practice wisdom and compassion in their raw forms. We focus on many deities in our rituals. The most common is Guru Rinpoche, who went to Tibet to re-enliven Buddhism. To align with him is to align with all the states of all the Buddhas. In the deity transmission, you sit with a ritual master, probably in a group, and he becomes that energy distribution. If it's about compassion; he becomes a living ball of compassion. Your job is to let that into you and become like him. You let your body become like his body. You let your energies become like his energies, and you attempt to have your thinking become like his thinking in this state.

Then he is likely to give you certain stabilizing practices so that you can go away by yourself or in groups and do it over and over again until you become used to it. Until it becomes part of you. The most common stabilizing practices are mantra and sound. The next is visualization, to be able to see the forms, which are often painted in tankas, very complicated cloth paintings. And sometimes the practice is represented in mandalas, which are colored pictures, symbols that are meant to touch you in a way that is subconscious and the essence of what's going on. Sometimes they will use scents, songs, sitting or standing positions, movements of the hand or body. In the yogas the teachers will ask you to do specific things inside your body.

The first stage is called the "wang" (or "empowerment"), when the teacher gives you this energy, makes it available to you. It may take a long time for you to be able to germinate inside yourself the seed of compassion. You do have it; it's there. So the teachers pour in a whole lot of compassion and speed the process up. The Vajrayana practices give you a boost. If it somehow sticks in you, your practicing it during a daily or weekly regimen will keep it alive, and it'll start to have effects on you in your everyday life.

A Tibetan Buddhist's daily practice might include attempts to embody a state or visualizations of a deity or chanting. One of the beliefs is that the sounds themselves have effects on the body, and so chants are particular symbols or sounds to make the body more available. The more modern teachers also want us to know what we're doing, at least as best as our brains can, so they often require us to chant in English as well as Sanskrit and Tibetan.

The relationship with teachers is complex. Among the things ritual masters did in Tibet was to travel around doing empowerment after empowerment, getting groups of people together and handing out the goodies, or going into retreat and practicing for all of us. In the west it's been somewhat different because those who have good language skills have been willing to confront our thinking.

Not only do they confront what we think, but they also confront how we think it. We've already concluded things that are inadequate for what they teach. Since most of us are not yet able to know what it is the teachers see, how this place really works, they double-bind our thinking so that we can no longer fool ourselves. In the west we tend to "know" how it all works by thinking in descriptions. Quite often more western teachers will link opposing thought patterns which don't fit, and we're left to resolve the quandary. In the process of attempting resolution, we often experience a lot of mind-opening.

There is another approach in which the student and the teacher are in closer relationship, more individual time is spent with the student, and the teacher is willing to be less formal and more loving, more demonstrative of his love and willing to act in ways that attract the body-mind of the student so that they can hang out together as buddies. With Gyalsay Rinpoche this included everyday life, washing up, cleaning house, making ritual paraphernalia, and "doing shoppings," as he would say. This is the most dangerous relationship of them all. My experience with Rinpoche shows what can happen when you're in that sort of relationship. Because, you know, they're really not your buddies; they're there to help. And the more available to them you are, the more they will help. But they won't help you in the ways your ego expects. So it's not the same as going out with a dear friend and having a good time. It's a lot more complex.

In these relationships a word, a thought, a glance, a moment of ignoring or one of moving towards can often have enormous meaning, and the student can benefit greatly. I can remember many times when Rinpoche seemed to get bored with what I was saying half-way through, and it was up to me to work it out: where did I change direction, what did I do that had created this response? I became extraordinarily sensitive to him, and his responsiveness became very, very fine, which other people wouldn't have noticed, but I was working with him all the time. On the outside it looked like two buddies hanging out together, and on the inside I was always being chopped up and looked at. I was doing it; I was looking at myself. He wasn't hurting me or doing anything to me.

But I recognized his powers and his freedom. He had the freedom not to act in expected ways with a lot more freedom than I did, and he could change direction in an instant. It surprised me over and over again; logically my body-mind was expecting to move a certain way, and he would change direction subtly and easily. I would be utterly dumbfounded. I would catch myself in a body expectation, not a thinking expectation, of doing it a certain way. All of a sudden we would be doing it a different way, and I couldn't imagine how that would be possible because my own internal assumption was so clear in another direction.

The freedom such a teacher has is an enormous teaching. It comes from internal flexibility, which I'm not very good at even talking about. My current state is much more rigid than his. Compared to other folks, I'm not rigid generally, but, compared to an enlightened being, I'm seriously rigid. This sort of relationship is not the same as sitting in a class when he's doing a teaching or having a discussion about dharma. But, as you get closer to them, these sorts of things happen.

Everything Rinpoche was teaching me will be useful in the bardo, the place between death and rebirth which is very important from the point of view of Tibetan Buddhism. Each person has a set of bardos all of his own, and they're very well described by Sogyal Rinpoche in *The Tibetan Book of Living and Dying*. Generally speaking, what happens in the bardo is that you lose your body, but you carry an awful lot of your unfinished stuff. You can imagine how many feelings, thoughts, wants, displeasures and pleasures you have. When you become unembodied, they lose their order and their hierarchy of value, so you tend to be flooded by them and they have a lot of power. It's like putting flavoring in cake batter. It goes all the way through the cake; it doesn't just stay in one part of the batter. That's what happens with every thought, attitude and emotion; so you're really swept. Also the effect of each thought is like pushing when you're weightless; it's very amplified.

In death you move through a series of bardos. It's a very busy time, and it's difficult to process it all without a lot of skill. You lose a lot of the things that are precious about being human. There is no space in the bardo; there's no order. You have no ability to contain things. The best thing you can do there is to give yourself over to the relationship with your guru, the Buddha, the forces that are really interested in your becoming enlightened. But, as you can imagine, a jealousy, an attachment, a wish, a lover or whatever creates larger effects in the bardo. So keeping any intention of guru relationship clear amongst all that washing around is very difficult.

But if you *can* do that, the potential to become enlightened in a bardo is quite high. It's much more difficult, but you can, during the time of death, become enlightened. Everyone can do that, no matter what else is going on. One of the things about having a good life and being able to do some of these practices is that you learn to hold on, even in the bardo, to some of the skills that will help you become enlightened: transformational practices, watching yourself move from jealous to less jealous, from angry to less angry, from loving to wider loving, from romanticized attachment to caring about someone without having to subsume yourself into it. All the skills that you learn in deity practice in a body will be helpful to you there. So when one of the teachers or one of the energies comes to offer you help in the bardo, you'll be able to recognize it. And you'll be able to do some of the things that will hold the space clear enough for their energy to be effective with you, for you to be able to follow their energy, even though it's a very busy and tumultuous time.

This is true after every lifetime. If it does work out and you are able to follow a teacher into one of the Buddha lands, you will not be compelled to re-embody and, when you do re-embody, it will be with the intention of being helpful rather than of a personal satisfaction like getting something right or wrong, hurting somebody, loving yourself, or whatever. All that will be gone when you do finally re-embody.

You move through different bardos after every death unless you short-circuit the process by going to a Buddha land. I have no idea what the Buddha land is like. But it's not a bardo. There are several Buddha lands. One fits each of us best, and they're supposed to be pretty cool places to hang out. When you come back into human life from a Buddha land, you maintain connection with it. There is some suggestion that certain masters actually are in a Buddha land at the same time as they are embodied. Once I was talking with a teacher, and he suddenly started to laugh uproariously. He told me he had been playing a board game with an 11th century master in a Buddha land, and, as he was talking with me, he had just won the game. It's not an either/or phenomenon.

There are two parts to making a good death. One is what you do in the bardo. The other is what you do as your body is dying. Since we're not able to predict our bardo experience, it seems best to do as much—burn as much karma—as we can while dying. I think my dad had a good death, and he was as paranoid as all get out when he died and very uncomfortable, but he came out of it for a moment and talked about how indulging in his paranoia was his choice. Then he went back into the paranoia, and my sense was that he was burning off something he'd had all his life. It didn't look comfortable or pretty, and I'm not an expert in this. But his death feels complete to me, unlike other deaths about which I keep wishing things had happened differently, that more had happened. I can't say that his death was useful to him, but it looked like it to me. It looked horrible to my family, and they all thought it was a terrible death. They're not Buddhists, and I don't know who's right.

I doubt that planned death works. I don't think it can make any difference because you'll take everything with you. I'm absolutely convinced it's only as good on the other side as you can make it here. There's no escape, there's no place to go to, there's nothing to get out of. If you don't do it here, you'll do it next time, or you'll do it in the bardo. That's all there is to it. There's no getting away from it.

Compassion and wisdom are always the goals toward which we try to progress, and attachment is always one of the major hindrances. There are many different forms of attachment. Attachment and revulsion are different sides of the same coin. Expectation is an attachment. The body—each being different—is attached to certain outcomes. Your body might be attached to knowing why things work the way they do. You might be attached to knowing how one gets control. Or you might be attached to having your reality taken into account. People consider these reasonable things for human beings to want, but they are attachments from the Buddhist point of view. And we are not against achieving them, if there's a simple way to do it. If a human's going to do better at waking up by being rich than by being poor, then it's fine for that person to be rich. If it gives you more time and calms your fears so that you can practice, then abundance is fine.

Whatever your issue is, if it can be taken care of easily, and if it doesn't have to kill a lot of other people and create a lot of disturbance, then it's okay. If a T-shirt will make you happy, have that T-shirt; now use the happiness for the practice. That's basically the philosophy. If giving you a T-shirt is going to prevent six months of misery and in giving you that T-shirt there's an opportunity for six months' practice, that's a doubly good thing. It's all right if you're just happy for six months because Buddhists favor happiness over misery. If having the T-shirt also makes you available for practice, if that's your preference and where your current development is, then that's fine, too. But if you end up spending six months having to get T-shirt after T-shirt after T-shirt, then that is not so smart. It becomes a compulsion, an obsession, or a delusion that T-shirts are the way to happiness. For Buddhists, that's not so supportable.

We are very much in favor of things like good food, good company, warmth, love, family, good neighbors, and good friends. We're not about having to push through or go without. Whatever works efficiently to keep the being available for the transformation process—it's just a matter of making sure these things don't become the point in itself. If you happen to be born into a precious lifetime, but get caught in the feeling of needing more, more, more, that's as big a problem as that of the person who lives in poverty who can't get enough water.

One of the important things to keep in mind, connected with the notion of attachment, is that everything always changes. That's the nature of it all, from the Buddhist point of view. You never put the same hand in the same stream. It's always new water, new sensation, a new hand. Everything is impermanent. We're on the wheel, we're in the process of being reborn, we're in the process of dying. Nothing is going to stay stable. Our belief that there is stability is a trick of the mind, a delusion. It's an attachment in that we want to have control, understanding, whatever we decide will stop our being frightened and allow us to keep the world still so that we feel comfortable. But that's not the nature of the world. So we keep reminding ourselves that nothing ever happens twice. And what you think is happening isn't because you have only seen a piece of the puzzle. You are the blind person who touches the elephant at one end and thinks that's the whole elephant. When you think you know what's going on, you really don't. You only know a piece of what's going on, and that piece may be infinitesimal, one pixel in the big picture. No matter how right you've got it, you haven't got it right. And that's a pretty disturbing piece of information.

Another important piece of information is that, if the universe is changing all the time, then there are many possibilities you haven't been able even to consider. The shorthand version is that just about everything is possible at any moment. The third thing that is useful to know is that Buddha is not strained. He is not pushed. He doesn't create anything. There is no effort. There is discomfort, but it's not made into a problem. So add these three things up in terms of your path. Continually recognize that everything is changing, that what you think is happening isn't happening, that everything is possible, and, at that point, relax. If you could hold all those pieces together, you would be moved to wake up pretty quickly. And that's what Tibetan Buddhism is trying to help us do.

I'd like to give you some idea of how my relationship with Rinpoche helped with this. I can only talk about it in terms of what it has done for me, this particular body-mind, so the stories are somewhat personal

and don't necessarily generalize. That is always the case. Guru interactions are always very specific, and generalizations about them tend
to be wrong. I would go so far as to say that there is no single purpose
for every individual in Buddhism. There are lots of books about living
a life that doesn't get you in too much trouble, learning to notice what
is and isn't good for you, all kinds of strictly relative goals. But, as far
as I can tell, for only a very few people is there serious consideration
of awakening right now.

My relationship with Rinpoche was specific to my path, and, at the
same time, gives some of the flavor of being in relationship with a guru.
It's different from other relationships. Rinpoche opened me to the idea
of possibility itself, and it took time to let myself accept the idea that
the world and myself and this lifetime weren't as limited as I had supposed. These days, if something catches my attention because it is out
of the ordinary, I look at it as a possible guru intervention at the same
time that I look for an explanation such as "I fucked up" or "Someone was mean to me." I do this because the world has proven over and
over again to be different from what I decide it is. That means I can't
only trust my own perceptions or conclusions. I need to include the
knowledge that I have been wrong before and that new information may
be on its way to undo my current beliefs.

If I don't do this I will miss the new information or feel upset, be-
trayed or attached by it. Judgment is the most common mistaken reaction. Remember that, for Buddha, upset or discomfort does not equal
a mistake. The practitioner is on the edge of becoming subversive. Being
subversive is not an unusual position for gay men and women and particularly now for the gay culture. Although we're resistant to the idea,
being homosexual has until recently been inherently subversive. That
gives us gay men and lesbians stamina for the dharma, the body of
Buddhist knowledge.

Guru interactions seem innocent, easy. It was wondrous, being able
to live in the same house as and spend time daily with a man who always seemed different from anyone else I had ever met. But I now see
my life as much larger than before I met Rinpoche. In fact, I see it as
a dauntingly large project. The work that needs to be done intrapsy-
chically or within this organism to prepare myself for the continual journey is mammoth. Before meeting him I was a little bored. I felt I was
too successful, as a physician and as a man in relationship with another
man, owning a house and finding a place in society. Now I see myself
as just a small piece that needs lots of attention and work to be able to
approach the skills that he had.

The first instruction he gave me was that it would be good for me

The Venerable Gyalsay Rinpoche, a highly attained and recognized Tulku in the Sakya tradition of Tibetan Buddhism, was born in Nangchen in 1950. Nangchen is in Eastern Tibet and is part of the province of Kham. His four brothers are all recognized Tulkus, each of different lineage, and his mother was said to be a highly attained practitioner. All the sons escaped from Tibet to India after their mother died and as the Chinese invaded the local province when Rinpoche was six years old. Gyalsay Rinpoche had his lineage seat in a monastery in Dhirru, Tibet, and Bir, India. He graduated from the Sakya College and was a student of His Holiness Sakya Trizin, current head of the lineage. He died in 1992.

to be more compassionate. I had thought I was nice as I could be. I thought I did everything as caringly as I knew how. But I didn't know what compassion meant. Having been brought up in Australia, I had no cultural context in which to know what compassion could be. I didn't know that it meant sometimes being fierce and sometimes ignoring people's beliefs. I began to see this from the way Rinpoche dealt with other students. He showed me intentionally.

Often it was not as I expected it to be. I would bring people along to meet him and, out of my love and respect for him and for them, I would assume that they'd do very well together, but frequently that was not the case. I usually got negative responses from my friends. For example, two of my friends from the sangha, the family group of Buddhists, told me I was further along than Rinpoche, I didn't need him and should start teaching by myself.

I would ask, "Rinpoche, why don't you work with this person, why don't you heal him, why don't you fix him, why don't you invite him to do meditation with you, why don't you show him some of the practices?" What I was really asking was, "Why don't you like him?" Rinpoche said things like, "He's not ready yet," "There's different work to be done," "He doesn't have sufficient qualities to do that particular practice," and so on. But he didn't make himself attractive to them. He was not excluding these folks; he was simply not wasteful. For most of my life up until then I had felt that everybody should have everything: everyone gets a go at everything; you deal with it if you don't make it, and, if you do make it, you get it; everybody deserves all the opportunities there are.

Now I started to understand that there was a way of seeing what the right opportunity was to offer somebody. I was not so far along, but I did see Rinpoche averting a lot of wasted time, energy and pain. For the first time I recognized the value of being able to see a wider reality and how deeply kind it is. Buddhism has a very long view. The teachers are not frightened of death. They see it as inevitable. They don't mind when people die feeling ripped off. They don't seem to feel frustrated. They plant a seed that might take root in the next life or the life after that and might flower ten or fifteen lives after that.

I would find myself manufacturing fantasy, say, dissociating myself from my concerns, going around being kind, pretending that I didn't really matter, as if that would awaken me. But living with Rinpoche showed me that that wasn't okay, either. He exercised. He did strenuous prostrations. He worked out. He was concerned about his weight. He talked about body functions. He talked about how he felt and what his body was like. He related to how I spoke about my body and would show concern and love around those issues.

And at other times he showed utter disrespect and lack of interest when I became over-involved. I learned to feel what he would support and what he wouldn't support and used that to turn to myself and look at my intention. It became more important to me to sense my relationship with him than it was to have my own diatribe or preciousness. At least, that is true when I catch it; I don't catch it all the time. And I am, of course, continually horrified by how preciously I view myself and to what a great extent I am self-involved. I think that the ripening of the effects of my relationship with Rinpoche gives me the ability to include this truth about myself.

Being with Rinpoche was not predictable. I couldn't psyche out what he was and wasn't going to pay attention to, and how he would behave with people didn't match my expectations. That's not to say that he wasn't insistent and steadfast. For example, Rinpoche's insistence helpfully supported me as a gay man; I was often ravaged with sexual impulses that included him, and these pleased him. That's not to say that he was at all comfortable with the idea of homosexuality originally. When I asked him about being gay, he told me it had no meaning in terms of spiritual practice. That was somewhat insulting because being gay is obviously special. He didn't ratify the specialness, was never very interested in gayness being special in any way. I would hear from others close to Rinpoche that he felt socially inept around the issue of being gay. He didn't know what it would be like to live in San Francisco for a couple of months in a gay household in a gay community, and he wondered whether this was a strange or unusual thing to do. These are not uncommon thoughts. Most people are not ravingly anti-gay, but are probably very ignorant about gayness. He was ignorant and had some fear and concern about it.

One of the validations of Rinpoche's ability to be what was necessary was mirrored when a Lama of high stature, but not Wisdom Mind, came to stay with us. He wanted to see if we could set up a center in our house in the middle of the gay ghetto in San Francisco. He had the same education and training as Rinpoche so I expected he would be as easy to work with; alas, it was simply not so. I suppose one should take into account the fact that he arrived on the Women's Night of June Gay Pride Week when thousands of topless dykes strolled past us both, locked out and sitting on the front stoop, for several hours. Even so, his homophobia and unresolved sexual urges made him totally unavailable as a teacher. He couldn't even consider a center in the Castro because he had the feedback that many Asians were afraid to be seen here.

The recognition that even this Lama with his enormous storehouse

178 / Anthony E. Richardson

of Vajrayana knowledge and experience, teaching in many Asian cultures, would be of very little help to my gay friends has led to the discussion of what would be the best teacher in a gay context. Many of us hold His Holiness the Dalai Lama in high esteem especially since he has agreed to the possibility that the Buddhist admonition to anal or oral sex is probably culturally based. We already know that cultural bias at a practical level so it is not news to us. What many of my friends are waiting for is a gay teacher with Wisdom Mind to include our sexuality in practice. In my own experience this has not been necessary because my sexuality and my primary relationships strengthened and my gayness shone more as a direct effect of being with my straight identified guru. Not everyone does best with a relationship like I had with my teacher and I can see how it will be likely easier for many of us once we have such a teacher. After all my friends are only asking for the inclusion that Rinpoche afforded me.

But his response to me was different. He acted as though he believed fully that I was okay. He was willing to go past his own cultural comfort zone because it was useful to me, and because he loved me and wanted me to have what I needed to wake up, even if it included an energy that he would not normally hold. Then he learned very quickly. He didn't learn to accept gay as anything special or meaningful. The only thing he said was that there were a number of gay men he came into relationship with who were good students. Without a quiver around the issue of gay or not gay, socially acceptable or not socially acceptable, his criteria was, "Hmm, here's another place where there are students to whom I am able to be of more help because of their availability." Gyalsay Rinpoche was really happy to use any opportunity that could kick things along. In retrospect, I've concluded that there's useful potential in having to be different from the dominant culture; it can lead to more availability for unusual states. This is both a vulnerability and an asset. I've seen Rinpoche use it in a number of different situations.

My relationship with him was unlike any other in that it was always edgy. I was always very pleased to see him. I was always swept in the presence. I always felt some melting. It's difficult to talk about this without turning into such a devotee of love that it seems as if I lose all ability to be objective. He was like honey. He was always like dipping into warm honey. Very strange experiences would arise for me: changes in perception, changes in time, in the sense of waiting or expectation.

At times with Rinpoche I was so happy I couldn't ask a question, I would feel I was not being a good student if I couldn't come up with a topic. It wasn't like a normal social conversation. We had a degree of honesty and ease, but I also felt great terror. That terror is amazing to me. I loved him so, and yet I would go out of my way not to go over and see him, not to spend time with him, to find something else to do. What I was with him was so disruptive of how I knew my life that I would continually have to go away to find out who I was in the old sense. Yet I couldn't stay away. I had to go back, and there I was in terror, wanting to withdraw, wanting not to be demanding or ask too much of him, wanting not to tell him about what was going on for me, but needing to find some way to at least show up.

I'm pretty competent in most of my relationships. I'm a psychiatrist; it's my trade. But I was utterly inept in this relationship, because this one wasn't about competence. Ineptness is one of the things that happens, and it's very scary, and a little like how it is in a loving sexual relationship. You never know what's going to happen. You never know where it's going to take you and what it's going to do. It took me to many different places and gave me many different physical pains and confusing thought patterns and energy changes. The amount of energy I have in the day has changed, my sleep patterns have been disturbed, and stability is elusive.

This disruption of stability is a hallmark of a relationship with a guru. When I could mention it to him, he would be very kind, open and supportive. I remember one time when he was in Australia and I was in San Francisco, I called him to talk about an issue of distress, and he said, simply, the simple words, "I will help." I was so amazed that someone would help at this place of disruption. I understand about being helped when you feel bad, but this was beyond feeling bad. This was more about being terribly disrupted and not knowing how to stay with it. Now I know about getting help when disrupted or agonized so that the pain becomes less the issue and more an accompaniment, but I didn't then.

It's more than becoming a better human being. It's about becoming awake, able to see beyond humanness—yet I did also become a more useful human being, that's clear. I observe that people who hang out with these teachers, even in the most peripheral way, get to be much better human beings, much happier, more functional, more responsive, fuller, living more abundantly, feeling more aware of other sentient beings. And there are certain experiences that the human organism is designed to find satisfying, appropriate, happy-making, that at a certain level become no longer the point. So it's a matter of allowing yourself to be guided moment by moment without losing responsibility and allowing yourself to notice what is arising in the context of awakening without losing your humanity, but noticing when it appears to be getting tweaked.

These teachers are about our becoming fully awake. Once I was with Rinpoche, and I'd just heard a lot about Dzogchen which is a practice in which there is no form or actual shape and everything is dissolved into emptiness with the aid of a guru. I asked Rinpoche, "Is what we're doing Dzogchen?" while really thinking, "Or are we doing a special something reflective of my specialness?" With great skill, he turned to me and said, "No, what we're doing is starting." That experience of being deflated remains very important. Luckily, I was able to have enough humor to feel both the blow and the wonder of it.

I remember once having an empowerment from him before a retreat, and I noticed that I felt an upswelling of the floor sweep through me as though I was being carried in the surf. That night at dinner the room seemed to turn upside down, and I held on to the table in case I fell over. The following day I was racked with chills, and my spine felt frozen as though I was very frightened although I didn't feel scared. Several years later I asked him to do it again, he shook his head and said it was very hard, and I knew I had made it a special event and thus stopped it from being stable within me. Now sometimes the room moves, sometimes I get body-frightened, and it is just so.

Being out of relationship with Rinpoche when I would make manic attempts to please was much more painful than being slapped: to feel the love connection dissolve right before me when there was no reason for it except what I was, with no place to go, nothing to blame, no circumstance to make up. It was clearly my own change, of my own generating. And it has brought me to maintain a level of responsibility which deals with much more than what I do or how good I look to the world or how good my work looks on the outside.

One of the reasons we tell each other Rinpoche stories is to re-induce the recognition of what awakening is. I had an ongoing discussion with Rinpoche over a number of years about the idea that there are unseen forces which the teachers talk about freely. I couldn't understand. Did they mean a metaphor, a reality, a psychological projection, or what? In my psychotherapy practice, the people I saw who had felt haunted seemed to have a primarily psychological problem, and issues of powerlessness and victimization were common themes. So I had decided that the demon stuff was all bunk; that was my way around it. I told Rinpoche that I thought that demons were merely a movement of one's mind; he agreed, and I was safe. Next I told him I was afraid that I was not being compassionate to my patients when they felt demons arise because I felt contempt that they had created them, and he agreed. Now it was getting hard again. Finally I told him of my vision of a demon during a retreat, he told me that he used to know him in human form, and I was so confused that it has taken me a long time to recognize the teaching in it.

I was so confused. There was no clear statement of what was what, so it was less safe, less manageable, less absolute. There were two issues: safety and value. It seems true that human beings need both to feel comparatively safe and to have a value system in which some things are better than others. Rinpoche often said that there are some conditions that are better than others for a particular body-mind. That will always be true. Knowing that and responding to it are appropriate things to do. And pretending that it's not true is not appropriate. He also said things that utterly supported my idea that it takes a human being's attachment to a demon for the demon to be powerful in that person's mind or body. At other times he has told me that demons were simply things we made out of our own minds. At still others he told me that demons don't exist at all. And he also told me that demons were often attempts to help and that feeding demons quiets them.

So, in the process of having my thinking wobbled from side to side with him taking different views each time, I would feel crazy because I couldn't stabilize in one reality or another, and then I tried to add that there actually are better places, better situations for human beings, and that those better situations were important. It all came to a head at a fire ritual at which we were burning sesame seeds. The sesame seeds were being burnt in order to kill primitive beings to set them free from their primitiveness. Thousands of seeds were thrown into the fire as an act of liberation. At the beginning of the ritual I asked Rinpoche, "How come we can kill folks? We're not supposed to kill folks." And he looked at me and said, "They're just sesame seeds."

It was a long ritual so we had a break halfway through, and I said, "I'm loving throwing these." And he said, "Be aware that each one of them is a being unto itself and that you're liberating each being." My mind started to freeze. Finally I thought, "Well, then, I'll go the other way and I'll ask him why it's okay for us to liberate beings," and I asked, "How do we know that we're giving them a better opportunity than they already have?" And he said, "It's because we are loving them. It is because we are respectfully loving them as we liberate them." The concept of loving beings whom I had decided didn't exist seemed, all of a sudden, a great vulnerability to me. But, through my relationship with Rinpoche, feeling his active devotion to every sesame seed, my loving these beings somehow moved me, and my cage of beliefs was gone. If I had not had access to the glue of his devotion, I would have been ripped apart or would have had to reenact my earlier conclusions. I was not large enough, wise enough, possible enough to do it alone.

Making any real change seems impossible without the company of someone who is living more freely.

I'm also aware that it's not an easy task for an enlightened mind-stream to take a body. Rinpoche was very uncomfortable, and he stayed that way. He didn't really mind being physically uneasy, although he clearly felt pain. He was very sensitive to environments, and his body and his relationship with his body were not characterized by rest or ease. He said to me one time that inhabiting a body was extremely uncomfortable because of the compression and because it made him feel so stupid.

But they do it. They do it in order to be of help to us. And, you know, that piece of information alone has been very helpful with my old expectation that I was supposed to be comfortable. When you start to embody the sort of energies that Rinpoche is talking about, then bodily discomfort is a natural result. Our expectation is that some day we will rest or it will all be better. No, not at the body level. And it also lets me know our importance as students; if my teacher is willing to be in pain, maybe I should pay attention to my awakening also.

The teachers' bodies are happy even in the presence of discomfort because they are included in enlightenment. So one of the things I try to move toward is letting the tissues of my body know about awakening so that discomfort does not cause separation from Buddhahood. The teachers do not use their discomfort to define themselves. It is a natural part of their happiness, their helping us, that they are uncomfortable. And there is nothing unhappy about that.

I didn't see Rinpoche get involved in being uncomfortable. I would see him make responses to his discomfort which would not make him less or more uncomfortable; then he simply wouldn't pay much attention to it. He didn't make it mean anything. Very often he wouldn't mention it because the people around him would have made it mean something.

He didn't let me know he was going to die. I would have done everything I could have to stop him from dying. That's my attachment to his body. It was a great body. I liked it a lot. Particularly round and luscious. Certainly a body designed to seduce the pants right off me. Coincidence, do you think?

POEM BY TREBOR

I AM WRONG

Looking out the window
of an airplane
I start to cry
at how beautiful the world is
the pulled cotton of low clouds
green hills layered
like muscles
cities laid out in intricate designs
like tattoos on the skin of the earth
I could fall in love with you I muse, gazing at the body of the planet
    below me
To be a living thing is to have a crush on the world

Must it be unrequited love?
I cry and I cry Dzogchen*
the world is perfect
unquestionably perfect
—there is no doubt
and I am sad
for the suffering is this:
there is something between us
the world and I
a profound misunderstanding

So often we pass without hello

A fool, I am truly afraid that we are not one
and utterly convinced of the fear
unquestionably
—there is no doubt

And I am wrong
Perfectly, unquestionably, undoubtedly wrong

---

*Dzogchen, or Great Perfection, is the Tibetan Buddhist practice in which the generation and completion stages are effortlessly present. It is known as "perfection" because all the enlightened attributes of the three *kayas* are perfected in the stabilization of intrinsic awareness.

Leonard Zwilling (left) and Michael J. Sweet, Monona, Wisconsin.
Photo by Kalleen Mortensen

We Two Boys Forever Non-Clinging: Being Buddhist and Coupled

Michael J. Sweet

I A Personal View

Lenny and I had been together for three years when he went to live at the Buddhist monastery: he made no promise to return, and I felt devastated at losing the relationship that I had dreamed about since the dawning of my desires in puberty. We first met at one of the classic queer venues of the pre-Stonewall era, the fabled standees' line of the old Metropolitan Opera on Eighth Ave.[1] This didn't happen totally by chance; there was a go-between, my old high school friend Phil, a slightly closeted Irish Catholic, who had met this "interesting and acerbic Jew" at Fordham and thought that we would surely get along (he was more right than he imagined!). The meeting was like a thunderclap of good fortune—an attractive guy my age, brainy, witty, and musical; we hit it off immediately, and he invited me to visit him in farthest Rockaway to see his Oscar Wilde collection—this sounded very promising. I wasn't sure he was gay, nor did he know I was, but we immediately formed a very close friendship, spent all the time we could together. We whiled away the hours listening to Bach and Wagner, reciting Baudelaire and Swinburne, walking drunkenly through the city singing radical songs from the '30s, endlessly talking, and finally one fine spring morning falling into each other's arms with long suppressed desire. This was in the mid-1960s, in an America still intensely homophobic, and with few openly gay couples in evidence to serve as role models. I knew there was a gay subculture in New York, but imagined it in unappealing terms—bitchy, swishy, superficial, and alcoholic, a stereotype that was probably at least partly based on some of the realities of that era, as depicted for example in the play and movie *The Boys in the Band*. A lot of my fear was based on deep doubts about my own attractiveness and worth, and meeting someone like Lenny, who seemed to like me, was like a wonderful fantasy come true.

MICHAEL SWEET's biographical note can be found on page 13.
   This article is a revision of "Together on the Path: Gay Relationships in a Buddhist Context," published in Robert E. Goss and Amy A. S. Stongheart (eds.), *Our Families, Our Values: Snapshots of Queer Kinship* (New York: Harrington Park Press, 1997):114–27.

So how was this idyll shattered, and what did Buddhism have to do with it? Six months after becoming lovers, we found our own place, a fifth floor walkup apartment, a hovel with the bathtub in the kitchen, in an ancient tenement on East 3rd St., on the Lower East Side of Manhattan. Away from our parents' homes at last, we loved it, and immediately got involved with the burgeoning "hippie" counterculture, in which being gay was accepted as either no big deal, or a groovy defiance of straight society. We were both marking time in college, but LSD and other psychedelics were everywhere, and proved much more engrossing than Latin or the English metaphysical poets. With psychedelics came the opening to a new world "beyond the doors of perception" in Blake's memorable phrase. The experience might best be described as "mystic," an ineffable state by definition; a recent description characterizes it about as well as possible, as "a hidden dimension of human consciousness in which the dichotomies of normal awareness are transcended in an intense experience of unity or community with a hidden reality of presence."[2] I'd read about Zen of course, and had been quite inspired by Kerouac's *Dharma Bums* and Ginsberg's queer Buddhist-Hindu mystical rants, when I was a teenager. But with direct experience came an intense desire to find out more about this higher reality, and we started reading the few books then available, going from Tim Leary's loopy psychedelic take on the *Tibetan Book of the Dead*, to Evans-Wentz's theosophical interpretation of the same book, to Alexandra David-Neel's exciting tales of flying lamas. By 1966 we had found our teacher, Geshe Wangyal, a Kalmyk Mongol from the Crimean area of Russia, who had spent forty years in Tibet and was the first Tibetan Buddhist monk in America to teach Buddhism to Americans.

Geshe-la, as we called him ["geshe" is the Tibetan "Doctor of Divinity" degree; "la" is a Tibetan suffix denoting respect and affection] was a most extraordinary person. His own main teacher was the influential and mysterious Buriat Mongol lama Agvan Dorzhiev, a chief advisor of the Thirteenth Dalai Lama, and a key figure both in the revival of Buddhism among the Mongols in this century and the "great game" of Central Asian politics.[3] Geshe-la taught Buddhism in the ordinary manner, reading and explaining texts with his students, but he taught even more powerfully in his everyday interactions, which could manifest themselves as immensely compassionate or exceedingly wrathful, but in all cases were meant to increase the student's awareness of his or her egocentricity and neuroses. In the apt words of one of his closest disciples, Jeffrey Hopkins: "He taught untiringly and was both the most beautiful and the most terrifying person I have known. To live with him was to live with emptiness."[4] This method of teaching in everyday life resembles the tales of some of the Zen masters, of Tibetan teachers such as Marpa (the guru of the great mystic poet Milarepa), as well as of certain twentieth century teachers such as Gurdjieff and Fritz Perls.

Unlike the generally xenophobic Tibetans, Geshe-la was curious about other peoples and cultures, and travelled extremely widely, in China and India, and even made a rare journey (for a Tibetan monk at that time) to England in the 1930s, with his student and friend, the gay English explorer, scholar and musician Marco Pallis. Anticipating the Chinese suppression of Tibet, he emigrated first to Northern India and then to the United States, in 1955, to minister to the Kalmyk community in New Jersey. He also taught Mongolian at Columbia University, and began to teach Buddhism to American students, over the objections of Mongol traditionalists. As a man of the world of great sagacity and practicality, he was a consummate "people-knower" and was well aware that a number of his students were gay, lesbian, or bisexual—this was a matter to which he seemed to assign no importance. He had enormous charisma, and his first teachings to Lenny and me, unlike the mystic secrets we had anticipated, were blunt injunctions to get away from drugs, especially LSD, find jobs, and show some compassion for our parents—coming from him these words were effective, as they would have been from nobody else; we saw him as the embodiment of Enlightenment.

Geshe-la always characterized spiritual development as a process to mature human beings; or as he phrased it, to "ripen" (which in his pronunciation, rhymed with "pippin"). Unfortunately, maturation can't be rushed, so despite his influence, and my beginning to study Tibetan language and to do some elementary Buddhist practice, I was still a highly immature, insecure, self-centered kid at that time. Lenny drudged away at a straight job at an uptown bank, and was the principal financial support of our whole scene; we'd moved "uptown" to 4th St. between Avenues A and B, a large apartment with a floating population of two to four friends who lived with us, and various people crashing temporarily or just hanging out. Lenny would come home from work and find us listening to loud rock, jazz, Tibetan or Indian music, talking foolishness, smoking hash, lounging around—all he wanted then was a little peace and privacy, but we just urged him to "cool out," get high, and teased him for being so "up-tight." Lenny didn't have the behavioral skills to assert himself then and just became more and more depressed and anxious; finally, he fled to the monastery, as the only way out of an intolerable situation.

A couple of months without him brought me to my senses. I'd realized how unaware of his needs I'd been, how utterly insensitive—this was a sobering insight, after I'd imagined, with the grandiosity of the young fueled by the hubris of that self-celebratory era, that I was a Bodhisattva (a Buddhist "saint," totally devoted to the needs of others!). I visited him out at the monastery a few times—I was further alarmed once by someone joking about how Lenny and one of the female students should "get married"—and I gave him assurances that things were really going to change if he came back home. After he decided to do so, we were sitting with Geshe-la one evening, and he looked at us and said: "You two must stay together; you must help each other." We both agreed, and have always considered that our true "wedding"—we pledged our commitment in front of the person whom we considered a Buddha. It must have stuck, for thirty years later we are still together, and rather happily, which seems a near-miracle in these times.

In the rest of this essay, I'd like to look at how Buddhism can be a positive part of other lesbigay couples' lives, by examining the attitude of traditional Buddhist cultures toward queer people and same sex friendship and sexuality, and looking at Buddhist ways of relating to others. I'd also like to briefly review some of the challenges facing Buddhism in its confrontation with contemporary forms of queer identities and relationships.

II Leaving Home and Finding the Chosen Family

Through almost all of its history, in the many cultures in which it flourished, Buddhism has decisively rejected so-called "family values." The basic paradigm is found in the life story of Śākyamuni, the historical Buddha. He is depicted as a very sheltered young man of wealth and high status, already married with a young son, when his first view of sick, aging, and dead people took away his pleasure in family life— and the sight of a homeless mendicant gave him hope of a way out. For Śākyamuni, no less than for the Jesus of the Gospels,[5] the biological family was an impediment to spiritual growth, to be renounced if possible; the very name for the traditionally crucial step in Buddhist practice, entering the monastic state, literally means "leaving home." I have occasionally been asked about the "Buddhist marriage ceremony," and I have to tell people that this did not exist *per se* in traditional Buddhist societies, because marriage was not considered a religious occasion.[6] It was mainly with the development of modern forms of Buddhism influenced by Western (primarily Christian) models that specific marriage ceremonies have been created and enacted by Buddhist clerics.

The privileging of those who renounce social forms and obligations is not unique to Buddhism, but has deep roots in Indian society. It is not difficult to understand the motivation for such renunciation, given the rigidly hierarchical and rule-bound nature of the traditional Indian family, which requires the subordination of all individual needs to increasing the prestige, wealth and connections of the kin group. Women especially are treated as commodities, judged by the size of their dowries, future earning and childbearing capacity, and other hard-eyed considerations. One can sense the joy of the early nun who wrote that "I'm free/free from kitchen drudgery/no longer a slave among my dirty cooking pots . . . and I'm through with my brutal husband. . . . I purge lust with a sizzling sound—POP/'O happiness,' meditate upon this as happiness."[7] But the Indian renunciant is rarely a solitary figure; the Hindu *sādhus* (wandering ascetics) are organized in distinct groups, and a noted gay South Asian specialist with extensive field experience has asserted (in a private communication) that homosexual behavior is rather widespread among these groups. The Buddhist monks and nuns were pledged to celibacy; nevertheless, they wandered in same-sex groups of brothers or sisters in the Dharma, led by a preceptor or abbot/abbess who fulfilled the parental role. They had found a new family, with rules to be sure, but whose objectives were quite different from the one they had left: to support each other's spiritual development, having cut the attachments to wealth and lust connected with the worldly family. Within a few hundred years most Buddhist renunciants were settled in monasteries or nunneries, and the monastic community clearly functioned as a surrogate family, taking care of its members and inheriting their property at their death. There seems at least an analogue here to the lesbian or gay man who must often "leave home" to escape the abusive norms of the heterosexual family, and who then finds support from a chosen family of queer brothers and sisters, which can nurture that person's full human potential.[8]

III   Friendship and Sex in Buddhism

Having grown up queer in a Jewish working class "non-observant Orthodox" milieu, with its overpowering emphasis on marriage and family, Buddhism was the very breath of freedom for me. Not only is reproductive heterosexuality not compulsory, it is not even seen as particularly desirable for those wanting to "wake up" to reality and spiritual growth. Homophobia is a non-issue in Buddhism—all sexual attachment is regarded as an unhealthy psychological factor, because it is thought to lead to selfishness, anger, envy and other painful results—but the gender or genders to which one is attached is not of any significance. Buddhism has no sternly parental creator-god to get angry at harmless human diversity. Consequently, Asian Buddhist societies have never seen the murderous persecution of queers found in the West—in Thailand, Sri Lanka, Japan, and Tibet same-sex sexual behavior was and is widespread, among laypeople and monastics, and this is not problematic, as long as the layperson fulfills his or her obligation to marry and produce children, and liaisons do not create a public scandal.[9] This acceptance of same-sex love, albeit in a way that seems closeted to present-day gay sensibilities, may be a part of the reason that so many lesbigays have found a congenial spiritual home in Buddhism: ranging from well-known openly gay Buddhists such as the poet John Giorno, the late Allen Ginsberg and Roshi Issan Dorsey (a former drag queen and speed freak who became a Zen abbot),[10] to a number of lesbian and gay academics in Buddhist Studies (of whom the most prominent and public is perhaps Jeffrey Hopkins of the University of Virginia), as well as to the rank and file members of many American Buddhist centers, which, at least in my experience, have a significantly higher percentage of queer folks than is found in the general population.

In Asia it was gender transgression which was stigmatized, rather than same-sex sexuality per se; this was especially true regarding males who adopted the behavior, dress, and/or the receptive sexual activity "proper" to women. Such people were considered as a "third sex" in India from ancient times and were regarded as being disreputable and déclassé, although also at times as having special magical potency. They were generally ridiculed and devalued, but accepted as part of society, like the female prostitutes to whom they were sometimes compared.[11] The Buddhist attitude toward this group was a negative one, clearly from the point of view of expedience; they were barred from becoming monks or nuns mainly to protect the reputation of the monastic community. If the lay community, on whom monastics depended for their food and other necessities, came to see Buddhist monasteries as a hotbed of queer sexuality, this would endanger the whole monastic order and its spiritual goals.[12]

Among monks and nuns, any penetrative sexual behavior was considered grounds for expulsion from the order. Non-penetrative acts were considered lesser and expiatable offenses, and one odd group of Tibetan monks, non-scholarly types who acted as police, security guards, musicians, and other important but low-status roles, justified their notorious romances with handsome youths on the grounds that they practiced only intracrural intercourse.[13] Although same-sex relationships and sexual behavior were found in monasteries from China and Japan to Tibet, and were tolerated if not exploitative or too scandalous, they were nevertheless seen as falling short of the ideal of celibacy, distracting the monk or nun from the singleminded devotion to spiritual development and the welfare of others considered appropriate to renunciants.

In contrast to homosexual behavior, same-sex friendship and companionship were highly valued in Buddhist culture. The popular literature of tales and fables, known to both laypeople and monastics, is consistent in its misogynist portrayal of wives and female lovers as lustful, unfaithful, sinful, etc., and its view of marriage as a sink of misery for both women and men. Friendship, on the other hand, is extolled in the highest terms, the model being the exemplary love and devotion of Buddha's closest attendant, Ānanda (see my essay on him in the present volume). The ideal form of friendship is considered to be that of the "virtuous friend" (*kalyāṇamitra*), who is motivated by the desire for the happiness and welfare, and especially the spiritual development, of his or her companion.

IV   Homophobia in Buddha-land

While the attitude toward gay people in the Buddhist milieu, both in Asia and in American Buddhism, is a model of acceptance compared to the prohibitions and persecutions of the desert monotheisms, I would not want to leave this subject giving the impression that homophobia doesn't exist. Particularly in America, where fear and hatred of queers is in the environment from our earliest years, simply becoming a Buddhist doesn't erase deep-seated prejudices. Lenny and I, in fact, once had a horrendous experience of homophobia (and anti-Semitism to boot), in our extended interactions with a notable American Buddhist, and a recent autobiographical account gives a devastating view of internalized homophobia in a prominent Buddhist teacher.[14] A public example of this phenomenon occurred after Jeffrey Hopkins was interviewed in *Tricycle*, relating among other things some of his personal experiences with gay sex in a Buddhist context, and giving an excerpt from a gay tantric sex manual that he had written.[15] This interview provoked a flood of angry letters and cancelled subscriptions in the next issue (Fall, 1996), one writer going so far as to say that gays "have no right to live in the United States under any circumstances." To those who later wrote to the magazine that this hate mail was intolerant and contrary to Buddhist values (which it clearly was), the otherwise ultraliberal editor replied with a sanctimonious statement saying that those who are against homophobia were just as intolerant as the 'phobes,[16] showing once again the sad reality that queer-hatred is the only remaining socially acceptable form of prejudice in the U.S.; it is inconceivable that *Tricycle* would have provided a forum for similar hateful letters about Asian, Hispanic or African Americans.

V Ways of Relating

How can Buddhism be relevant to contemporary gay people in couples and other relationships, who are grappling with the perennial problem of "how can we get along?" I believe that the answer, or part of it, lies in the side of Buddhism that encourages prosocial attitudes: starting with generating proper concern for one's own happiness and freedom from pain, one extends this feeling to one's parents, friends, and other benefactors, and eventually even to neutral and hostile people, cultivating joy in others' happiness and an impartial attitude.[17] This can help transform the initially selfish infatuation that we feel for people, wanting them all to ourselves, wanting to control them, into a true caring for and knowing the person as s/he is. These are the two kinds of love distinguished by William Blake in his poem "The Clod and the Pebble" (in the *Songs of Experience*). The first "seeketh only Self to please/ To bind another to Its delight/ Joys in another's loss of ease,/ And builds a Hell in heaven's despite." The second, like the lovingkindness and compassion encouraged in Buddhism "seeketh not Itself to please,/ Nor for itself have any care,/ But for another gives its ease,/ And builds a Heaven in Hell's despair."

Added to these social emotions is the basic Buddhist premise that the Self is an ever-changing dynamic system, lacking any permanent core. The combination of this view with love and compassion is a way to synthesize seemingly diametric opposites—a warm loving concern with detachment, which includes accepting the autonomy of others. This may seem like a tall order, and it is, but it certainly can be an ongoing ideal, given the necessary awareness and practice to sustain it. Such an attitude leads the way to true intimacy, and a solution to the commonest hassles I've seen in couples that I've known personally, or worked with in couples therapy: alienating each other with criticism or control, inability to hear each other, the fear of the other partner taking pleasure in friends or recreation that one doesn't like, and seeing the partner's changes or differences, the latter usually the very basis for the attraction, as a rejection of oneself.

I think that fundamentally it has been the willingness to work at accepting each other's many changes, along with our supportive chosen family of gay and nongay friends, that has helped Len and I stay together and continue to evolve over the past thirty-four years, and this seems a commonality in other successful relationships that I have encountered. While acceptance and mutual caring and concern are crucial to any relationship, gays and lesbians may have some advantages in developing these attitudes. The pride and self-acceptance that has come with gay liberation has broken down much self-hatred, fear and rejection of other gay people, and enabled us to come together as a caring community, especially in response to the AIDS crisis. We can remember and use the pain of our oppression to increase empathy for others, and we are hopefully not bound by traditional heterosexual concepts of marriage as ownership and control. I think of a nongay friend, who recently confided that he hates going to large social gatherings, "but I have to, my wife drags me to them." Middle-class heterosexual norms require couples to be together in social settings, under the penalty of shame and gossip; queer couples seem more free to be individuals in relationships, rather than inseparable halves of a whole.

VI   The Wheel Keeps Turning: Buddhism in the Gay '90s and Beyond

Asian Buddhisms in America have interacted with our culture and values to create new varieties of American Buddhism; this is inevitable—religions are always in the process of change, and the same kind of adaptation occurred when Buddhism encountered other already-developed cultures, such as in China. How will American Buddhism deal with l/b/g Buddhists, and with gay Buddhist relationships, which are very different in form and content from anything known in traditional Asian societies? Some have already opted for assimilationist acceptance, similar to the liberal Christian or Jewish denominations that celebrate same-sex unions and welcome gays into their congregations. For example the Soka Gakkai movement in America, an outgrowth of the Japanese Nichiren school, has approved marriage ceremonies for same-sex couples, the first Buddhist denomination to do so. Two representatives of Buddhist groups testified in favor of same-sex marriage in Hawai'i, and the Dalai Lama opined in an interview that gay relationships were fine, as long as the people involved "did not have any vows" (i.e., were not monks or nuns).[18]

However, while the aforementioned are all positive gestures, to accept loving monogamous gay/lesbian couples is not much of a stretch for Buddhists, since there are no theological grounds for not doing so. The challenge will be more in dealing with the queerer side of our community: the many non-exclusive relationships (probably the majority among gay male couples), group relationships, S/M, and so on. The one clear rule in traditional Buddhist lay sexual morality is the prohibition of adultery (although even that doesn't formally apply to people who haven't taken special lay vows); non-adulterous sexual play among ordinary laypeople is generally ignored in Asian Buddhist societies.

However, this view of adultery is clearly "conventional," that is, non-absolute and situational, based on the realities found in premodern Asian societies, predicated on the culture of marital ownership. To stealthily have sex with someone else's partner was seen as akin to using his oxen or milking his cow without his permission. Whether this would apply in a more open model of relationships, in which people did not consider their lovers or partners as property, needs to be the object of discussion among Buddhist ethicists, and among queer Buddhists in general; some have already taken up this question, usually moving in the direction of a more situational view of sexual misconduct, depending on the intention of the sexual act and its effect on oneself and others.[19] In my personal experience, having an open relationship can be freeing and enriching, enabling mutually satisfying loving contacts with a wide variety of people. It can also be quite frightening, and has forced me to confront my own selfishness and egocentricity, and given rise at times to paranoid thinking and strong "negative" emotions such as anger and jealousy. Whether it is better to use such negative thoughts and emotions as part of one's spiritual practice, confronting them with mindfulness and non-attachment, or to simply avoid them as much as possible by having a monogamous relationship (which can of course give rise to other negative feelings) is a dilemma for each individual and couple to settle for themselves dependent on their personality styles and values, including their Buddhist beliefs.

A further question relates to monasticism. While mainstream traditional Buddhism has considered the monastic life as nearly the *sine qua non* for the higher development of ethics, contemplation, and wisdom, American monks and nuns have been rather few in number, with fewer still who remain permanently in the monastic life. My purely subjective impression is that a fair number of these American Buddhist monastics, unlike their Asian counterparts, have at least in part chosen the celibate life as a retreat from sexuality and its conflicts, often (but not always) from gay and lesbian sexuality. This is a phenomenon one of our friends has called "the saffron closet"—immersion in Buddhism, as a layperson or a monastic, as a strategy to avoid confrontation with one's forbidden or feared sexual orientation. Such avoidance is contrary to the Buddhist values of insight and self-acceptance, and terribly damaging to the individual's ability to relate genuinely to others in the world. I've known some folks who have emerged from these saffron closets, and managed to joyfully connect to others emotionally and sexually, while maintaining their Buddhist identity and practice. Recent years have seen the growth of groups that are specifically devoted to providing support for gay male and lesbian Buddhists; the most prominent of these has been the Gay Buddhist Fellowship, a nationwide nonsectarian gay male group based in San Francisco which organizes group practice, teaching, and community work, and Maitri Dorji, a New York City based group of gay men and lesbians associated with the organization founded by Chögyam Trungpa. It is to be hoped that American Buddhism will continue to provide affirming spaces for gay people to develop as individuals and in multiple kinds of relationships, as part of a loving spiritual community, and that gay individuals, couples, and groups will evolve creative solutions to the challenges of being both queer and Buddhist.

NOTES

[1]See Wayne Koestenbaum, *The Queen's Throat* (New York: Vintage Books, 1993) for a dishy account of what the opera line meant to young gay men in the '50s and '60s.

[2]Jeffrey Kripal, *Kali's Child: The Mystical and the Erotic in the Life and Teachings of Ramakrishna* (Chicago: University of Chicago Press, 1995):20.

[3]For the fullest, though still inadequate account of Dorzhiev's life, see John Snelling, *Buddhism in Russia* (Rockport, MA: Element, 1993).

[4]Quoted in *Snow Lion Newsletter and Catalog*, Fall 1994, p. 29.

[5]See for example, the gospel accounts in Matthew 10:35-37, 48-50, Luke 9:59-60.

[6]Buddhist monks and nuns are not entirely removed from the laity of course, and do perform some rituals relating to lay life, such as funerals or house-dedication ceremonies, but their role in marriages, if any, was rather peripheral. See Heinz Bechert and Richard Gombrich (eds.), *The World of Buddhism: Buddhist Monks and Nuns in Society and Culture* (New York: Thames and Hudson, 1984):14, 188.

[7]Translated by Anne Waldman and Andrew Schelling, "Songs of the Elders: From the Buddha's First Disciples," *Tricycle*, 5(2), Winter, 1995, p. 48

[8]See for example the life stories related in John Preston's *Hometowns: Gay Men Write About Where They Belong* (New York: Dutton, 1991), and in the book he edited with Michael Lowenthal, *Friends and Lovers: Gay Men Write About Families They Create* (New York: Dutton, 1995).

[9]For example, in the Tibetan Buddhist cultural area, Owen Lattimore reported that Mongolian Buddhist monks justified same-sex sexuality on theological grounds; see his *Nomads and Commissars* (New York: Oxford University Press, 1962):211. A young Japanese spy who lived disguised as a monk in Tibet also reported widespread homosexual behavior among lamas; see Hisao Kimura, *Japanese Agent in Tibet: My Ten Years of Travel in Disguise*, as told to Scott Berry (London: Serindia, 1990). Two modern prime ministers of Thailand have been

widely known for their same-sex orientations, without damage to their political careers (Peter Jackson, personal communication, October, 1995). For sympathetic tales of Japanese Buddhist monks and their love for young men see Ihara Saikaku, *The Great Mirror of Male Love*, trans. by Paul G. Schalow (Stanford, CA: Stanford University Press, 1990).

[10]See Daishin David Sunseri, "Stories About My Teacher Issan Dorsey Roshi," and Issan Dorsey Roshi, "Mindfulness Is Not a Part-Time Job," both in Winston Leyland (ed.), *Queer Dharma: Voices of Gay Buddhists* (San Francisco: Gay Sunshine Press, 1998):149–59.

[11]For detailed information on queer identities in classical India, see Michael Sweet and Leonard Zwilling, "The First Medicalization: The Taxonomy and Etiology of Queerness in Classical Indian Medicine," *Journal of the History of Sexuality* 3 (1993):590–607 and Leonard Zwilling and Michael Sweet, " 'Like a City Ablaze': The Third Sex and the Creation of Sexuality in Jain Religious Literature," *Journal of the History of Sexuality* 6 (1996):359–84. For the best study to date of the contemporary Indian transgender/third sex group, the *hijras*, see Serena Nanda, *Neither Man Nor Woman: The Hijras of India* (Belmont, CA: Wordsworth, 2nd ed., 1999).

[12]See Leonard Zwilling, "Avoidance and Exclusion: Same-Sex Sexuality in Indian Buddhism," in Winston Leyland (ed.), *Queer Dharma: Voices of Gay Buddhists* (San Francisco: Gay Sunshine Press, 1998):45–54.

[13]About this group, the Dop-Dop (*Idab Idob*), who were found in the vast monastic universities of Central Tibet, see Melvyn C. Goldstein, "Study of the Ldab-Ldob," *Central Asian Journal*, 9 (1964):123–41.

[14]Robert K. Hall, "Homophobia and Spiritual Teachers: A Coming Out 'Affair,' " in Winston Leyland (ed.), *Queer Dharma: Voices of Gay Buddhists* (San Francisco: Gay Sunshine Press, 1998):239–46.

[15]Mark Epstein, "In the Realm of Relationship: Mark Epstein Interviews Jeffrey Hopkins," *Tricycle*, Summer 1996, vol. v, no. 4, pp. 53–58.

[16]Helen Tworkow, "Editors View: Whaddya Mean 'We,' " *Tricycle*, Winter 1996, vol vi, no. 2, p. 4.

[17]This practice is described in detail in many popular books on Buddhist practice; see for example Geshe Kelsang Gyatso, *Universal Compassion* (London: Tharpa Publications, 1988) and Pema Chödrön, *Start Where You Are: A Guide to Compassionate Living* (Boston: Shambhala, 1994). For a psychotherapeutic application of these attitudes, see Michael Sweet and Craig G. Johnson, "Enhancing Empathy: The Interpersonal Implications of a Buddhist Meditation Technique," *Psychotherapy*, 27 (1990):19–29.

[18]On the controversy caused by the Dalai Lama's comments, see Dennis Conklin, "The Dalai Lama and Gay Love," in Winston Leyland (ed.), *Queer Dharma: Voices of Gay Buddhists* (San Francisco: Gay Sunshine Press, 1998):351–56.

[19]For example Robert Aitkin, a prominent nongay Zen Buddhist abbot and activist, stated in his testimony to the Hawai'i Commission on Sexual Orientation and the Law on Oct. 11, 1995 his view that the Buddhist precept of not engaging in sexual misconduct, usually taken to apply to adultery, means that "self-centered sexual conduct is inappropriate. . . . Self-centered sex is exploitative sex, non-consensual sex, sex that harms others." [Taken from a reprint of his testimony posted on the Internet, from khush@flux.mindspring.com., Jan. 6, 1996]. This is also, as might be supposed, an intense object of discussion among gay Buddhists themselves, a topic often discussed in the newsletter of the Gay Buddhist Fellowship; see, for example Jim Wilson, "The Precept About Sexuality," *Newsletter of the Gay Buddhist Fellowship*, April, 1999, pp. 1–6.

III

GAY FICTION ON
BUDDHIST THEMES

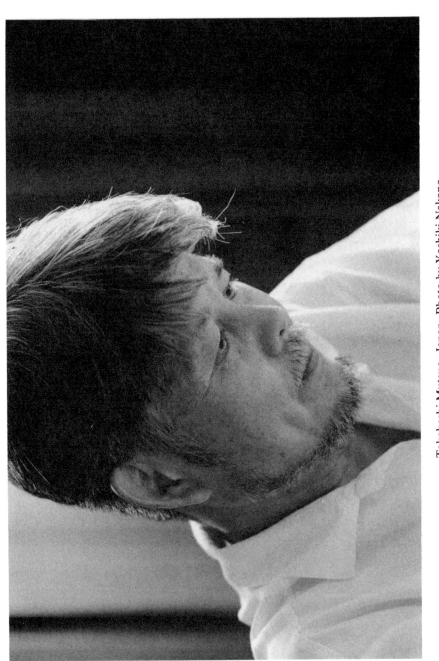

Takahashi Mutsuo, Japan. Photo by Yoshiki Nakano

Zen's Pilgrimage

Takahashi Mutsuo
Translated by Jeffrey Angles

Biography of Takahashi Mutsuo

Ever since the Japanese writer Takahashi Mutsuo (1937–   ) published his second anthology of poetry *Bara no ki, nise no koibito-tachi (Rose Tree, Fake Lovers)* in 1964 to national literary acclaim, he has continued to turn out a large number of anthologies of poetry which have received widespread attention. To date, Takahashi has written well over two dozen volumes of poetry including *Kono yo arui wa hako no hito (This World or The Man in the Box,* 1998). He has been the recipient of a number of important literary prizes in Japan, such as the Rekitei Prize, the Yomiuri Literary Prize, the Takami Jun Prize, the Modern Poetry Hanatsubaki Prize, and the Shika Bungakukan Prize. Recently in 1997, the architect Dani Karavan honored Takahashi by selecting him to write two tanka (a thirty-one syllable form of traditional Japanese poetry) to be inscribed on an important public monument near Nagai Stadium in Osaka.

Though Takahashi has been most visibly active in the realm of poetry, he also frequently crosses the barriers of literary genre. A bibliography of his publications immediately reveals that in addition to his Western-style and Japanese-style poetry, he has also written novels, Nō and Kyō-gen plays, reworkings of ancient Greek dramas and epic poetry, count-less works of literary criticism, and even an opera libretto. His fictional works include the 1972 collection of novellas *Sei sankakkei (The Sacred Triangle)* and the 1974 novel *Zen no henreki (Zen's Pilgrimage).* Taka-hashi's most recent publications are the 1998 anthology of poetry men-tioned above and the critical work *Yominaoshi Nihon bungaku shi (Rereading Japanese Literary History,* 1998), which has generated a great deal of attention in the literary academy.

A large number of Takahashi's poems, especially those dating from before the mid-1980s, are available in English translation. Translator Hiroaki Sato has published in the U.S. three anthologies of Takahashi's work: *Poems of a Penisist* (1975), *A Bunch of Keys* (1984), and *Sleep-ing, Sinning, and Falling* (1992). He has also translated for a CD col-lection of Takahashi's poems entitled *Voice Garden* (1996), in which Takahashi reads his work to musical accompaniment composed by Takahashi Yūji. Translations by Sato and others are also available in the Gay Sunshine Press publications *Orgasms of Light* (1977), *Gay Roots Volume 1* (1991), and *Partings at Dawn, An Anthology of Japanese Gay Literature* (1996).

Takahashi presently lives in the seaside city of Zushi, ten kilometers to the south of Yokohama.

Jeffrey Angles (1971–   ), translator of this text, has spent a number of years living and studying in Japan. Presently, he is at Ohio State University writing a dissertation on homosexuality in twentieth century Japanese literature. His M.A. thesis, completed in 1997, examined Takahashi Mutsuo's early, longer works and includes several original translations. He has also translated several short stories, including a homoerotic story by the writer Inagaki Taruho, for a forthcoming anthology of modernism in Japanese literature.

Translator's Introduction
Jeffrey Angles

Takahashi Mutsuo's works, especially those written before the mid-1970s, deal extensively with a number of tightly interrelated themes, specifically homoeroticism, the relationship between the individual and the sacred, the incomplete and void nature of the individual, and the resulting search for psychological completion. Frequently in these early works, Takahashi employs the rhetoric of religion to describe the dynamics of sexuality. For instance, the works *Homeuta* (*Ode*, 1971) and *Sei sankakkei* (*The Sacred Triangle*, 1972) depict the existential relationship between the individual and the object of erotic desire while frequently employing images and motifs from Catholicism. In a recent conversation with the present translator, Takahashi stated that it is the responsibility of the individual writer to come to grips with the worldviews and philosophies that have shaped human thought and to react to these frameworks in order to produce his own ideas. In his early works, this process is particularly visible. In them, Takahashi repeatedly borrows the framework of religion in order to depict the relationship between the internal, psychological world and the external, physical world as they come together in the sexual act.

The 1974 novel *Zen no henreki* (*Zen's Pilgrimage*), is the longest of Takahashi's fictional works to date and the only work thus far which depicts homosexuality in an explicitly Buddhist framework. This fantastic and often extremely funny novel is loosely based upon the classic Buddhist tale "Entry into the World of Reality" found within the

Flower Garland Sutra. This ancient story follows a young boy named Sudhana as he travels about India in search of enlightenment. Along the way, Sudhana encounters a large number of prominent philosophical teachers who then serve as his teachers.

Takahashi's clever reworking also involves a young man, an eighteen-year-old boy named "Zen," short for Hokkai Zenzai (written with the characters meaning "Dharma-world virtuous treasure"). When the novel begins, Zen leaves his hometown for the big city of Tokyo, and on the train there, he has the first of many explicit, homoerotic encounters. The conductor of the train is an ancient man who calls himself Monjū Bosatsu, the Japanese name for the bodhisattva known in Sanskrit as Mañjuśri. As they ride towards the capital, the mysterious conductor gives Zen an extraordinary blow job, meanwhile somehow managing to explain, despite his full mouth, that homoeroticism is one means to enlightenment. According to him, Mahāvairocana, the main deity of the Shingon Buddhist pantheon, is actually a gigantic phallus in space that spews cock-shaped UFOs towards all the planets in the universe. This enormous penis, located on the far side of an infinitely vast stretch of space, is the source of all energy in the cosmos. So that humankind might achieve unity with this primeval being, all men have been equipped with genitalia in Mahāvairocana's image, the use of which can induce ecstatic enlightenment. In accordance with this iconoclastic explanation, Monjū Bosatsu substitutes the word *Mahāvairocana* wherever the word *penis* would appear, starting a tradition that persists throughout the novel. As the train pulls into Tokyo, Monjū Bosatsu instructs Zen to wander through the erotic underground of the city, using his Mahāvairocana to study the mysteries of the universe.

Throughout the rest of the novel, Zen roams through porno theaters, gay bars, saunas, and other sites of homoerotic activity, engaging in a number of bizarre adventures along the way. Like Sudhana in the *Flower Ornament Sutra*, Zen encounters various eminent "teachers," but Zen's experiences, unlike all but a few of Sudhana's, are always explicitly erotic in nature. Each chapter describes a month-long series of titillating escapades, each in a different location. At the end of every chapter, Monjū Bosatsu visits Zen in order to deliver a report on his spiritual progress and to interpret Zen's recent experiences in the light of Buddhist philosophy and history. Finally at the end of the novel, Zen achieves liberation and is united with the great Mahāvairocana that is the source of all life.

In this final chapter, Takahashi draws explicitly on the sexual practices of Tantrism, a brand of esoteric practice preserved most notably in Tibet. Tantra involves exercises designed to transform the ordinary into the divine by weaving an enlightened universe in the place of the present world of suffering. It teaches that sex is nothing to shy from, and in fact, it uses sex in some practices to reproduce the bliss of Nirvana. Sexual union is understood as the merging of opposite or disparate elements and parallels the sort of communion that should be present in the state of enlightenment. By laying these ideas over the history of Japanese Buddhism and by weaving them into his light-hearted connection between Mahāvairocana, UFOs, and a huge, glowing phallus, Takahashi produces an iconoclastic and amusing melange of ideas that relate Buddhism and homoerotic sexuality.

Below is a translation of the concluding chapter of *Zen's Pilgrimage*. Prior to this chapter, Zen unintentionally kills a man and is thrown naked into jail. Over the next month in detention, his cellmates repeatedly assault him. In fact, during one particularly rough bout of anal sex, they manage to knock loose a cherished talisman, a golden ring that Zen has swallowed to keep safe. When Zen then uses the toilet, the ring slides out and is washed away, leaving him feeling alone and without any protection in the world. After a month in jail, Zen is taken before a judge, who despite Zen's actual crime, convicts him only of public indecency. Zen has started to manifest symptoms of venereal disease, and when he is returned to the cell after sentencing, all the other prisoners shun him. In a moment of hallucinatory fever, he imagines that his body has turned into a large number of orifices that are all being penetrated simultaneously—a vision foreshadowing images that surface in the section below. Upon waking and experiencing a feeling of utter dejection, a warden informs Zen that he is being released. The translation below picks up as Zen is walking nude and dazed from the jailhouse.

Zen Is Reunited with Monjū Bosatsu; Passing through the Intermediate State, Zen Becomes One with Mahāvairocana

Finally free after weeks in the cell, Zen descended the stone steps of the police station. Spread before him as if in greeting was an expanse of sky so brilliant and blue that it made his eyes smart. Yesterday when he had been chained to the other prisoners like a bead on a Buddhist rosary and led to and from the courtroom, a terrible blizzard had been in progress. It was unlike any he had ever seen before, but today, not even a single flake was left in the entire landscape. Had all of it disappeared overnight? The snow, however, was not the only thing that had disappeared. The rows of houses and stores that should have stood before the police station, the billboard advertising vitamins, and even the buildings clustered in the distance like trees in a forest had all vanished. Looking across the vast, empty expanse of the plain before him, even the edges of the field itself melted into the intensely cerulean sky.

This couldn't be Tokyo, could it? Zen had once seen pictures of the charred ruins of Tokyo in a magazine containing photos of the city after the March 1945 air raid, the biggest of the Pacific War. What Zen saw, however, was nothing like that. The pictures had showed a city full of scorched trees, blackened roof tiles, and buildings reduced to skeletons. The rubble formed a series of mountains and valleys that undulated sharply in topography. None of those mountains and valleys, however, were present in the landscape before Zen, since needless to say, there were no skeletal buildings or heaps of rubble in sight. The weeds and grass covering the surface of the plain were proof that what had been there before had not recently been leveled. The grasses rustled as a scarcely perceptible breeze rippled through them, stirring them just enough to catch and reflect the sunlight. It was as if some primeval plain predating human habitation had appeared to occupy the land in front of him. Not only was there no place like that in Tokyo, there was probably no such place in all of contemporary Japan.

Since the landscape did not belong to the outside world, he figured he had to be standing in the midst of some landscape that was previously hidden inside him. Somehow, his inside world must have transformed into the external world. If so, he must have incorporated what was formerly outside into his internal world. But what did it all mean?

What was this inside-out world, this inside-out Zen all about?

"I'm out in the middle of the wilderness! No sign of civilization anywhere," Zen thought as he descended the stone steps. Just as he reached the bottom step, however, an ultra-modern train suddenly appeared before him. Zen found he was standing on the open-air platform of a train station, but strangely there was not a single soul in sight! He was confused. Then, with equal abruptness, a boy appeared between him and the train. Was he even ten years old? He hardly came up to Zen's chest. Most astounding, however, was the fact that he wasn't wearing even a stitch of clothing.

What a beautiful body! The boy's limbs were richly fleshed out, yet there wasn't a trace of the unhealthiness of excess weight. As the boy stood there, his bare feet spread out squarely planted on the ground, every part of his body seemed to glow with a look of pure innocence. The priestly, shaven head that sat atop his chest wore a beautiful smile. Indeed, Zen wondered if a lovelier smile was even possible—that's how beautiful it was. Though the package between his thighs was of an adorable, appropriately boyish size, its round head poked candidly forth with the brazenness of an adult. It too wore a grin no less happy than the shaven head above it.

"It's Śākyamuni of the Flower Festival!" Zen realized. When he was young and still living in his birthplace on the shores of Kyūshū, he had celebrated the birthday of the Buddha every April 8. In front of even the tiniest temples stood small statues of the infant Buddha covered with canopies woven from the flowers of the milk vetch plant. Invariably, the statue stood in the middle of a basin containing sweet tea and a small ladle. Children would come to give a few coins in offering, press their hands together, and scoop up some of the sweet tea with the ladle to pour over the statue. Then, they would take home in glass jars and small sake bottles the sweet tea that had washed over the nude, infant Buddha.

It had been the longest time since Zen had thought about this, and these memories carried Zen back to the contented, warm world of his childhood. Standing there in the breeze, the light spilling across the land, and the blue of the sky, Zen felt happiness well up within him. He felt as if his very being were melting into the landscape to become one with it. It was as if the life he had led over the last year, the terrible life that began that day when he ran away to Tokyo after graduating from high school, had been nothing but a dream. He had also completely forgotten his years in grade school so all that remained was the memory of his preschool days. As he stood facing the nude Śākyamuni, he was so oblivious to his surroundings that he felt as if he had come to inhabit a petite, boyish body just like the Buddha of the Flower Festival before him. The boy's youthful form was all he perceived.

Zen's body, however, was nothing like that of the brilliantly shining child before him. Over the course of the last year, he had made his way through the degenerate, corrupt sea of earthly desire. After coming to Tokyo, he had wandered on a pilgrimage through places reeking of wickedness and depravity, slipping from place to place as rapidly and easily as a backgammon piece sliding over a game board. On top of that, he had committed murder and been tossed into the lockup. Even the most severe punishment was not enough to wash him clean. Day after day, night after night, he had accepted the sexual affronts of his cellmates, and after it was all said and done, the only charge that the judge brought against him was the petty charge of public indecency. He had contracted some incurable disease that caused even his cellmates to ostracize him, and his entire body had degenerated into a monstrous collection of holes. Finally, he was chased even from jail. Yet in the midst of his filthy, wretched, and naked state, a single part of his body—the Mahāvairocana between his thighs—stood flawlessly erect with the full splendor that it had displayed ever since he had got up that morning. Zen knew this to be the case, yet he could not bring himself to let his gaze drop to the member standing erect at his groin.

Śākyamuni, still smiling with his entire body, continued to stand before Zen. Though the petite Mahāvairocana between the boy's thighs was still that of a young boy, its shiny round head and splendid erection resembled at least in form that of an adult. Zen wondered if the Mahāvairocana of the statues of Śākyamuni of the Flower Festival had one of these erect, round cockheads, which looked so much like the shaven head of a priest. No, he stopped himself short. The infant Śākyamuni before him was indeed Śākyamuni himself. He had come as a harbinger of the future adult Śākyamuni, and it was therefore not without reason that he should have an erect Mahāvairocana with a round head like all other adults.

As a general rule, the Śākyamuni statues that are used in the Flower Festival depict the Buddha with one hand pointing upward and the other downward, a position that indicates that he alone is holy throughout heaven and earth. This Śākyamuni, however, used his upward-pointing index finger to point in the direction of the train while the downward finger turned towards Zen. As Zen tried to unravel the meaning of these rather unbecoming, angular gestures, Śākyamuni began speaking to him. His voice was extraordinarily charming.

"Get on, Sudhana."

"Huh?"

"You are Zenzai, aren't you? I've come a long way to meet you."

"Meet me?"

"I am serving as the guarantor for Hokkai Zenzai, who was convicted of the crime of public indecency. I was the one who paid the five thousand yen for your fine, and now I'm here to welcome you out of jail."

So that was it. Now that Zen thought about it, he remembered the judge yesterday in court telling him that he would have to pay a fine and have a guarantor to vouch for him if he wanted to be released. Be that as it may, Zen had no memory of ever having met a funny little boy like the one before him. The precocious tone was so unbefitting the sweet face attached to it! Really! What a know-it-all, just like an old man in the body of a ten-year-old! Had this baffling little priestling really come to serve as his deputy, let alone his guarantor? Someone else must have taken on the responsibility and sent over this strange little guy as his representative. If so, then who was his real patron? Try as he might, he couldn't think of a soul who might be willing to serve as his patron. But wait, what about that fellow Monjū Bosatsu? Could he be the one? He had to be. There was no one else who would be willing to step in and save him.

"That means you and Monjū Bosatsu are . . . ?" Zen's voice trailed off in confusion.

"One and the same. I'm Monjū, the Bodhisattva Mañjuśri himself!"

"You're pulling my leg. He's a lot . . ."

"Older? Little kid, decrepit old man—we're both the same person. There's a text called the *Sūtra of Heroic Valor*, which tells of a buddha known as Ryūjujō Nyorai who lived innumerable kalpas ago in the infinitely distant past. It states that he lived to the age of 4,400,000 years before entering Nirvāṇa. He was a previous incarnation of Monjū Bosatsu, so you might say that I'm an old man all right! Another account speaks of me as a boy. It says after an infinite number of eons have passed, I will once again enter the world as a tathāgata. This means that even though I may appear to be just a baby priest, as a matter of fact, I am only the tiniest invisible seed of a child. But let's set this tiresome logic aside, shall we? Monjū Bosatsu transcends all time and space. He is ever-changing, and at the drop of a hat, he can take on the form of an old man, boy priest, or whatever he sees fit."

There was no reason to believe that an ordinary ten-year-old could manufacture such convoluted logic. The boy had to be Monjū, just like he said. Still, in his heart, Zen simply could not believe that the man he had met on the train—the one who seemed to be going on a hundred but who now, believe it or not, was supposedly four million plus—could possibly be the ten-year-old standing before his very eyes. No way could he believe it. What was all of this about? If the old man was Monjū and the boy was Monjū, how many more Monjūs were there running around? Just as Zen slipped into confusion once again, the kid turned around, squatted on the ground with his back turned to Zen, and right before Zen's eyes, stuck his buns out like a kid wanting someone to wipe him after using the potty. He had a truly splendid bottom, a round, plump, and white *manjū* filled with bean-jam. Yes, a real live *manjū*! It had to belong to Mañjuśri! Deep within his heart, Zen suddenly knew that this really was Monjū Bosatsu. A year ago, when he was in the conductor's room of the special express bound for Tokyo, the ancient conductor had stuck out a derrière so meaty and perfect that it seemed impossible that it belonged to such an old man. On that occasion, Zen had also been struck by how much the guy's ass looked like a bean-filled bun. Nonetheless, the knowledge that the boy before him was indeed Monjū Bosatsu came so suddenly that Zen didn't even have time to remember that incident on the train a year ago. There before his eyes and deep within his consciousness, the old Monjū Bosatsu had been supplanted. The only Monjū Bosatsu was the Monjū Bosatsu before him.

What was this ultra-modern train that the young Monjū Bosatsu was telling him to get aboard? Monjū answered before Zen even had a chance to ask. Though his voice was just as sweet as ever, it still contained a power that left Zen with no choice but to obey. The mysterious utterances leaving the boy's mouth were precisely the sorts of things that he would have expected from the old Monjū Bosatsu, but Zen was so overwhelmed that the thought of the old Monjū never entered his mind. He found himself completely wrapped up in the words of the young figure before him.

"So you're wondering about the train, eh? The train is called the *Tantrayāna*. In Sanskrit, *Tantrayāna* means 'the Secret Vehicle.' The reason for the name is that this train is really a time machine, and we've got to go back 2,500 years into the past on it. Actually, it travels through space as well as time, but we'll talk more about that later. Now, imagine that this time machine is carrying you back 2,500 years to ancient India. On the banks of the Nairañjanā River is a village called Bodhgayā, and growing there is a somewhat tallish tree of the variety known as the pippala. Now, imagine a great, naked cock curving gently upwards as it sits in the shade of the tree's heart-shaped leaves. This Mahāvairocana is the Buddha Siddhārtha Gautama who has just attained enlightenment. It is King Śuddhodana's son, the prince of the Śākya clan. In the process of becoming one with the great one, he has taken on the form of the great, infinite Mahāvairocana in the farthest reaches of space, transforming himself into a gigantic, erect penis.

"After attaining enlightenment, the Buddha wanders the country preaching the way to enlightenment and buddhahood. Naturally, a group of followers gathers around him. Śāriputra, Mahāmaudgalyāyana, Mahākāśyapa, Aniruddha, Subhùti, Pūrṇa, Kātyāyana, Upāli, Rāhula, and Ānanda were his ten great disciples. In addition to them, however, a whole group of monks gathered around him. I sincerely doubt whether or not they understood the truth of Siddhārtha's enlightenment. To be honest, I don't think they understood anything at all, and that's why they continued to clamor around him at Jetavana-vihāra, Veṇuvana-vihāra, and all the other places where he preached. Let me give you a metaphor to describe the sight of them jostling around him. They were the very image of a crowd of mini-Mahāvairocanas, each still shrunken inside its foreskin. These little cocks, however, surrounded a big, bold Mahāvairocana sitting perfectly poised with its naked head held up high.

"With all of his followers jostling about, Siddhārtha passed into Nirvāṇa beneath a sāla tree along the Hiraṇyavatī River at Kuśinagara. Immediately, his followers began arguing about the truth of enlightenment of which he had spoken. They came up with all sorts of different takes on it; 'The Dharma and the Self exist together,' 'The Dharma is, and the Self is not,' 'Only the dharma of the present is the absolute reality,' 'Within the present dharma are the Five Aggregates, which are absolute reality, and the Twelve Places and Eighteen Worlds, which are provisional reality,' 'Even within the Five Aggregates, only the dharma of the priesthood is true, and the vulgar dharma is illusory,' and 'There is no absolute reality, only present manifestations.' But no sooner would someone disagree than someone else would come along with another opinion. Before long, Buddhism had split into six sects and twenty branches. Now, a new group of followers ran out of patience with these little cocks trapped in their foreskins. They stopped arguing about the fragmented teachings Siddhārtha had left behind and instead started concentrating on the meaning of enlightenment, looking for the real thing and not just its reflection. As bodhisattvas, each one of them sought the path to becoming a buddha and a tathāgata. Their teachings did not adhere slavishly in principle to Siddhārtha's scattered words and phrases. Proudly, they spoke of themselves as 'The greater Vehicle,' the *Mahāyāna*, which transports people to true enlightenment, and they ridiculed the other followers of the six sects and twenty branches by calling them *Hīnayāna*, 'The Lesser Vehicle. If you ask me, Mahāyāna philosophy is perhaps less objectionable than Hīnayāna, but it's really six of one and half dozen of the other. If you think of Hīnayāna as a foreskin-covered cock, then at best it is a dick that is only slightly revealed, or revealed halfway at the most. The real meat doesn't show through.

"Both Hīnayāna and Mahāyāna, whichever one you want to talk about, are both too caught up in the story of the historical Buddha and Tathāgata Śākyamuni. As for the true Buddha and the true Tathāgata, there is one and one alone—the great Mahāvairocana who has existed for innumerable kalpas, who has existed for such unfathomably long periods that he must seem immortal to any ordinary, mortal being. Between your thighs is another Mahāvairocana that you can use to become aware of him and give him concrete expression. A man who does so, and who thereby becomes a Mahāvairocana himself, is himself a buddha and a tathāgata. Śākyamuni was simply one such man."

If Zen had been thinking objectively as he looked at this little monk spouting profundities in his extraordinarily innocent voice, the whole sight would have been strange indeed! But he was completely overcome by Monjū's air of authority. The young monk appeared to Zen as a blessed vision, and he considered himself unworthy of it. A moment ago, the sweet figure had reminded him of the statues of the infant Śākyamuni he had seen at the Flower Festival. Since the historical Śākyamuni that the young monk was going on about was the Buddha and Tathāgata, it only made sense that the young Monjū Bosatsu, who was explaining these things, should so closely resemble the young Buddha. After all, Monjū too was an enlightened one and a tathāgata.

But that was not the only reason Zen was awe-struck. In the midst of the young Monjū Bosatsu's speech to his undeserving listener, he had used the word "Mahāvairocana." Right then, Zen's eyes dropped unconsciously to the Mahāvairocana between Monjū Bosatsu's tender thighs, where they remained glued. As the boy's philosophizing grew more impassioned and powerful, his cute, compact Mahāvairocana grew bigger and bigger with each word. By the time that he broke off his speech, he was equipped with a splendid, adult-sized tool that towered from his groin.

All of Zen's attention was now focused entirely on the Mahāvairocana. It was as if Monjū Bosatsu had completely transformed into a giant, speaking Mahāvairocana to which Zen lent his ears. Facing Zen all the while, the young Monjū Bosatsu-Mahāvairocana stepped nimbly back into the raised, open door of the train he had called the *Tantrayāna*. Zen tried to follow him, but the step at the foot of the door was unexpectedly high, and there were no holds that he could use to hoist himself up through the open aperture. He was stuck outside.

He did not know what to do, so he resorted to the only thing that he could think of. Sticking out in front of him was Monjū's penis. Zen parted his lips and teeth into two neat, little rows and took the organ deep into his throat. Immediately, his tongue wrapped itself around the point where the shaft and head of the boy's Mahāvairocana came together, then he tightened his lips and teeth firmly against the base of the boy's tool. To Zen's astonishment, the Mahāvairocana lifted him into the air. An instant later, he found himself aboard the train.

How would one go about describing the strange sights on board? He had expected the car of the train to be long, narrow, and rectangular. From the outside, it had looked that way, just like a car on any old train, but when he was actually on board, he began to wonder if he hadn't been mistaken. The interior was spherical, or to be more precise, it appeared to be in the shape of a lotus bud just ready to open. It was almost as if the young Monjū Bosatsu and Zen were inside a covered dish designed so that the two halves came together to form the elaborate lotus shape. A thick weaving resembling a Gobelin tapestry enveloped the ceiling and floor, and embroidered all over it were what seemed to be an infinite number of buddhas. Monjū stood on one of the embroidered buddha images, and Zen knelt in front of him with the Mahāvairocana still in his mouth. At that moment, Zen was overcome with a strange sensation. He felt as if his mouth were holding not just the boy's Mahāvairocana but also all of the countless buddhas embroidered on the floor and ceiling as well.

Zen was in a position that was the exact opposite of one year ago. That was when he had spread his legs wide and thrown his head back while Monjū worked his mouth over Zen's Mahāvairocana. Now, however, it was Monjū whose legs were spread and whose head was thrown back allowing Zen to manipulate his Mahāvairocana. Yet what was different was that a year ago when Monjū Bosatsu had pressed his two full cheeks in around Zen's Mahāvairocana like two attendant figures flanking a central statue of a Buddha, he was still somehow able to keep prattling on and on. Now, however, even though Zen wanted to ask about the Buddhas on the ceiling and floor, all his energy was given over to the Mahāvairocana in his mouth. He could not utter a sound, much less a word, even if he had tried.

Yet as if in response to the question in Zen's eyes, Monjū began to speak. Meanwhile, he spread his legs, planting his feet firmly on the ground. Lacing his fingers together behind his neck, he threw back his head.

"You'll be surprised to find that these throngs of Buddhas are woven in an intricate order. You've heard of maṇḍalas, right? These are two of them right here. The floor on which we are standing is covered with the Womb-World Maṇḍala, and on the ceiling is the Diamond-World Maṇḍala. The former is derived from teachings in the *Flower Garland*

Sūtra and the latter is based on the *Diamond Peak Sūtra*. To be even more specific, the Mahāyāna maṇḍala-world of earthly and physical things as described in the *Flower Garland Sūtra* is elevated to higher level in the Tantrayāna maṇḍala-space of heavenly and spiritual things, as described in the *Diamond Peak Sūtra*. Thus we can say that Tantrayāna grows out of Mahāyāna. I told you before how Mahāyāna emerged in opposition to Hīnayāna during the endless debate over the historical Buddha's fragmented teachings. Now, within Mahāyāna there were also some who were dissatisfied, and so a few of them left that school of thought too. They may not have been able to consciously articulate their dissatisfaction, but when it came right down to it, they felt that Śākyamuni Buddha's profound enlightenment could not be transmitted through language in some simple way. After all, it had taken him six years and forty-nine days to attain it! Buddha's enlightenment was by its very nature a mysterious, unknowable secret; therefore, it should come as no surprise that it couldn't be conveyed through words. A secret is a secret. Though the secret was never explicitly revealed, Śākyamuni Buddha was somehow able to enter the mysteries of the great fountainhead from which arise all buddhas of the three worlds—present, past, and future. He became one with the Buddha, the great and benevolent Mahāvairocana, that transcends all time and space. Through his participation in these secrets, Śākyamuni was able to make the secret of enlightenment his own, even though the fundamental secret of the Buddha remained hidden. This is the key to Tantric Buddhism.

"The seeds of this philosophy are present in Hīnayāna as well. Even Hīnayāna had a number of adherents who, while belonging to Hīnayāna, distanced themselves from endless interpretation and debate. Instead, they devoted themselves solely to fervently repeating incantations and the names of people present at various sermons. Out of these practices grew a canon of mystical incantations and maṇḍalas. The Womb-World Maṇḍala, which places the Mahāvairocana Buddha at the center, developed out of the concept of the Lotus-Womb-World as explained in the *Flower Garland Sūtra*. The pattern of the Diamond-World Maṇḍala then developed as the Womb-World Maṇḍala was elevated to a higher level. About that same time, the two central texts of Tantrayāna, the *Great Sun Sūtra* and the *Diamond Peak Sūtra*, came into existence.

"In a nutshell, that is how Buddhism developed from Hīnayāna into Mahāyāna and then into Tantrayāna. Yes, Sudhana, my friend, we might be able to tell a similar story about you. They say that the development of the one mirrors the development of the whole. Ontogeny follows phylogeny. That's what I'm trying to say. Let's take a look at your past. Take the train that you used to take every day to school. You might say that was the *Hīnayāna*. The special express on which you stowed away to go to Tokyo was the *Mahāyāna*, and now the super-express that you and I are riding at top speed is the *Tantrayāna*. Understand?''

When he heard the words "stowed away," Zen remembered the old man Monjū Bosatsu. He had completely forgotten him since the old Monjū Bosatsu had transformed into this new, young form. For the first time, he became fully aware that his position vis-à-vis Monjū Bosatsu had undergone a complete reversal. A year ago he had been the one serviced by Monjū, but now it was he who was doing the servicing. How astonishing! Of course, this was not the first time that he had attended to the pleasure of another. Every night for weeks in jail, his mouth, his hands, his thighs, and even his ass had been called upon to satisfy his cellmates' need for pleasure, or rather, their need for release. No matter how he looked at it though, he had been forced into servicing them. But what about now? He might argue that only his mouth had been impressed into service, but his hands were helping too. Though he might object that he was ignorant of what he was doing, wasn't he making subtle use of his coiled tongue, raised teeth, and puckered lips to ride the waves of his partner's pleasure?

Zen tried to pull away from the young Monjū Bosatsu's Mahāvairocana. He wanted to stand up from his cramped position to look out the window and see where the train that he was on—or, rather, he had been put on—was headed. According to Monjū, this was the *Tantrayāna*, but where on earth was the *Tantrayāna* taking him? Even though he wanted to free himself from the Mahāvairocana, he found that he could not. It was not because his lips, teeth, and tongue had locked onto the young Monjū Bosatsu that Zen could not let go. No, he could not free himself because the Mahāvairocana was somehow sucking him in. Monjū continued talking as if he had all the time in the world, keeping Zen sucked into his crotch all the while.

"Now you know how Hīnayāna gave birth to Mahāyāna, and how Mahāyāna gave birth to Tantrayāna. Now, you're probably wondering what the 'Tantra' in 'Tantrayāna' refers to? What is the true nature of the great secret that we mentioned earlier? These are tough ones. Of course the eight patriarchs of Shingon Buddhism—Dainichi Nyorai, Kongōsatta, Ryūmyō Bosatsu, Ryūchi Bosatsu, Kongōchi, Fukū Sanzō, Keika Ajari and Kōbō Daishi—knew the answer. They all knew, but since their position called upon them to carefully keep the secret until the end, they did not transmit it by using words.

"Of course, this doesn't mean that there has never been an attempt to elucidate the secret and pass it on. Tantrayāna, 'The Secret Vehicle,' was taken to China where it became Shingon Buddhism, but it also remained in India. The Indian branch considered sexual energy to be the fount of all creation, and accordingly, this school of thought is called the *Śakti* or 'Sexual Energy' sect. The practitioners of Śakti placed so much emphasis on sexuality that they openly affirmed the appetites of the flesh, but the sect eventually collapsed after becoming entangled in a web of obscenity. It was not the only sect to fail though. Not a single branch of Buddhism managed to survive in India. The Śakti sect went into decline, taking with it all of the depravity associated with its name, but the true Śakti teachings were carried to Tibet by the Indian teacher Padmasambhava, whose name, incidentally, means 'Born from a Lotus.' From then on, the Śakti teachings thrived as a form of Tibetan Buddhism. Once the purest strain of Buddhism, and thus the purest essence of India, had been carried to the far side of the Himalayas, it felt, in a way, like Tibet had become another India. We must, however, not place too much emphasis on Tibetan Tantrayāna and forget about the 'Secret Vehicle,' which made its way to Japan through China.

"What I mean is this. The real substance of India and the original nature of Buddhism were condensed into Tantrayāna, the 'Secret Vehicle,' part of which remained in Tibet and part of which was transmitted to Japan. In order to understand what the Tantra of Tantrayāna and the secret of the Secret Vehicle really are, we have to try fitting together esoteric Tibetan and Japanese Buddhism like pieces in a jigsaw puzzle. In doing this, we must take into account a very important sūtra: the *Prajñāpāramitā in One-Hundred and Fifty Verses*. It begins with a description of the seventeen 'purities' of a pure bodhisattva. A bodhisattva will manifest purity in exquisite bliss, purity in the arrow of desire, purity in touch, purity in the bond of love, purity in sovereignty, purity in seeing, purity in rapture, purity in love, purity in pride, purity in adornment, purity in mental abundance, purity in clear light, purity in bodily rapture, purity in form, purity in sound, purity in smell, and purity in taste. Each of these characteristics is indicative of sexual rapture. Some people say that these 'purities' are mere metaphors or just descriptions of the pure state that accompanies the rapture one experiences in seeking enlightenment. That is not true. The rapture of seeking enlightenment and the rapture of sexuality are one and the same. There is no distinction between them. A piece of our jigsaw puzzle falls into place. If, for a moment, we were to acquiesce and accept that they are simply metaphors, then the metaphors were so aptly chosen that they describe their subject matter perfectly.—See my timing is perfect. We've arrived."

But where on earth were they? Though Zen feared that the Mahāvairocana in his mouth would grow longer and longer and rip his jaw from its hinges or jam his throat full, he managed to somehow stand up halfway, even though the inescapable Mahāvairocana stayed firmly planted in his mouth. From this new vantage point, he saw that a horizontal strip of windows circled the circumference of the lotus-shaped room, right where the Womb-World Maṇḍala ceiling and the Diamond-World Maṇḍala floor joined to form the lotus-shaped space. Outside, he spied a two-storied temple gate with a round sign that read "The Monjū Hall of Wisdom." In the distance, he could see the main building of the temple as it stood in the midst of a marvelous mountain seascape. There, stretching into the middle of the sea was a narrow, sandy path, green with the pine trees growing along its length. Though Zen had never seen it before in person, the landscape was familiar enough from postcards that he recognized it as Ama-no-Hashidate or "The Bridge to Heaven," one of what was popularly known as the Three Great Landscapes of Japan. That would mean that this strange train, rectangular on the outside but lotus-shaped inside, had sped across the great distance between Tokyo and here without stopping. What speed! Ah, but of course, Zen thought to himself. This is the *Tantrayāna*, which surpasses both the *Hīnayāna* and *Mahāyāna*. His awe for the young Monjū Bosatsu grew.

"You've got it, Zen. This is Ama-no-Hashidate on the Sea of Japan, and this particular spot is named for me. See the address on the temple? 'Ama-no-Hashidate, Monjū Koazakirito.' No doubt you're wondering why we came straight here and not somewhere else. The answer to your question is hidden in a poem written four hundred years ago by an old monk named Eiyū, who belonged to the Tatchū Nyoze Monastery of Ken'ninji Temple in Kyoto. He was visiting Ama-no-Hashidate when he composed the following poem: *Hashidate no matsu no fuguri mo iriumi no nami mote arau Monjushiri ka na.*

"At first glance, you might think the poem means something like this:

"Even the pinecones of the evergreens at Hashidate
Are washed by the waves of the inlet—
Ah, Mañjuśri!

"The poet sees the pinecones that have fallen from the trees at Ama-no-Hashidate and are floating in the waters of the inlet. He then raises his eyes to take in the Monjū Hall of Wisdom in the distance. Moved by the beauty of the place, he utters a plaintive sigh to express the depth of his emotion. Read in this way, the poem describes the tranquility of the scene. However, there is also another meaning hidden in the poem.

The second meaning rests on two puns. The word *fuguri* or 'pinecone' can also mean 'testicle,' and the Sanskrit version of my name *Mañjuśri* contains the word *shiri*, which means 'behind' in Japanese. Reading the poem with this twist, the two meanings overlap to produce something like this: 'Starting with your erect cock, I suck in even your two balls, which lap and wash inside me. Ah, the ass, with its power to embrace all things is as great as the compassion of Mañjuśri!' See, it's all about dick and ass.

"The place where we now are is the famous 'Low-Gated' Monjū Hall, which along with Abe Hall in Yamato and Natori Hall in Ōshū, ranks as one of the three greatest sites in Japan dedicated to me. Legend states that this particular Monjū Hall was built during the distant Age of the Gods, during which the Bridge of Heaven itself was created. Long, long ago, the two deities Izanagi-no-Mikoto and Izanami-no-Mikoto hung a ladder from the Plain of Heaven and descended to earth. There, by the seashore, they pledged themselves to one another in matrimony. It is said that the ruins of the fences that surrounded the house where they lived became the lumber for the Monjū Hall. Part of the ladder that they had suspended from the Plain of Heaven broke off, and it fell into the water to become the famous spit of land known as Ama-no-Hashidate.

"Don't you think there's something odd about this story? Well, there is! Why would the beloved home of Izanami and Izanagi become a temple dedicated to Monjū? That's because I, Monjū Bosatsu, was Izanami, and Izanagi was my *śakti*. Look at the ceiling. Each of the tathāgatas and bodhisattvas embroidered on the Diamond-World Maṇḍala is embracing a female being. These female beings are called *śakti*, and they are embodiments of the divine, creative force. Tibetan practitioners of Tantrayāna sometimes draw maṇḍalas like this, with all the tathāgatas and bodhisattvas locked in sexual embrace with their female śakti counterparts.

Now, there is a second meaning hidden in the myth of Izanagi and Izanami, just as there was in the poem about Ama-no-Hashidate. The myth that Izanami and Izanagi descended from the Plain of Heaven on a ladder disguises the underlying, true story. I, Monjū Bosatsu, flew here to earth from outer space with my śakti in a cock-shaped UFO. Together, we came from the Great Beyond of the great beyond, from the Fountainhead of all fountainheads, from the Reality of realities, from the great phallus of purple gold, Mahāvairocana. Do you remember how a year ago I told you a story on the special express about how a phallic UFO fell on Mt. Kinpu in Yoshino? Well, Ama-no-Hashidate and Mt. Kinpu weren't the only places where these UFOs landed. Flying cocks—small ones, large ones, and every size in between—landed throughout all of ancient Japan. They touched down everywhere from the southernmost island to the northernmost province, and the temples that now are found all over Japan were constructed on their landing sites. People don't know this of course so they attribute the founding of the temples to great teachers, saying idiotic things like 'Gyōgi built that one,' or 'Kōbō Daishi started that one.' But come on! Do they really think that Gyōgi or Kōbō Daishi, great men though they were, could walk all over Japan like that?

"Now, where were we? Ah yes, I had just finished talking about the connection between this place and myself, Monjū Bosatsu. Now that the *Tantrayāna* has brought us here to Ama-no-Hashidate, we're going to continue on a little trip through the sea and kick up a few waves on the way. We're setting out for India! You realize, however, I can't tell you which India we are going to. There are three Indias: the one we see today on the map, the little 'India' that was created on the far side of the snow-capped Himalayas when Buddhism was taken to Tibet, and the abstract 'India' of the fundamental truth that lies beyond even what was created in Tibet. Unfortunately, I can't tell you where we're headed, but to get there, we need to change our trajectory."

Monjū Bosatsu turned to change the train's direction. Simultaneously, Zen suddenly was liberated from the Mahāvairocana that he had been holding in his mouth for so long despite all of his efforts to separate himself from it. Once it was gone from his lips, however, what wretchedness, solitude, and despair he felt! He had never experienced such feelings before. They made him realize just how wonderful the thing that had filled his mouth really was.

There was, however, no time to linger over the wondrous qualities of the cock that had just left his mouth. Monjū extended his hand, spun Zen around, and pushed him down by the nape of his neck. Now, Zen's ass stuck up in the air, just as Monjū had shown his to spark Zen's recognition soon after meeting. In one smooth stroke, Monjū plunged his Mahāvairocana, which had grown even more impressive than the adult-size tool he had a moment ago, deep into Zen's ass. The violence of the thrust should have been excruciating, but to the contrary, it filled Zen with seemingly endless pleasure. Though his ass still remained just an ass, it felt as if Zen's orifice had become a living lotus that joyfully accepted its violator. Inscribed within the petals and pleats of this lotus of flesh was a maṇḍala ablaze with bodhisattvas, each locked in embrace with its śakti. Each and every one, though as numerous as the grains of dust in the universe, radiated an ecstatic smile as if caught up in rapture.

Just then, that was when it happened. To quote the sūtras, it was something "so strange and absurd that it cannot be described in words, something that astonishes the heavens and makes the earth tremble." The pleasant force that he had been feeling in a vague, abstract way— could it be?—suddenly made itself distinctly felt in the lotus orifice in his face and in the tip of his Mahāvairocana. Monjū had divided into three bodies, each of which was now simultaneously pressing into a different orifice, filling Zen's asshole, mouth, and Mahāvairocana at once. But that was not all. Something else had also occurred—something even stranger and more indescribably absurd, something even more astonishing and earth-shaking. Zen realized that he was no longer simply experiencing the pleasure of his own asshole, mouth, and Mahāvairocana. He also felt the rapture enjoyed by the Mahāvairocanas themselves as they plunged in and out of the three orifices. He felt the same pleasure experienced by Monjū Bosatsu himself. At the same moment that Monjū divided into three bodies, Zen, the recipient of his penetration, too had divided into three bodies, and both Monjū Bosatsu and Zen were feeling the ecstasy of the other. The two were engaged in the Tantric principles 'being one another, entering one another' and 'subject and object passing through one another.' They had become embodiments of a pleasure as multi-faceted as an eight-faced, six-armed Buddhist statue. As they panted and groaned, their voices became the mantra *a-hūṃ, a-hūṃ* filling the air.

The panting and groaning seemed like it would continue forever, yet in the midst of it, Zen heard the voice of Monjū. He realized it wasn't the young Monjū Bosatsu's voice but the hoarse speech of the older Monjū Bosatsu, who had burst forth from the innocence of the former's youthful form. The voice brought back with it a wave of nostalgia.

"Zen! Zenzai? The state that you feel throughout your body is the most buddha-like of buddha states, the most tathāgata-like of tathāgata-states. You are experiencing Nirvāṇa itself! Sūtras preserved deep inside the Lamaist palaces of Tibet—sūtras from the Tantrayāna tradition, also known as the 'Diamond Vehicle' or the 'Vehicle of Supreme Yoga'—speak of the 'Single Body of the Buddhist Follower.' They speak of the Brahman, or the universe that surrounds us, as the greater Self. They also talk of the Ātman, the self that is in the universe, as the Smaller Universe. The Brahman, or Greater Self, is represented by seven lotus flowers layered upon one another. Likewise, the Ātman, or Smaller Universe, is also shown as seven layers of lotus flower. Now, what are the seven lotuses of the Ātman? From bottom to top, they are the Murādhāra Chakra, Svādhiṣthāna Chakra, Maṇipura Chakra, Anāhata Chakra, Viśuddha Chakra, Ājñā Chakra, and Sahasrāra Chakra.

Each chakra corresponds to a part of the anatomy: the perineum, genitals, navel, heart, throat, third eye, and brain. It is said that the goddess Kuṇḍalīni is enshrined in the lowest of these seven lotuses, the Murādhāra Chakra, and she is the source of life. The concept of a life-giving sexual embrace became associated with her, thereby making her the equivalent of the śakti of the Śakti 'Sexual Energy' Sect. Hence, we can speak of Kuṇḍalīni and the śakti in a single breath.

"So what is Kuṇḍalīni-Śakti anyway? To answer this question, it's best to look at where Kuṇḍalīni is situated. Kuṇḍalīni resides in the Murādhāra Chakra or the perineum, as it is known in medical terms, right? But here, the story gets a little more complicated. The word for perineum in Japanese is written with two characters meaning '*to meet*' and '*yin.*' Now, when yin and its complement yang come together, yin meets yang and yang meets yin, right? The perineum or '*meet yin*' could therefore also be called '*meet yang.*' My point is that the Murādhāra Chakra is where the two cosmological principles come together. If you touch your perineum with your fingertip, you'll see. Right there is where the yin, represented by the root of the rectum, and the yang, represented by the root of the genitals, separate. It is in the Murādhāra Chakra that the yang of the Svādhiṣthāna Chakra and the yin of the Kuṇḍalīni go their separate ways. Therefore, it's right on track to say that the second chakra, namely the Svādhiṣthāna Chakra, and all the others, are no more than parts of the Murādhāra Chakra. Of course, that which diverges must return to its source and become one once again. Yin and yang, concave and convex, yoni and linga—all must come together again. This is the basic teaching in Kuṇḍalīni-Śakti worship.

"There is a pitfall here that threatens to lead us astray, however. There is a tendency to assume that, when the old texts talk about the yoni and the linga coming together, they are talking about different things becoming one, namely the union of the opposite sexes. That's not correct. The yoni and linga are actually the yin and yang within a *single body.* They are the anus and the penis—no, to be more precise, they are all the yin elements and all the yang elements, which are represented in turn by the anus and the penis. The sensations associated with these yin and yang elements throughout the body develop from the penis, mouth, and rectum. When these yin and yang elements combine, they open the lotus flower of the seventh of the seven chakras—the Sahasrāra Chakra located on the top of the head where the individual and universal meet—and we connect to the Brahman or the Greater Universe. In this way, the self that is the Ātman and the universe that is the Brahman penetrate and move through one another, one becoming all and all becoming one. They enter the mode of existence in which all phenomenal things are mutually unhindered and interfused and thus create an inexhaustible cycle of interdependence. In this way, they give rise to the most buddha-like of buddha-states, the most tathāgata-like of tathāgata-states: true Nirvāṇa.''

So, then, who was the boy known as Zen? Who was Monjū Bosatsu? The two had become one. The yang pushing its way in belonged to Zen as much as to Monjū; and the yin accepting it belonged to Monjū as much as to Zen. No, the story was even more complicated than that. As the yang pushed in, so did the yin, and as the yin accepted, so did the yang. When the words ''Zen! Zenzai?'' were enunciated at the beginning of the speech, they had sounded like ''Monjū! Monjū?'' Who was speaking? Zen or Monjū Bosatsu? And who was listening? It was impossible to say. Where once there had been two, the only thing remaining was an unbounded, unknowable, and indescribable feeling of bliss. Monjū Bosatsu spoke, and Zen listened—or perhaps it was Zen who spoke and Monjū Bosatsu who listened.

"Okay, Zen! Okay, Zenzai? The unusual nature of your name *Hokkai Zenzai*, meaning 'Virtuous Treasure of the Dharma World,' determined your fate from the beginning. You were destined to set out on a pilgrimage in search of the true way. Now look how far your journey has brought you! You left the *Hīnayāna* behind in your hometown. You rode the *Mahāyāna* special express to Tokyo, where you spent a year. There you passed through the Ten Stages of the Bodhisattva as explained in the *Flower Garland Sūtra* and through the Ten Stages of the Spirit as described in the *Secret Maṇḍala Teaching*. Now you are riding the *Tantrayāna*, the 'Diamond Vehicle,' the 'Vehicle of Supreme Yoga.'

"The section 'Entry into the Realm of Reality' in the *Flower Garland Sūtra* ends like this: 'Then, the young Sudhana gradually came to possess, like the Bodhisattva Samantabhadra, oceans of desire to save sentient beings. He came to equal footing with Samantabhadra and all the other enlightened ones, and his body filled all worlds. He matched him in penetration, practice, perception, and divinity. He attained equal mastery at turning the wheel of the Dharma, at rhetoric, and at articulation. He became his equal in powerful fearlessness, residing on the same footing with the enlightened ones and feeling their great compassion as his own. He became the peer of all enlightened ones in miraculous emancipated freedom.'

"In this passage, the word 'Samantabhadra' could just as well be replaced by the words 'Mañjuśri,' or 'all buddhas,' for Samantabhadra, Mañjuśri, and all the buddhas are equal in terms of enlightenment. What I'm saying is that this line from the 'Entry into the Realm of Reality' could be describing you, my boy, right now. At this very moment, you are equal to Mañjuśri, to Samantabhadra, and to all the various enlightened ones. You are equal to the Buddha of buddhas, the Tathāgata of tathāgatas, the Life Force of life forces, the True Reality of true realities, the shining phallus in the infinite great beyond of space, the Great Principle which is space itself—Mahāvairocana.

"As a matter of fact, it was this morning, right when you left the jail cell that you achieved Nirvāṇa and an existence equivalent to that of Mahāvairocana himself. The *Tantrayāna* coming to pick you up in front of the police station this morning and all of the other things you have seen since then have been mere projections of your own internal state. No sooner were you riding the *Tantrayāna* than an intense force propelled it from the jailhouse and drew it to the Monjū Hall of Wisdom at Ama-no-Hashidate. At that point, the earth's gravity released us, and without even realizing it, we rose from the surface of the earth. The ancient bridge between heaven and earth at Ama-no-Hashidate carried us into the heavens, and the *Tantrayāna*, like the erect penis that it is, stood up and immediately headed for Mahāvairocana. Yes, at this very moment, we are flying towards Mahāvairocana, whom I referred to before as the abstract idea of India, the location of the fundamental truth of Indian Buddhism. We are flying faster than the speed of sound or the speed of light through the Intermediate State.

"The Intermediate State serves as a buffer between the world of the living and the world of the dead. The seventeenth section of the *Treatise on Mahāvairocana* states, 'It is after death and before life, thus coming and existing in between the two. It is the state of absorption of desire and form. For this reason, it is called the Intermediate State.' The eighth section of the *Abhidharma Storehouse Treatise* explains, 'The five aggregates in the transitional state between life and death represent what is known as the Intermediate State. Because it does not extend to all places, the Intermediate State is not Life.' What I'm saying is that you died once you completed the Ten Stages of the Bodhisattva and the Ten Stages of Spirit on the path to wisdom. This morning, you passed away at the height of your abjection.

"Now, the dead must spend forty-nine days in the Intermediate State. Why forty-nine days? Doesn't that sound familiar? Siddhārtha Buddha, one manifestation of the Mahāvairocana Buddha, sat in meditation on the banks of the Nairañjanā River in Bodhgayā beneath a pippala tree for forty-nine days before finally achieving awakening. Likewise, the dead must wander for forty-nine days through the Intermediate State before being reborn into a new life. There are two ways that one can be reborn. One can either re-enter the revolving cycle of the Six Paths through existence or one can be released into Nirvāṇa. The entrances to the Six Paths are, in ascending order, the womb of beings in hell, the womb of hungry ghosts, the womb of animals, the womb of asura warriors, the womb of human beings, and the womb of devas. As a being passes through the paths, each time it is reborn, it aims for a higher womb so that it can enter the higher level and be closer to Nirvāṇa. Of course, aiming for Nirvāṇa means aiming for Mahāvairocana. At the moment that Siddhārtha Buddha achieved awakening, he achieved unity with Mahāvairocana. That much is clear. When he dedicated himself to the hermit's life after leaving his mother Queen Māyā and his wife the Princess Yasodharā, he left behind all things even remotely related to the womb and the cycle of rebirth.

"Now where was I, Zen? While I have been talking, Zenzai, time has been slipping away moment by moment. It is now the forty-ninth day since we left Ama-no-Hashidate. At this very second, the cock-shaped train *Tantrayāna* is shooting forward, carrying your Ātman towards Brahman—the Brahman of all Brahmans, Mahāvairocana. The seven lotuses of the seven chakras are opening. Come, Zen! Come to Mahāvairocana, Zenzai! Do not be hampered by the hands that come to hold you back. Do not be obstructed by the wombs of the Six Paths. Aim for the single, shining entity! Become one with Mahāvairocana!"

Suddenly, the bud-shaped ceiling and floor opened, creating an enormous aperture in both places. Through the hole in the ceiling, five more lotuses were visible above, making a total of seven open lotuses. A powerful gust of wind blew through the hole in the floor of the lotus enclosure, blowing the occupants through the holes of the other lotuses into the emptiness of the Intermediate State.

Who was it floating there? Was it Zen? Was it Monjū Bosatsu, Samantabhadra, or some manifestation of all the buddhas and bodhisattvas? At any rate, at some distance away, there floated an awe-inspiring sight, a giant cock complete with two testicles and a rectum. The tip of the phallus was spewing forth smaller sets of penises, testicles, and rectums or linga embraced by yoni-śakti, each of which was a small replica of the original. As these smaller sets shot forth, they looked like sperm shooting quickly and powerfully from a great being in orgasm. These linga rushed away with tremendous speed, disappearing from the range of visibility. Surrounding each lingum and yoni was a golden nimbus that resembled the golden ring Zen had inadvertently flushed down the toilet in his jail cell. The golden bands of light of fifty-some of these haloes overlapped as they flew into the distance, led by the cocks and rectums inside them.

The spiritual, supernatural entity that was no longer Zen, Monjū

Bosatsu, Samantabhadra, nor any of the other buddhas or bodhi-sattvas—the entity that one could only call the Mahāvairocana heading for Mahāvairocana—pressed forward on its way. Meanwhile, through the eye that was its entire body, it could see through the Worlds of the Ten Directions. There were no longer any heavenly bodies or nebulae around it, only the small and large cock-shaped UFOs zooming in every direction. Each of these phalluses had its own hue of light—a white of dazzling clarity, a yellow of brilliant saffron, a red of radiant scarlet, a bluish-green of resplendent teal, and so forth—indicating that each represented its own level of spiritual power.

Circling among the phallic, cigar-shaped UFOs were a number of flying saucers reminiscent of the female genitalia in their flatness. As the saucer-shaped UFOs approached the cigar-shaped UFOs, they revealed a gigantic set of closed lips. These lips would open and a wet tongue slide forth to suck in the phallic UFOs; however, once they understood that the phallic UFOs were stubborn in their resistance, the lips immediately bent into a frown and flew away. How many flying saucers were turned away? Before long, every single flying saucer had left the area, leaving nothing but the cigar-shaped UFOs. Each and every one now glowed with a bright, white light that revealed the intensity of its heat and radiance.

The entity that was no longer Zen, Monjū, nor all of the buddhas and bodhisattvas—the Mahāvairocana heading for Mahāvairocana—radiated an unstinting white light that grew all the more dazzling. Gradually, its head pushed its way into the waves of the increasingly brilliant sea of clear, white light. As it progressed, its color and light melted away until it finally vanished from all sight.

QUEER DHARMA: VOICES OF GAY BUDDHISTS, vol. 2
is published in paperback and limited hardcover editions.